hamlyn

THE OFFICIAL
MANCHESTER CITY
HALL OF FAME

GARY JAMES

First published in Great Britain in 2005 by Hamlyn,
a division of Octopus Publishing Group Ltd
2–4 Heron Quays, London E14 4JP

ISBN 0 600 61282 1
EAN 9780600612827

A CIP catalogue record for this book is available
from the British Library

Printed and bound in Spain

10 9 8 7 6 5 4 3 2 1

Contents

4   Foreword by **Bernard Halford**

6   Introduction

9   **1978–1983 AWARD** Joe Corrigan

19   **1911–1927 AWARD** Tommy Johnson

29   **1966–1971 AWARD** Tony Book

39   **1928–1935 AWARD** Eric Brook

49   **PANEL AWARD** Francis Lee

57   **1984–1991 AWARD** Paul Lake

67   **1936–1950 AWARD** Frank Swift

77   **1972–1977 AWARD** Colin Bell MBE

87   **Pre-1910 AWARD** Billy Meredith

97   **PANEL AWARD** Peter Doherty

105   **1992–2002 AWARD** Niall Quinn

115   **1951–1957 AWARD** Roy Paul

125   **PANEL AWARD** Mike Summerbee

133   **1958–1965 AWARD** Bert Trautmann OBE

143   **LIFETIME ACHIEVEMENT AWARD** Roy Clarke

151   **PRE-1950 AWARD** Sam Cowan

159   **POST-1950 AWARD** Alan Oakes

167   **LIFETIME ACHIEVEMENT AWARD** Ken Barnes

174   Index

176   Acknowledgements

FOREWORD by Bernard Halford

From boyhood in the 1940s Manchester City has always been my team, and I've had the privilege to see some of football's greatest players wearing our blue shirts. Back in the immediate postwar years, City boasted many great and talented stars, and it was always so exciting attending Maine Road. By the mid-1950s I had already seen such wonderful stars as Bert Trautmann, Ken Barnes, Roy Paul, Roy Clarke, Bobby Johnstone and many more, in their prime.

Of course, the most successful period for the Club began in 1965 with the appointment of manager Joe Mercer and his assistant Malcolm Allison. Within five years of starting their work, Joe and Malcolm had guided City to promotion, the League Championship, the FA Cup, the League Cup and the European Cup Winners' Cup. City feared no one, and Maine Road became the greatest place to be for fans and players alike.

At the Hall of Fame Awards 2005 we gave an award for Outstanding Achievement to Malcolm, and to Joe's widow Norah, in recognition of that great period and the success of the Mercer-Allison partnership. It was appropriate that, on a night dedicated to the players, their significnt roles in City's history were remembered.

Since the end of the Mercer-Allison period, we may not have found the same level of sustained success but we have unearthed many exciting players over the years. Some of these have become celebrated international players, others have achieved cult status all, have brought enjoyment to City fans.

The Manchester City Hall of Fame was created to recognise the achievements of City's greatest players. It's a wonderful idea and I was extremely pleased when I was asked to chair the selection committee, although I must say that the role is also a very difficult one. We have had many truly great players over the years and selection is always a difficult process. We try to ensure that we follow the wishes and choices of the fans wherever possible but, being a passionate supporter myself, sometimes it's very difficult to select one player above another. Bobby Johnstone, for example, is one player I am very keen to see recognised, but then I also appreciate that the 1950s – like the '30s, '60s and '70s – was a very strong period.

The Hall of Fame is an opportunity for us all to remember the great moments from our own footballing lives. Contained within this book are wonderful memories of my time at City, but also other remarkable moments from Billy Meredith to local hero Paul Lake.

This book has been written to highlight in detail the careers of all the Hall of Fame players, and I'm delighted that Gary James, a man whose initial work created the Hall of Fame, has written this book. I've known Gary for quite a few years now, and like me he shares a strong desire to see every period of City's history awarded the highest level of respect. His earlier works have all proved interesting, well written and informative, and I'm sure you'll agree that this book continues in that same vein.

Clearly, what makes this story though are the players themselves, and we at City are very supportive of our Former Players' Association. Originally set up by predominantly 1950s players, the Association includes players from the 1930s through to the Premier League era, and its committee works extremely hard to keep in contact with former players from every period. Naturally, it's vital the Association continues to attract new members as time moves forward.

I've enjoyed my 30 or so years working at City and my lifetime of support for the Club. There's always been something special about City, and at various times throughout my life this Club has given me tremendous pleasure. Enjoy the book and never forget what these players – and the hundreds of others who have played for our Club – have achieved and what enjoyment they have brought.

Of course, time moves on and personalities change. Fifty years from now a whole new batch of players will have come and gone, but I believe there will always be something magical about Manchester City and the players already inducted into the Hall of Fame.

Club Secretary Bernard Halford at the inaugural Hall of Fame Awards.

Bernard Halford
Club Secretary and Chair of the Hall of Fame Committee

INTRODUCTION

This book highlights the lives and careers of the 18 players inducted into the Manchester City Hall of Fame since its creation in 2004. It also provides potted histories of those great City players who narrowly missed being inducted during the first two years of the awards, and gives a statistical breakdown of City season by season during each time period.

Before delving straight into the stories of these players, it is worth highlighting the history and reasoning behind the Hall of Fame. The key aim of the Manchester City Hall of Fame is to recognise those players who have made a significant contribution to the history of Manchester City. That contribution may have been in the form of helping the team to win silverware, or it may have been made by players achieving iconic status due to their efforts and rapport with supporters.

The original idea for the Hall of Fame came from discussions I had with senior figures within the Club during the development of the award-winning Manchester City Experience – the Club's museum and stadium tour. As I was planning the museum it soon became clear that the Experience focus had to be on the overall story of the Club, and that there had to be something else to recognise the players. I considered how other sports organisations around the world recognise their star performers, and so the concept of the Hall of Fame was born. As far as I'm aware City are the first League side to honour players at such a prestigious ceremony. Other clubs have similar concepts, but none is of the stature of City's.

Once the decision was taken to create the Hall of Fame, the specific details had to be determined. It was clear that proper recognition of players throughout City's history was needed and so the history of the Club was divided into 11 time periods. A shortlist of stars from each period was created based primarily on the views of myself, secretary Bernard Halford and Kevin Parker from the Official Supporters' Club. Supporters were asked to vote for one player in each time period, and those votes determined the first 11 entrants. However, it was also clear that during certain periods, most notably the 1930s and the late 1960s, City possessed a large number of extremely strong, successful candidates. A further three awards were therefore created to ensure proper representation.

To determine the additional three entrants, and for the future development of the Hall of Fame, a panel of experts was created. With strong support from the *Manchester Evening News*, which became the official sponsor of the Hall of Fame, a panel was created made up of long-serving secretary Bernard Halford, Radio Five's City-supporting broadcaster Susan Bookbinder, *Manchester Evening News* representatives and, importantly, there was to be a different supporter each year selected by the *Evening News*.

In addition to the three panel awards, it was also decided that a Lifetime Achievement award should form part of the Hall of Fame. Around the same time discussions took place between Club officials, myself and Hamlyn on the production of this book.

The first Gala Dinner was held in January 2004 and was a huge success thanks to the efforts of the hosts, Susan Bookbinder and John Stapleton, and many Club officials, in particular Rosie Bass, Bernard Halford and Danny Wilson. The following year the decision was made to retain the quality of the Hall of Fame by limiting the awards to three main categories – pre-1950, post-1950 and a Lifetime Achievement award. On this occasion nominations for the two time periods came directly from supporters, with a shortlist of six players created. The panel debated the merits of each player and agreed with supporters that those who had received most votes should be inducted. They also debated the merits of several contenders for the second Lifetime Achievement award.

The February 2005 Gala Dinner was also a major success and, as well as the three main awards, special awards were presented to Malcolm Allison and Norah Mercer, Joe Mercer's widow, in recognition of the glory years under Mercer and Allison in the late 1960s and early 1970s, and another award was created for the greatest City goal of all time as voted by attendees at the dinner. Paul Dickov's memorable equaliser in the 1999 Division Two play-off final at Wembley won this primarily because of the importance the goal has had on the Club's recent history.

The research and writing for this book commenced immediately after the first awards, with the aim being to capture the stories of these great players. On a personal level I had already been fortunate to interview some of these men and their families, and by using those interviews, modern-day interviews, contemporary reports and also the Manchester City Experience archive, I have tried to convey the importance of each player. Many of these players have achieved phenomenal success, while others became cult heroes because their stories touched supporters. All are important to the fans.

City have been blessed with many great players since their initial formation as St Mark's Church side in 1880. Hopefully this book helps to celebrate the roles many of them have played in ensuring City's development over its 125-year history. I hope this book entertains and that you enjoy reliving some great moments and stories.

Gary James

NOTE ON THE TEXT
The layout of this book has been designed to match the order and time periods of the players who were inducted into the Hall of Fame, rather than forming a chronological story. Within each section the time period for which the player has been inducted is detailed as part of the chapter heading rather than the player's own career dates. As an example, Joe Corrigan's career forms the first section as he was the first to be inducted, and the dates corresponding to his award (1978–1983) are included with the chapter heading. Statistical information on City's performances and career details of other players during that period are also included.

Panel awards and Lifetime Achievement awards are referred to in the chapter headings where appropriate.

Paul Dickov celebrates scoring 'that goal' in the 1999 play-off final.

Joe Corrigan

Joe Corrigan's City career is an inspirational story for any young goalkeeper. He achieved great success with the Blues and became a regular member of the England squad. However, there were also significant setbacks along the way that he overcame through determination and a desire to prove himself. A very popular figure, Joe was idolised by the Maine Road faithful.

Joe Corrigan
1978-1983 AWARD

Rugby Roots

Manchester-born Joe went to Sale Grammar School and enjoyed participating in sporting activities. However, the school curriculum put more emphasis on rugby than on football and Joe's opportunities to develop as a footballer were limited. He did excel as a second-row forward for the school rugby team and that must have helped improve his general co-ordination and ball-handling skills, even if the ball was a different shape.

After school he became an apprentice at AEI, an engineering firm, and played for their football team, sometimes as a centre half. Joe remembers this period well: 'I went to Sale Grammar School and there was no football at all. I played rugby union for the school and for Cheshire, and I guess that helped my ball control, catching ability etc. Despite this, I always wanted to be a 'keeper and I played football at any opportunity really. When I started as an apprentice at AEI in Trafford Park the chance came to play for the works side and I played at centre-half. I had no choice about that – I wanted to play 'keeper. I guess my size made me a defender.

'Then one day I had to go in nets at half time and I suppose I must have looked all right because I was encouraged to go for a trial. Both City and United were contacted, and a reply came from Maine Road within a fortnight.

'United offered me a trial as well, but once City showed the interest they did I turned them down. I wanted to be loyal and City had faith in me. That mattered a great deal.'

Impressed with Joe's general aptitude for the game, Harry Godwin, City's chief scout, asked him to sign for the Club's youth team and he joined a set-up that included Tommy Booth and Ray Hatton – boxer Ricky Hatton's father.

'City signed me that night, after my first trial,' says Joe. 'It was the sort of situation you would never have today.'

It was manager Joe Mercer who signed Joe as an amateur that September of 1966. Joe remembers fondly this period of his goalkeeping career and of the roles played by Joe Mercer and Malcolm Allison in creating the right environment. 'There was such a great atmosphere and the best thing about Malcolm Allison was that he treated every player the same. It didn't matter if you were in the first team or the B team. I was only a kid but I could tell Malcolm was a great coach. He was more like another player than management. Joe used to be the front man – the ambassador. He was the manager and we all knew it. Together the pair worked perfectly.'

A Testing Start

Joe turned professional on 25 January 1967. A little over eight months later, an injury to regular goalkeeper Harry Dowd, coupled with new signing Ken Mulhearn being cup tied, allowed Joe to make his first-team debut in the third-round League Cup tie against Blackpool on 11 October 1967. Clearly, his elevation to the first team a month before his 19th birthday was a major test and, for City, a major gamble, but the Blues had no real choice. The game itself ended in a 1–1 draw, with some reports suggesting that a more experienced goalkeeper would have saved the Blackpool goal. Joe still retained his place for the replay a week later and City defeated the Seasiders 2–0.

At this stage of his career it was inevitable that Joe's spell as number one was a temporary one and for the fourth-round League Cup tie a fit Harry Dowd returned to action, while Ken Mulhearn had established himself as the first choice for League games (he had signed for the Blues in September 1967). Mercer and Allison had found it difficult determining which goalkeeper – Mulhearn or Dowd – was their number one. Injuries, inconsistency and nerves all seemed to play their part in limiting each player's spell. Mulhearn made most appearances during the 1967/68 League Championship-winning season, while Dowd seemed to be the preferred choice during 1968/69. Joe was really the third choice and this made it difficult for the young goalkeeper to be given first-team experience, but he was determined to learn and did so during a spell away from Manchester. 'I had three months on loan at Shrewsbury under Harry Gregg, the ex-United 'keeper,' says Joe. 'Even though I only played reserve games, I learned so much. Harry was tremendous, a man who knows what 'keeping is all about and who was one of the all-time greats himself. Up until then, my career had been at a stalemate. Within a couple of months of coming back, I made my full League debut.'

Rapid Progress

That full League debut for Joe came in a 2–1 defeat at City's bogey team Ipswich Town on 11 March 1969, with Mike Doyle scoring the consolation for the Blues. He made three further appearances that season – in 1–0 defeats at mid-table Nottingham Forest and at eventual champions Leeds United and then in a 1–0 victory over Liverpool on the last day of the season. Although City's fortunes varied during these games, it's fair to say that Joe Corrigan played well. That win over Liverpool was Joe's first clean sheet in the League. 'Those games gave me the chance to really show what I could do. Luckily, I did okay and the next season, with a lot of pushing from Malcolm, I was City's first choice.'

Player Career Statistics
Appearances

JOE CORRIGAN

Position
Goalkeeper 1966–83

Typical Height and Weight
1.92m (6ft 4½in)
92kg (14st 7lb)

Born
Manchester, 18 November 1948

League Debut
Ipswich Town (away)
11 March 1969

	LEAGUE		FA CUP		FL CUP		EUROPE		TOTAL	
	App	Gls	App	Gls	App	Gls	App	Gls	App	Gls
1967/68	0	0	0	0	2	0	-	-	2	0
1968/69	4	0	0	0	0	0	0	0	4	0
1969/70	34	0	1	0	7	0	8	0	50	0
1970/71	33	0	3	0	1	0	6	0	43	0
1971/72	35	0	2	0	2	0	-	-	39	0
1972/73	30	0	5	0	1	0	1	0	37	0
1973/74	15	0	1	0	0	0	-	-	16	0
1974/75	15	0	1	0	0	0	-	-	16	0
1975/76	41	0	2	0	9	0	-	-	52	0
1976/77	42	0	4	0	1	0	2	0	49	0
1977/78	42	0	2	0	7	0	2	0	53	0
1978/79	42	0	2	0	5	0	8	0	57	0
1979/80	42	0	1	0	4	0	-	-	47	0
1980/81	37	0	8	0	6	0	-	-	51	0
1981/82	39	0	2	0	4	0	-	-	45	0
1982/83	25	0	3	0	3	0	-	-	31	0
TOTAL	476	0	37	0	52	0	27	0	592	0

'Both finals were tremendous thrills, real "Roy of the Rovers" stuff; the League Cup win over West Bromwich Albion especially. Here I was, three years after playing Sunday football and school rugby, at Wembley.'

Joe's progress was rapid, especially since Ken Mulhearn had been bought by Mercer and Allison to be the first choice. Joe was still only 20 when the 1969/70 season began, and the Blues were proving to be the most successful side in the country. It is unusual for any side at the height of its powers to make such a young goalkeeper their number one. It was especially unusual in that City already possessed two established medal-winning goalkeepers.

The opening game of the 1969/70 season saw the Blues beat Sheffield Wednesday 4–1 and Malcolm Allison started to tell the media and anyone else who cared to listen that Joe would be 'as great as Swift'. Most thought this was typical Allison hyperbole but over the years Joe would find himself rated in the same bracket as Frank Swift and Bert Trautmann, two of his great predecessors in the City goal. Joe, in common with them, would also go on to become one of the Club's longest servants.

On 15 November 1969 Joe played in his first Manchester derby match. It was a thrilling 4–0 victory for the Blues and was summed up by the Manchester United reporter David Meek as the most one-sided derby of all time. That wasn't exactly true but for Joe it was a significant match, watched by over 63,000 at Maine Road, and the first of his 26 derbies – a total that no other player has matched while with City.

'Roy of the Rovers'

That 1969/70 season proved to be a rather mixed one in the League, with the Blues finishing a disappointing tenth. However, in knockout competitions City ruled, reaching two finals – in the League Cup and the European Cup Winners' Cup. Joe's progression was moving at a pace no one could

have predicted and he played a significant part in City clinching both trophies. 'Both finals were tremendous thrills,' says Joe. 'Real "Roy of the Rovers" stuff; the League Cup win over West Bromwich Albion especially. Here I was, three years after playing Sunday football and school rugby, at Wembley.'

Those successes were followed by a call-up to the England Under-23 squad to play the Soviet Union and Joe appeared to be on the verge of a truly great career. He played exceptionally well during the first leg of the 1971 European Cup Winners' Cup semi-final with Chelsea and it seemed as if nothing could go wrong. Then disaster struck when he was injured and replaced for the second leg of the European Cup Winners' Cup tie. The Blues lost, Joe's replacement, Ron Healey, was credited with an own goal, and City's chance of success was over.

A Testing Time

Joe continued to be the preferred number one for the next couple of seasons but criticism was starting to be directed at him. Mistakes made him an easy target for supporters who were expecting more and, at one point, it was reported that Joe dreaded the thought of playing at Maine Road. There were even suggestions that he was thinking about giving up on the game. He certainly did not get an easy ride from the press and nobody seemed to think back to his great contribution during City's 1969/70 season.

Joe recalls those days philosophically: 'It's a part of football that will never go away. I have no bitterness about it. In fact, I think I was lucky because the press were a little kinder back then. They would lay off a bit. I would hate to go through the same thing now. My view was that I was paid to do a job to the best of my ability. At times that wasn't good enough to get into the first team and I accepted that. It's alright moaning in the press or whatever, but you can't hide – especially in goal!'

Scottish Under-23 international goalkeeper Keith MacRae was signed from Motherwell in October 1973 for £100,000 and Joe's time as first choice seemed over, especially as MacRae was two years younger than Joe and deemed a much better prospect. 'I went on the transfer list in response to that signing,' says Joe. 'After all, it equalled the record for a goalkeeper at the time.'

Joe's chance was, though, to come again just as it looked likely he would have to leave Maine Road to resurrect his career. 'One thing that was a big help happened in 1973/74 when I broke my jaw and had it wired up for three weeks,' explains Joe. 'I lost about a stone in that time and felt really fit when I came back. That played a big part in keeping me down to 14–14.5 stone (89kg–92kg) – my ideal playing weight.'

Back on Form

A spell over Christmas 1974 didn't really show Joe at his best, but in the following March MacRae was injured and had to leave the field in a match with Leicester. With no goalkeeping substitutes in those

Joe makes a daring save at Maine Road watched by Ipswich's John Wark and City captain Paul Power.

Joe's Prime Time

Manchester City 1 Tottenham Hotspur 1. FA Cup final – 9 May 1981

Goalscorer Hutchison

City Team Corrigan, Ranson, McDonald, Reid, Power, Caton, Bennett, Gow, Mackenzie, Hutchison (Henry), Reeves

Attendance 100,000

Manchester City 2 Tottenham Hotspur 3. FA Cup Final Replay – 14 May 1981

Goalscorers Mackenzie, Reeves

City Team Corrigan, Ranson, McDonald (Tueart), Reid, Power, Caton, Bennett, Gow, Mackenzie, Hutchison, Reeves

Attendance 92,500

These two matches may not have brought Joe Corrigan a winner's medal but they did raise his profile nationally and bring him the accolade of Man of the Final. An enormous television audience worldwide witnessed this, the 100th FA Cup final, and the story of City's season captured a great deal of attention. The Blues had commenced the season with Malcolm Allison as manager but results, performances and a general air of doom and gloom made the first few months difficult. Then John Bond arrived in October and the atmosphere was transformed as City progressed to the League Cup semi-finals and the FA Cup final.

City were in control for most of the initial match at Wembley. Tommy Hutchison had put City into the lead in the 29th minute and the Blues had looked unstoppable. Danger did come from Spurs at times but Joe played magnificently and blocked any danger. Unfortunately, ten minutes from the end disaster struck. Tottenham were awarded a free kick 20 yards (18m) out. Osvaldo Ardiles tapped the ball to Glenn Hoddle, who curled it around the wall. Joe knew he had the shot covered but Hutchison somehow got in the way. The ball hit his shoulder and was diverted past Joe and into the net for Tottenham's equaliser. 'I'm sure Hoddle's free-kick was going wide,' says Joe, 'until Tommy got in the way and deflected it past me.'

Immediately after the equalising goal, Joe, clearly disconsolate himself, walked over to the devastated Hutchison, helped him to his feet and muttered a few words as he patted him on the back. At a time when blame would have been easy to apportion, the City goalkeeper thought more about the feelings of his team-mate than about the incident itself. That says a great deal about Joe's humanity.

The game went into extra time and with the score at 1–1 after 120 minutes, a replay was scheduled for the following Thursday. Joe and most of the City side received considerable praise in the media, with the *Daily Mail* stating, 'For what they are worth to the bewildered Tommy Hutchison, the defiant Joe Corrigan, the prodigious Nicky Reid and the inspiring John Bond, my sympathies are with City. At least they gave their all for 90 minutes and then dredged up a little extra for the additional half-hour. With the exception of Graham Roberts, Tottenham's approach was a disgrace.'

All neutrals seemed to share those views and City felt aggrieved. Joe himself would have preferred to have seen the game settled on the Saturday. 'For me the FA Cup final is all about the Saturday. The players are all hyped up, the fans are all hyped up, the television is all hyped up. The Cup final is meant to be

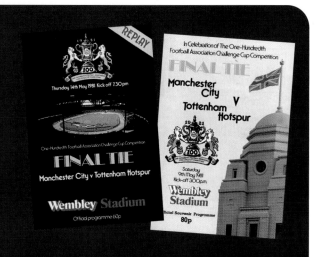

all about who is best on the day. I've no doubt that on the Saturday we were the better team. The second game did not feel like an FA Cup final.'

Despite Joe's views, the second game has become recognised as a classic. It ended 3–2 to Spurs but contained a couple of superb goals. The most famous one is Ricky Villa's 75th-minute Tottenham winner, but City fans will always remember Steve Mackenzie's 20-yard (18m) volley as a classic goal.

Tottenham, in the second game, put Joe under more pressure than he had been under in the first and he certainly performed heroically. In the years since the final, the story of Ricky Villa's goal has grown and grown, yet on the day itself it was the performance of City's brilliant goalkeeper that had won the acclaim. Joe's profile had been raised once again but undoubtedly he would have exchanged that to see City win the Cup.

Man of the Final Joe Corrigan makes a save from Tottenham's Garth Crooks.

days, Mike Doyle went in nets but for the following match Joe's opportunity to shine came again. The player was determined that if this was to be his City swansong he would give it his best shot. 'You have these situations in football,' he says, 'and have to battle away. If you give up, you not only lose the club you are at, you carry a reputation as a quitter. I was determined to at least go down fighting.'

Joe played the final ten games of the 1974/75 season and although results were mixed, both fans and the media were impressed with his form. The following season opened with him as City's first choice and in February 1976 he played in City's great League Cup final success over Newcastle. 'I thought this was the start of another great team at City. Dave Watson proved what a commanding centre-half he was that season. As a 'keeper it made such a difference playing behind two great centre-halves like Dave and Mike Doyle at Wembley. I remember the feeling of disbelief after I saw Dennis Tueart's incredible winner. Twelve months earlier I had been told I was useless. Here I was – a Wembley winner! It just shows what you can do if you're prepared to work at it.'

The amazing turnaround in Joe's career was the talk of football, and City fans fully appreciated the efforts their goalkeeper had made to re-establish himself. Supporters voted him their Player of the Year in 1976 – an amazing accolade considering the achievements of the other truly great players in the squad that season – and at long last the likeable goalkeeper had proved himself as one of City's best stars. Further supporter Player of the Year awards followed in 1978 and 1980, but the biggest honour of the 1970s had to be Joe's selection for England only a few months after the 1976 League Cup final.

England were playing in the United States as part of a Bicentennial tournament and Joe's opportunity came on 28 May in New York when he came on as substitute for Jimmy Rimmer. 'At half time of the Italy game Les Cocker, the trainer, told me to get stripped and come on as sub. We were 2–0 down at the time and, while I'm not saying I had anything to do with it, we won 3–2!'

Joe's Finest Fellow Citizens

During the period 1978–1983 the Blues were consistently one of football's four best-supported sides and had a pedigree few could match. They featured in the highly entertaining 100th FA Cup Final, defeated sides such as AC Milan in European competition, and generally proved to be one of the nation's glamour sides. However, the period did end with the Blues suffering relegation for the first time since the early 1960s.

GERRY GOW Tough-tackling midfielder Gerry Gow arrived at City in October 1980 after making 368 League appearances for Bristol City. From the moment he arrived, supporters loved his fighting spirit and determination to see the Blues succeed. He stayed in Manchester for only two years, making 36 League and Cup appearances, but during that brief spell he was one of the key forces behind City's transformation from struggling side to FA Cup finalists. He later had spells with Rotherham and Burnley, but he will always be remembered as one of John Bond's most important signings.

DAVE WATSON Many view Dave Watson as one of City's and England's greatest-ever central defenders. He was certainly a superb, granite-like figure for the Blues after joining them from Sunderland in 1975. Within a year of his arrival in Manchester he had helped City to League Cup success and in 1976/77 the supporters voted him their Player of the Year. While with the Blues he gained 30 England caps and in total he made 65 international appearances. A strong defender, Watson will always be remembered for being a rock for City between 1975 and 1979 and to many fans he remains the greatest of all central defenders.

PAUL POWER A tremendous captain, Paul Power was one of City's most consistent performers during this time period. He signed professional forms in 1975 and remained with the Blues until 1986. In between he captained City to the 100th FA Cup final, the League Cup semi-finals and to promotion to Division One in 1985. His best season was probably 1980/81, during which he led by example. He scored the only goal of the FA Cup semi-final with Ipswich and generally pushed the Blues forward at every opportunity. After leaving City he won the League championship with Everton. He may have had to wait until the twilight of his career but it was certainly a medal he thoroughly deserved.

MCFC statistics

	1978/79	1979/80	1980/81	1981/82	1982/83	Honours
League Position	15	17	12	10	20	FA Cup finalists 1981
FA Cup Round Reached	4	3	Final	4	4	
League Cup Round Reached	5	3	Semi-final	4	3	
UEFA Cup Round Reached	4	-	-	-	-	
Average Attendance	36,203	35,272	33,587	34,063	26,789	

ASA HARTFORD Scottish international Asa Hartford enjoyed two spells as a player at City. The first saw the midfielder play a key role in Tony Book's glamorous side during the 1970s, while the second saw him join John Bond's early 1980s side. Winner of 50 Scottish caps, 35 while with City, Hartford was a member of the Blues' 1976 League Cup-winning side. Always popular, he also joined City's coaching staff after his playing career had finished and had a spell as caretaker manager prior to the appointment of Steve Coppell.

TOMMY HUTCHISON Regarded by many as John Bond's finest acquisition, Tommy Hutchison epitomised the Club's resurgence under Bond during the 1980/81 season he was a dedicated consistent professional who always appeared supremely conditioned considering his status as a 33-year-old veteran. Hutchison helped the Blues to Wembley in 1981 and netted the 29th-minute opening goal. Sadly he also scored an own goal in that match, guaranteeing him an unusual place in Wembley history.

Tommy stayed with the Blues for less than two years, but during that time he made such an impression that fans still regard him as one of the most influential players of the modern era.

NICKY REID Another 1981 FA Cup finalist, Nicky Reid's first taste of first-team football came in the UEFA Cup tie with Borussia Moenchengladbach in 1979. Malcolm Allison gave him his opportunity and over the course of the following nine seasons the locally born player became a firm favourite with supporters.

The City squad photographed at the start of the 1979/80 season. Paul Power appears on the back row (second from right), while Nicky Reid is seen third from right on the middle row.

Joe went on to make a total of nine appearances for England but neutrals recognise that in any other era his tally would have been much higher and he would have been given more opportunity. England at this time possessed several fine goalkeepers – Ray Clemence, Peter Shilton and Phil Parkes – and manager Ron Greenwood tended to share the number one position between Clemence and Shilton, with Joe the third choice. Clemence was the more experienced of the three and was also playing regularly in Europe with Liverpool, as was Joe with City, while Shilton had been more used to relegation dogfights with Stoke at the time of Joe's debut. Joe's last appearance for England came on 9 June 1982, when he was 33 years old.

Moving Stateside

In 1981 Joe made another appearance in a Wembley Cup final. City lost the 100th FA Cup final in a replay to Tottenham but Joe had received tremendous praise for his performances in both matches. The Blues had also been very unlucky to lose the League Cup semi-final with Liverpool that same season.

Within two years of his heroics at Wembley, Joe had left City. He had become City's elder statesman and a much respected figure but the Blues had started to struggle financially. Expensive and largely unsuccessful transfers – City were the first side to buy three £1 million-plus players – during the late 1970s and early 1980s had an impact on City's ability to develop, and when the struggles came, senior players had to be sacrificed. Defeats against Southampton in the League Cup during November 1982 and Brighton in the FA Cup the following January meant the Blues were out of contention for any trophy. Manager John Bond left and his deputy John Benson was left in charge. 'I knew I was on my way,' recalls Joe. 'With the Club's financial position, City couldn't afford to keep the higher-paid players. I was very sad to leave.'

Joe was transferred for a surprisingly low £30,000 to Seattle Sounders in the North American Soccer League in March 1983 after making an overall total of 592 League, cup and European appearances – second only to record-holder Alan Oakes. Joe later returned to England with Brighton, and went on loan to Norwich and Stoke.

During the 1990s he became a highly sought-after goalkeeping coach, and in 2004, after spending several years at Anfield working for a variety of managers, Ian Rush asked Joe to become goalkeeping coach at Chester City.

As with Trautmann and Swift, Joe will always be remembered as a true Blue hero.

> In comparison with some players, I've not won that many awards at Manchester City. Not as many as some of the great players, but I do think that this is one of the best. I'm absolutely delighted. Thank you.

Joe Corrigan
collecting the Hall of Fame
award in January 2004.

Tommy Johnson

Tommy Johnson was a huge favourite with supporters throughout his 11-year career with the Blues. They recognised that, despite the fame and adulation, Johnson was from the same background as they were. For much of his City life he lived in the Gorton area of Manchester – a true working-class environment – and was often seen in the pubs and clubs talking and mixing with supporters.

Tommy Johnson
1911–1927 AWARD

Riveting Stuff

Tommy had spent his early life living in the town of Dalton-in-Furness. At the start of his working life he became an apprentice rivetter, working in the shipyards at Barrow while playing football for local sides Dalton Athletic and Dalton Casuals. He was a keen young player, with impressive goalscoring ability.

Around 1918, City full-back Eli Fletcher spotted Tommy and urged the Blues to sign this exciting 17 year old. Tommy joined City in February 1919 and he immediately made an impression during that final season of wartime football.

Once the full League programme resumed in August 1919, Tommy had to wait for his opportunity to impress in Division One. His chance did not arise until the following February but when it did he scored both goals in City's 2–0 defeat of Middlesbrough and immediately became a favourite with the fans.

Regal Progress

Tommy retained his place for the following six games, the last of which became a landmark moment in the history of Manchester sport. City's meeting with Liverpool on 27 March 1920 became the first provincial match to be attended by a reigning monarch, when King George V visited City's Hyde Road ground. 'For a young man of 18 to make his mark with a great League debut,' comments his son Alan, 'and then only five weeks later be introduced to the King says a great deal about how his life had changed. When something like that happens you can't help but develop a strong bond with the people and the Club that helped to make it happen.

'Throughout his life he would talk about the day he met the King. Unfortunately he didn't score that day, but City won 2–1 and, apparently, the King was very happy with that result. I suppose, if I think about it, meeting a member of royalty back then was even more special than today because, other than the occasional photo in a newspaper, you would never see the King. Nowadays we see royalty on television all the time, but back then there was nothing. There was more mystique about them.'

The Maine Man

After the King's visit, Tommy lost his place in the side as manager Ernest Mangnall searched for his best strike force. It wasn't until the 1922/23 season that the striker could be regarded as a regular, when he played in 35 of City's 42 League games and scored on 14 occasions.

On the opening day of the 1923/24 season Tommy netted in the Maine Road stadium's inaugural match. It was, says his son, Alan, 'Another very, very proud moment. Horace Barnes scored the first, but for my father's name to be linked forever more to Maine Road's first game is wonderful. When the ground staged its last match in May 2003 Dad's name was back in the spotlight and I was even interviewed by the television companies. Eighty years earlier I doubt he thought he'd be remembered in that way.'

That same season Tommy played in his first FA Cup semi-final – City lost to Newcastle in Billy Meredith's last match – and two years later in his first FA Cup final. It was the first appearance at Wembley for a Manchester side and attention was high, particularly as City's opponents were

'You can't help but develop a strong bond with the people and the Club that helped to make it happen.'

Lancastrian rivals and 1904 Cup final opponents Bolton. Sadly, a single goal from Bolton's David Jack settled the game. Worse was to follow for Johnson and company when a week later the Blues became the first side to reach Wembley and be relegated to Division Two in the same season.

Despite City's troubles, Tommy's career was developing well and on 24 May 1926 – just over three weeks after relegation – he made his England debut at inside left against Belgium in Antwerp. England won 5–3 with Tommy scoring once. Over the course of the following six years he was to appear in a further four internationals – all of them victories. He scored a brace in two internationals – the first against Wales at Stamford Bridge in 1929 and the second against the famous Spanish goalkeeper Ricardo Zamora at Highbury in 1931.

A journalist described Tommy as 'an inside forward with a left foot shot few players have equalled and a penchant for the telling cross-field pass'.

Record Breaker

During 1926/27 Tommy broke the 20 goals a season barrier when he scored 25 goals in 38 League appearances, including a hat-trick in the 8–0 victory over Bradford on the final day of the season. Another goal would have brought promotion on goal average but 12 months later Tommy celebrated as City returned to Division One as champions.

It was the following season that Tommy became recognised across the country as a major striker when he managed to score a Club record 38 goals in 39 League appearances. Five of those goals came in one incredible match with Everton at Goodison when City defeated the home side 6–2.

The 1929/30 season was to be Tommy's last at Maine Road despite a goal in the opening game and his role as the fan's favourite. There were plenty of magical moments from Tommy. The Manchester derby of October 1929 saw one of Tommy's most memorable performances. According to the

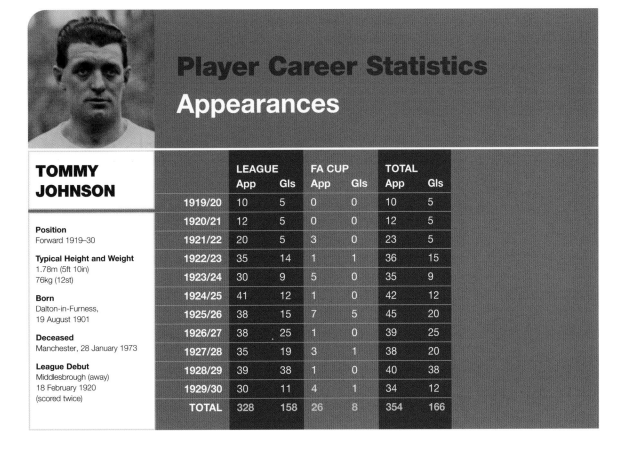

Player Career Statistics
Appearances

TOMMY JOHNSON

Position
Forward 1919–30

Typical Height and Weight
1.78m (5ft 10in)
76kg (12st)

Born
Dalton-in-Furness,
19 August 1901

Deceased
Manchester, 28 January 1973

League Debut
Middlesbrough (away)
18 February 1920
(scored twice)

	LEAGUE		FA CUP		TOTAL	
	App	Gls	App	Gls	App	Gls
1919/20	10	5	0	0	10	5
1920/21	12	5	0	0	12	5
1921/22	20	5	3	0	23	5
1922/23	35	14	1	1	36	15
1923/24	30	9	5	0	35	9
1924/25	41	12	1	0	42	12
1925/26	38	15	7	5	45	20
1926/27	38	25	1	0	39	25
1927/28	35	19	3	1	38	20
1928/29	39	38	1	0	40	38
1929/30	30	11	4	1	34	12
TOTAL	328	158	26	8	354	166

MCFC statistics

	1911/12	1912/13	1913/14	1914/15	1919/20	1920/21	1921/22	1922/23	1923/24
League Position	15	6	13	5	7	2	10	8	11
FA Cup Round Reached	2	2	4	3	2	1	3	1	Semi-final
Average Attendance	24,625	24,000	27,000	21,000	25,240	31,020	25,000	24,000	27,400

	1924/25	1925/26	1926/27	Honours
League Position	10	21	3 (in Div 2)	FA Cup finalists 1926
FA Cup Round Reached	1	Final	3	**Other Significant Events** Move to Maine Road in 1923; football played on a regional basis during First World War (seasons 1915–1919).
Average Attendance	29,000	32,000	30,848	

renowned Manchester journalist Ivan Sharpe writing in the *Athletic News*, 'Johnson should have been a fairly happy man. He has the credit of making the match come to life. It was going to pieces early in the second half when Moore thoughtlessly pulled up while appealing for offside and Johnson – with his right foot – scored and set the game alight.'

Out of Time

The game with United ended in a 3–1 City victory but it also saw one of the more controversial moments of the season, when the referee blew for full time a good two minutes before time was actually up. This was particularly galling for Tommy as he netted the ball after an amazing run just at the moment when the whistle went. Ivan Sharpe gave his entertaining thoughts on the incident in his match report, 'When Thomas CF Johnson was a boy he dreamed of playing for a First Division team, and like every youngster, of playing at centre-forward.

'On his night of nights he was playing against his own club's deadly rivals, and over 100,000 eyes were riveted upon him as he darted through the defence – "Go on Johnson!" – dodged this man and that man, drew out the goalkeeper, dribbled the ball round the other side's last hope and with the roars of the delighted populace acclaiming his performance, rolled the ball through the untenanted goal. I have not asked him, but I know it's true, because every schoolboy gets those midnight, alone-I-did-it goals.

'But isn't it a hard world? The once-in-a-lifetime goal dribbled around the goalkeeper on the aforesaid deadly rivals' very own ground all came true in this battle of Manchester, and the referee said the time had expired a moment before the ball had crossed the line! And that's not all. Time had not expired.

'The day he was told he was leaving he was absolutely stunned. He had no idea he was going to leave and he certainly didn't ask to go.'

My watch and every watch around me – plus the carefully compiled record I invariably keep of the minutes of the passing show – definitely established that the referee was two and a half minutes too soon. And this is making no allowance whatever for lost time.

'How curious that the referee got in a muddle with his minutes on the day the clock goes back. He provided the last "rows" of summer!'

Toffee Transfer

The following March, Tommy was transferred to Everton for £6,000. The supporters were furious. Petitions were written. Demonstrations took place and a boycott of the Blues was even threatened but there was nothing the fans could actually do to stop the transfer to Everton.

Club officials felt Tommy's transfer would soon be forgotten but a careful review of attendance figures for the period do suggest his departure to Division Two side Everton had a detrimental impact on support. During 1927/28 and 1928/29 City were the best-supported side in the entire League. During 1929/30 they attracted the second highest League average (33,339), but the following season – the first without Tommy – they dropped to fifth position with an average of 26,849. This was the Club's lowest average for eight years.

The supporters were not the only ones who were dissatisfied with the transfer. Tommy was too, as his son Alan confirms. 'The day he was told he was leaving he was absolutely stunned. He had no idea he was going to leave and he certainly didn't ask to go. We lived in Park Avenue, Gorton, at the time and

The City team *c.*1920. Tommy Johnson is seated third from right. Other notable stars include Max Woosnam (behind Johnson), goalkeeper Jim Goodchild (wearing cap) and Tommy Browell (seated third from left).

Tommy's Prime Time

Everton 2 Manchester City 6 – 15 September 1928

Goalscorers Johnson (5), Brook

City Team Gray, Ridley, McCloy, Barrass, Cowan, McMullan, Austin, Marshall, Johnson, Tilson, Brook

Attendance 47,871

This was one of City's most remarkable games of all time. The season had started with only one win in four following promotion and everyone had expected more. The gulf between Division Two and Division One, they thought, was not particularly great and players such as Johnson had been expected to tear into opponents just as they had done in the lower division. The fifth game of the season saw fans and officials get their wish. This was the day City not only delivered but, thanks to Tommy Johnson, exceeded expectations.

According to manager Peter Hodge, writing in the Manchester City match programme a few days after the game, 'From the commencement of the season, we have asked for patience. We did not expect that our team would be able to settle down right away but all along we have had confidence in the side and this, we think, we are entitled to say was thoroughly borne out at Everton a week ago.

'The result was sensational, and all the more gratifying in so far as it put our goal record on the right side, but what pleased us most of all was the play of the team. We could not wish for anything better. We were very glad indeed that there were so many of our supporters present, and we have been delighted with the letters of congratulation we have received.

'We only wish we had the space to publish them, and the eulogistic remarks that were made by the officials of the Everton club: they were very laudatory indeed. Suffice to say, however, that everyone was immensely impressed and it could not have been otherwise.'

Naturally, the 6–2 scoreline was deeply satisfying, but was also incredible considering the events surrounding the match.

The City team arrived at Manchester Central Station, the modern day GMEX centre, in plenty of time and ready to catch a train that would get them to Goodison a good 55 minutes before they needed to be there. However, the rail journey commenced nine minutes late and by the time the train arrived in Liverpool it was running at least 30 minutes behind

City 1923/24 (back row from left to right) Pringle, Donaldson, Mitchell, Cookson, Fletcher, (front row) Sharp, Roberts, Johnson, Hamill, Barnes, Murphy. This line up played together only once – away at Aston Villa on 29 August 1923.

schedule. Worse was to follow, as the *Athletic News* explained. 'The players, who had made such necessary preparations as they could for stripping in the saloon, were delayed at the ground. The taxis into which they were hurried to Goodison Park could not get through the crowd and some time was lost through the skip containing the outfit having to be pushed a considerable distance along the approaching road.'

Eventually, City managed to get on the pitch about nine minutes after the game was due to start and, after considerable pressure from the referee and other officials, the match kicked off straight away. Reigning champions Everton took the lead in the first minute while Johnson and his team-mates were still trying to prepare themselves.

Shortly before half time City pulled a goal back and then in the second half the away side were in dominant form. The key man was undoubtedly Johnson, who proved his ability to turn a game, with an incredible performance. He scored five goals, including one penalty, in the 6–2 victory and gained many admirers from Goodison.

According to the City programme for the following match, 'The chairman of the directors of the Everton club was only too ready to acknowledge that it was a long time since they had been so thoroughly beaten, and not only in the result, but in the play.

'It was a great triumph for us and one that was all the more meritorious having regard to the experience we had before the match. As is well known, we arrived late and the start was delayed nine minutes, but the fault was not ours.'

The FA launched an inquiry into City's late arrival and the Blues were ultimately fined, but for Tommy Johnson this was the match that cemented his name. He ended the season scoring 38 goals in 39 League appearances – a club record that still stands today and is unlikely to be broken.

A rare action shot of Tommy (attacker on right) against Newcastle in a City shirt *c.*1928.

he didn't want to go, but he had met Dixie Dean, the great Everton star, a few times and, because of Dixie, he felt that if he had to go somewhere it was better to go where he knew someone.'

Life in Liverpool

After City, Tommy's career developed further. Everton won the Division Two Championship at the end of his first season and followed that with the Division One title 12 months later.

Inevitably, the Goodison fans loved having Johnson in their side. As a technically gifted player Tommy proved to be a difficult man to play against. Regularly he would transform a match through one dynamic moment and while playing alongside Dixie Dean, perhaps Everton's most famous player of all, Tommy became the perfect foil for the great striker.

In 1933 Tommy appeared in his second FA Cup final, ironically against City, and became the first man to wear the number 10 in a final. The FA had decided to use shirt numbers on a trial basis and Everton were numbered 1 to 11 in what became the traditional manner, with sequential numbering running across the pitch, so that City wore numbers 12 to 22 (Eric Brook wore 12 and goalkeeper Len Langford wore 22).

Although Tommy had a relatively quiet game by his standards he did help Everton to a 3–0 victory.

Tommy's Finest Fellow Citizens

Throughout the 1910s and 1920s the City side contained many star players. Although trophy success was limited there were many high points with players of note featuring in every position.

ELI FLETCHER In defence, left-back Eli Fletcher was one of the Club's most consistent players. He joined the Blues in 1911 and remained a first-team player until 1926, during which time he made a total of 326 first-team appearances. In 1919 he became City's captain and was one of the main figures behind Tommy Johnson's development in Manchester. In fact, rumour has it that Fletcher had at one point, in 1919, threatened not to re-sign for the Blues unless they signed Johnson. Always versatile, Fletcher played 11 games in goal for City's Central League side during the 1922/23 season as he tried to regain fitness following cartilage problems.

JIM GOODCHILD In goal during most of this era was Jim 'Naughty Boy' Goodchild. Goodchild was City's rather entertaining goalkeeper who had a reputation for challenging refereeing decisions, hence the slightly humorous adaptation of his surname. In between his debut in 1912 and his last appearance, on New Year's Day 1927, Goodchild was a popular presence in Manchester.

Naturally, as with so many players during the time, the First World War affected his career, but postwar Goodchild was one of City's steadiest performers and in the 1926 FA Cup final he won much praise for his great performance.

The most humorous aspect of his career was his reluctance to be seen on the football field without his goalkeeping cap. According to one story, Goodchild's cap was once knocked off at a corner-kick, causing the goalkeeper to search frantically for his cap rather than the ball. The reason for that was that the large cloth cap hid a head that was 'as bald as a billiard ball'. The only other time Goodchild was known to be seen at Hyde Road without his cap was when the King visited in 1920, when it was a case of either appearing unpatriotic or revealing the secret.

HORACE BARNES One player from this period whose name will forever be linked with that of Johnson is forward Horace Barnes. Barnes, like Johnson, scored in Maine Road's opening match in August 1923 but, unlike Johnson, Barnes arrived in Manchester after a major transfer – from Derby County. The sum – £2,500 in 1914 – made it the record transfer fee of the period and proved both the player's quality and City's determination to bring quality to Manchester.

According to one story passed down through the generations, Barnes once hit a 35-yard (32m) free kick with such force that the ball broke both wrists of the opposition goalkeeper when he tried to punch it clear. Barnes was recognised as having one of the most powerful shots in the game at the time.

Barnes scored 125 goals in 235 first-team appearances – a similar ratio to that of another star striker from this period: Tommy Browell.

TOMMY BROWELL Browell, who joined the Blues from Everton in 1913, scored 139 goals in 247 games for City.

During the 1920/21 season, when the Blues finished as runners-up to Burnley in Division One, Browell became City's record scorer in a season when he netted 31 goals in 42 games. Only two men have surpassed this figure – Francis Lee with 33 in 1972 and Tommy Johnson with 38 in 1929.

Browell moved to Blackpool in 1926 and, according to his granddaughter, in later life he worked for the local bus company in the seaside town. It is known that many City fans would travel up and down the Blackpool prom trying to get a ride on Browell's bus. To them it was the highlight of their Blackpool break. Sadly he passed away in October 1955, two weeks before his 63rd birthday.

Both Horace Barnes and Tommy Browell had streets named after them as part of a 1977 Moss Side development.

FRANK ROBERTS Towards the end of Browell's City career, a former Bolton star was being groomed as his replacement. Frank Roberts arrived in Manchester for £3,400 in 1922 and left the Blues in 1929 after 130 goals in 237 appearances. By that time he had also been capped four times by England.

Another great goalscorer, Roberts was the leading City striker for three seasons and, like his colleagues Browell and Johnson, he managed to score five goals in a first-team fixture. Roberts' goals came in City's 11–4 victory over Crystal Palace in the fifth round of the 1926 FA Cup; Browell got his five against Burnley in October 1925 and Johnson in a famous match against Everton in September 1928. Understandably, Roberts was viewed as one of football's major stars at the time.

MAX WOOSNAM Max Woosnam was one of the most famous sportsmen of his generation, renowned for his all-round sporting prowess. At Cambridge University he excelled at football, cricket, golf and tennis. He found success as a doubles champion at Wimbledon and as a member of the Davis Cup team. He was also a tennis Olympic gold medallist.

In terms of football ability, Woosnam was an English amateur international, and he also captained the full England side in March 1922. He was a dedicated player and an archetypal English gentleman. He made 93 appearances for the Blues during a six-year career at the Club between 1919 and 1925 and, because of his status within the game, was made captain for the opening match at Maine Road.

Tommy Johnson, third player from right, waits in line to meet king George V at Hyde Road. Note that goalkeeper Jim Goodchild had removed his cap especially for the occasion.

After a total of 159 appearances and 64 goals, Tommy eventually crossed Stanley Park and joined Everton's great rivals Liverpool in February 1934. At Anfield he managed a total of 37 League appearances with his last ever game being a 3–1 defeat at Preston in April 1936. His last goal in League football had come several months earlier when his 74th-minute strike against Grimsby helped the Merseysiders to a 7–2 rout in September 1935.

Tommy the City Fan

After Liverpool, Tommy was made player-manager of Darwen and in the late 1940s he became licensee of a pub in the Gorton area of Manchester. Throughout his post-playing days he was a regular at Maine Road and during the highly successful Mercer-Allison years he, together with his former playing colleague Dixie Dean, became a very enthusiastic follower of Joe Mercer's side. According to his son Alan, Tommy was a dedicated City fan. 'At Everton he had a lot of success – he won more trophies than he had in Manchester – but City remained his club. In fact, after he'd left City he kept coming back to Maine Road and sometimes paid to stand on the Kippax side of the ground. He was often recognised and was usually congratulated simply for being "Tosh" Johnson!'

So why was Tommy Johnson so important to the history of Manchester City? Put simply, Tommy was a true fans' favourite, a player with the ability to excite and entertain while also keeping his feet firmly on the ground. Clearly his goalscoring exploits alone make him one of City's most important players but when his all-round contribution and entertainment value is considered, Tommy is without doubt a true Blue legend. 'It was a two-way relationship with the supporters, really,' says Alan, his son. 'They enjoyed his style of play and his determination but he also recognised their loyalty and commitment.'

Alan remembers his father being a familiar presence in the Gorton area. 'My father was proud of being an ordinary bloke. The players didn't get paid large wages and life at times was tough, and I think most of his neighbours and friends understood that he really wasn't any different from them. After he'd left City and joined Everton he would sometimes bring Dixie Dean to Gorton and the two of them would sit in the Plough or one of the other pubs chatting away. In fact, Dixie became as well known in the pubs of Gorton as my dad was!'

In 1977, four years after his death, a walk close to Maine Road was named in Tommy's honour. It was a fitting tribute to a man whose heart never wandered far from City.

Alan Johnson

son of Tommy, receiving the Hall of Fame award in January 2004.

' I don't know what to say. I know he'd be very proud. I'm proud and I know he was delighted to play with so many great footballers. When he won the record for most goals in a season, he never said it was his record because he felt it belonged to the entire team. Whenever they talked about it he always said that it was shared between 25 blokes. He said, "They all helped me to score, I only finished it." I'm so pleased with this recognition for him. Thank you. '

Tony Book

Tony Book's time as captain of Manchester City dovetailed with the Club's most glorious period of all.

He led the Blues to the League Championship, FA Cup, League Cup and European Cup Winners' Cup and became the first Blue since Bert Trautmann in 1956 to win the coveted Football Writers' Association Footballer of the Year award.

Tony Book
1966–1971 AWARD

Building a Career

Born in Bath in 1935, Tony remembers that football had always been important to him as a boy, 'My dad was in the Army, serving in India, and I moved out there with him when I was three. I stayed there until I was 11 and that's really where I learned the game, a lot of the time in bare feet. When I came back to England I played at school and with both Bath Boys and Somerset Boys as an inside forward. It was only in the Army that I became a full back. I was in the Royal Army Medical Corps and, like everything else in the military, you didn't get much of a choice. I was just told, "That's your position; just get on with it!".' The Army team included a League player called Frank Blunstone, who made 317 appearances for Chelsea. Blunstone organised a trial for Tony at Stamford Bridge but the opportunity to sign professional forms never materialised. 'When I was demobbed I got a letter from Ted Drake [the Chelsea manager], saying he didn't think I would be good enough but did say I might make the grade lower down the leagues!'

Following this rebuttal, Tony started playing amateur football in the West Country with a team from Peasedown and then with Frome Town. At Frome, Tony was paid as a part-timer and became involved in the building trade to help make his living, but his footballing career struggled to develop. 'We got knocked out of one of the preliminary rounds of the FA Cup and the players each got a letter saying the finances were bad and the club was preparing to let us go.'

Tony showed the letter to a fellow builder who happened to be a player with Bath City. One thing led to another and before Tony had a chance to think, he had become a Bath City player. He was to stay there for the following 11 years. During that period Tony was to meet Malcolm Allison. 'He breezed into the club to turn it upside down and set course for the Southern League title, plus a fine run in the FA Cup. When Malcolm left he did not forget me. One day a telegram arrived on the building site where I was working, laying bricks. It was from Malcolm asking me to leave for Canada immediately to team up with him in Toronto. We had a fantastic season with Toronto City, winning both the League and Cup. Then Malcolm returned to England and I went back to Bath.'

Strong Foundations

It wasn't long before Malcolm, installed as the manager of Plymouth, signed Tony for his new side. 'I was nearly 30 at the time and Malcolm told me to doctor my birth certificate so I could make the move! I had two great seasons with Argyle before Malcolm left. Soon after, he cropped up at Manchester City, and it wasn't long before I was packing my bags to join him. Even though I was a couple of months off my 32nd birthday, I had no hesitation in accepting his offer.'

Tony, supported here by Mike Doyle, was never afraid of competing for every ball.

Player Career Statistics
Appearances

TONY BOOK

Position
Defender 1966–73

Typical Height and Weight
1.78m (5ft 10½in)
73kg (11st 7lb)

Born
Bath, 4 September 1935

League Debut
Southampton (away)
20 August 1966

	LEAGUE		FA CUP		FL CUP		EUROPE		TOTAL	
	App	Gls	App	Gls	App	Gls	App	Gls	App	Gls
1966/67	41	0	6	0	2	0	-	-	49	0
1967/68	42	1	4	0	4	1	-	-	50	2
1968/69	15	0	6	0	0	0	0	0	21	0
1969/70	38	0	2	0	7	0	9	0	56	0
1970/71	33 (1)	2	3	0	1	0	7	0	44 (1)	2
1971/72	40	1	2	0	2	0	-	-	44	1
1972/73	29 (1)	0	5	0	2	0	1	0	37 (1)	0
1973/74	4	0	0	0	1	0	-	-	5	0
TOTAL	242 (2)	4	28	0	19	1	17	0	306 (2)	5

Tony's age did cause some concern, particularly for manager Joe Mercer, but Allison was quick to point out that Mercer had been a similar age when he had embarked on his highly successful spell as Arsenal's captain.

Tony made his City debut at the start of the 1966/67 season and he missed only one League game, through injury, during the following two seasons. His first season saw the Blues finish 15th and reach the sixth round of the FA Cup, which, for a recently promoted side, was a good record. 'We faced Leeds in the sixth round at Elland Road,' remembers Tony, 'and we hit them with everything we had. But Leeds grabbed a disputed goal and we lost.' That game brought a lot of attention City's way and it also brought them a great deal of confidence.

The former bricklayer was a major factor in the side's development and had already proved that Malcolm Allison was right to sign him. Joe Mercer was also delighted with Tony's performances. As he commented, 'I didn't mind him playing well and having plenty of skill, but what made me green with envy was his speed. I mean, it's not right for the over-thirties to be skinning the youngsters. It's meant to be a young man's game! We used to hear these First Division coaches shouting from the bench – "Take the old man on!" No chance! He was a great athlete.'

Captain Book

For the start of 1967/68 Tony was given the captaincy. 'We didn't start the season too well,' he admits, 'but we then won five games on the run,

'I had two great seasons with Argyle before Malcolm left. Soon after, he cropped up at Manchester City, and it wasn't long before I was packing my bags to join him.'

'I remember being carried off the pitch shoulder high at the end, but

my biggest memory has to be the large number of fans in the streets celebrating... It was a marvellous, wonderful night.'

which gave us a real boost. Then we had a difficult time over Christmas and New Year. Some people thought we might be losing our way, but by the time of the return game with United we'd got back to winning ways and were right up there with the leaders again.'

The game Tony is referring to is City's 3–1 defeat of United in March 1968. It was a crucial victory and left the Blues in second place, behind Leeds and ahead of United, with all three sides on 45 points and only nine games remaining. City, surprisingly, lost their next match, to Leicester, but they continued to be in with a shout until, on the final day of the season, they defeated Newcastle 4–3 in an amazing match to secure the Championship by two clear points from United.

For Tony, this was a marvellous achievement. 'I couldn't believe it as just two years earlier I'd been

playing part-time and was a bricklayer. I think in all my years in football the victory at Newcastle has to be my finest moment. I remember being carried off the pitch shoulder high at the end, but my biggest memory has to be the large number of fans in the streets celebrating. The number of cars and coaches coming back from Newcastle was tremendous and Malcolm at one point took to the street dancing! It was a marvellous, wonderful night.'

National Recognition

A tour of the States followed but this was beset with problems, especially for Tony, who suffered damage to his Achilles tendon. It looked as if his career was over, and he did miss the opening 25 League games, but in January 1969 he returned to action. It had been a difficult time, though. 'It was the low point of my playing career. We tried everything to get

MCFC statistics

	1966/67	1967/68	1968/69	1969/70	1970/71	Honours
League Position	15	Champs	13	10	11	Charity Shield 1968;
FA Cup Round Reached	6	4	Winners	4	5	League Championship 1968; FA Cup 1969;
League Cup Round Reached	3	4	3	Winners	2	League Cup 1970; European Cup Winners' Cup 1970
European Cup Round Reached	-	-	1	-	-	
ECWC Cup Round Reached	-	-	-	Winners	Semi-final	
Average Attendance	31,209	37,223	33,750	33,930	31,041	

it right. I had it in plaster; had cortisone injections; cortisone tablets; even deep ray treatment. If I had been younger they would have operated but because of my age the attitude was, wait and see what happens. I could have been out to grass.'

Tony's return to action captured the imagination of the public and the media, especially as he had guided the Blues to Wembley glory in the FA Cup. In fact a few days before the final Tony was voted joint Footballer of the Year, with Dave Mackay of Derby County, by the Football Writers' Association. Tony said at the time, 'To receive an award that my boss, Joe Mercer, and Stanley Matthews, Tom Finney, Bert Trautmann, and men of their calibre were given is truly astonishing. It is an honour for which the greatest credit goes to Joe Mercer, Malcolm Allison, and the team. I've had some wonderful help on the way.'

In recent years Tony has expressed the view that the judges had based the award on his performances over the Championship season as well as the FA Cup-winning season. This may well be true but his fightback following injury and his success on the field once he had returned were remarkable achievements in their own right. He may have deserved the award during the Championship season, but he certainly deserved it in 1969 as well.

European Adventures

Most players consider what success means to them in the days following a major triumph and Tony was no different. 'After each of our successes I told myself, "I'll never have to go back to bricklaying now." I just couldn't believe it. It was just like a dream and I didn't want to wake up. I just wanted it to go on. Success was the great thing about it and it kept me going.'

Further success came in 1970 when City won the League Cup by beating West Bromwich Albion and the European Cup Winners' Cup with a victory over Polish side Gornik. The first tie in the European Cup Winners' Cup saw the Blues win 6–3 on aggregate against Bilbao. Tony recalls, 'The newspapers had said that I'd done well but all this European football

Tony Book and Joe Corrigan take to the field for the second half of the Maine Road 1–0 victory over Ipswich, 28th February 1970.

was new to me. I'd never played in Europe before so it was a fresh challenge, and I enjoyed it.'

The 1970/71 season saw City progress in the European Cup Winners' Cup again but Tony received an injury at Derby and missed two important quarter-final games with old foes Gornik. The Blues still progressed but then came a tough tie with Chelsea. 'We fought hard in both games but we lost by a single goal both times,' says Tony.

Tony continued to play for the Blues until 1973, making his last League appearance on 29th September against Burnley. As his career neared its end he stepped down as captain, to be replaced by Colin Bell, but continued to be a key force. He certainly gave his all for the Club. In 1972 articles

Tony's Prime Time

Manchester United 1 Manchester City 3. Football League Division One – 27 March 1968

Goalscorers Bell, Heslop, Lee

City Team Mulhearn, Book, Pardoe, Doyle, Heslop, Oakes, Lee, Bell (Connor), Summerbee, Young, Coleman

Attendance 63,004

Tony Book's time at City saw many tremendous victories, but this match was vitally important as it set City up for the League Championship, and it was a sign that the balance of power in Manchester was shifting in the Blue's favour.

Under Mercer and Allison City had been reborn but everybody associated with the Club knew that the football world would only sit up and take notice once the Blues had started to achieve success in the Manchester derby. This Old Trafford match became vital, especially as United were reigning League champions and favourites to lift the title again. Sadly, the opening moments did not go City's way and Tony Book was involved. 'An unforgivable error on my part let in George Best early on with a mistimed backpass,' admits Tony. 'I knew I should have stopped him and what's more I knew that had I been alert I could have stopped him. It didn't need the groans of our fans to make me aware of what a zero rating I was getting because this was one meeting where neither side could afford slip-ups.'

Usually in these situations at Old Trafford, City would collapse and struggle to find a way back into the match and, for a while, the Blues were a little hesitant. Tony's colleagues helped him get his mind back on the proceedings. 'As captain my team-mates looked to me for example but on this occasion it was their attitude, their example, which promptly put behind me any thoughts of getting depressed about the incident.'

As Tony started to play a true captain's role again, City began to get the upper hand. Colin Bell began to control midfield; Mike Doyle won several important tackles; and gradually the Blues started to pressurise the Reds. After about 15 minutes Bell started a right-wing move and then ran several yards to reach the final pass and blast the equaliser past United goalkeeper Alex Stepney.

Tony rallied his side as the Blues now felt this could be their night. Further City attacks followed and then a Tony Coleman free-kick was curled into the box. Centre half George Heslop, who had never scored a League goal for the Blues, rose above all the United defenders to send a firm downward header past a groping Stepney and into the net.

United did try to get back on level terms, with Denis Law coming close at one point, but Tony had marshalled the defence well and there was no way United were going to find a way back into the match. In fact the Reds started to become ill-disciplined and when Colin Bell surged forward late in the match for what clearly would have been City's third goal, the United left back Francis Burns snaked out a leg and sent Bell crashing to the ground. Bell was stretchered off and would miss the next four games.

The Blues were awarded a penalty. According to the *Manchester Evening News* reporter Peter Gardner, 'It was a penalty all the way and Francis Lee duly made the final score 3–1. But it was a penalty City did not need. They had not only beaten United that night... they had murdered them.'

Tony's role as captain had been to ensure the Blues did not buckle and he felt delighted with the result, even if he still continued to blame himself for the opening-minute goal. 'By the finish City had played some great stuff and turned disaster into delight. That derby was a thrill to play in, despite my early reverse, and I rate it as one of the best games of football I have ever played in. In the last five or ten minutes we were just passing the ball about for fun. I remember even I kept it for something like eight passes in the corner.

April 1970 – Tony Book returns from Vienna with the European Cup Winners' Cup – the last major success of the Mercer-Allison years.

After such a great result, I really thought, and perhaps for the first time, that we had a real chance of winning the League.'

Another delighted man was Malcolm Allison, who had waged war on United since arriving in the city. He had vowed he would bring supporters hope and years later he looked back on this night with much affection. 'There was so much happiness among the City fans that evening. Years of humiliation had been, if not wiped away, eased. That night at Old Trafford the supporters of Manchester City walked out of the wilderness.'

Within two months the Blues had won the League Championship.

Tony's Finest Fellow Citizens

The late 1960s and early 1970s saw the Blues win the League Championship, the FA Cup, the League Cup and the European Cup Winners' Cup with a side that was packed with truly great players.

TONY COLEMAN Although winger Tony Coleman had a bit of a reputation as a wild character – Malcolm Allison described his signing as 'like the nightmare of a delirious probation officer' – he was a very popular player. Liverpool-born Coleman joined the Blues in March 1967 and was one of City's forwards during the 1967/68 Championship season and the 1969 FA Cup final. He joined Sheffield Wednesday in October 1969 after making 101 appearances for City.

GLYN PARDOE Glyn Pardoe has been one of City's most popular figures ever since he made his debut in 1962 at the age of 15 years and 314 days. Pardoe played for the Club in every position except goalkeeper and centre half and featured in most of the significant triumphs of the Mercer-Allison period. His greatest

moment came in the 1970 League Cup final, when he scored the winning goal. He did also suffer from serious injury – particularly in the Manchester derby of December 1970 when a devastating leg injury almost resulted in him losing his life. After more than 300 League appearances, Pardoe retired in 1976 and then embarked on a coaching career for the Blues. It was another excellent role for the Cheshire-born player and he is often credited with being one of the key influences behind the 1986 FA Youth Cup success. During 2005 Pardoe has been a regular at City games as summariser for BBC GMR.

NEIL YOUNG Inside-left Neil Young was the only goalscorer of the 1969 FA Cup final, opening scorer of the 1970 European Cup Winners' Cup final and highest scorer in the 1967/68 Championship season. Often

City pose in the red and black kit chosen by Malcolm Allison in 1969. From left to right (back row): George Heslop, Mike Doyle, Alan Oakes, Harry Dowd, Arthur Mann, Glyn Pardoe, Tommy Booth, Tony Coleman, (front row) David Connor, Bobby Owen, Colin Bell, Tony Book, Francis Lee, Mike Summerbee, Neil Young.

Book, chaired off the field by Pardoe, Booth, Lee, Doyle, Dowd and Bell.

overshadowed by the media interest in the triumvirate of Bell-Lee-Summerbee, Young was one of City's most consistent goalscorers during the Mercer-Allison period. A product of City's youth development system, Young signed professional forms in 1961, making his debut the following November. In 1972, after more than 400 appearances, he was sold to Preston for £48,000.

A period of conflict between the player and City followed in later years, before former team-mate Francis Lee became Chairman during 1993/94. Young was then welcomed back to Maine Road and City supported him with various testimonial events.

His return to the fold was thoroughly welcomed as many fans remembered manager Joe Mercer's comments about Young made in 1969: 'He has got more talent than anybody else in the club. Six foot tall, with a devastating left foot. His right foot works too.'

actually appeared suggesting he intended to go on until he was 50. Clearly, that was never likely but there was a spell when City fans and the media alike found it hard to accept that the player could ever retire. Tony told Peter Gardner of the *Manchester Evening News*, 'I feel in a frame of mind that has me thinking I can go on for another seven years at least! However, there is one thing I shall never do... stand in the way of youth. If I feel I just can't go on any longer then I shall pack up football. It will be a big wrench, but I will have no regrets.'

Moving into Management

The 1973/74 season saw Tony move into coaching and become new manager Ron Saunders' assistant. But his life was to take another unexpected turn when Saunders was dismissed in April despite taking the Blues to the League Cup final. Tony was asked to replace him and was put in charge for the final month of the season. He was manager for the infamous final match of the season when Denis Law netted a memorable winner against United at Old Trafford. City ended that campaign 14th and the following one in 8th place.

Tony's team once again proved to be kings of Manchester in 1975/76 when they annihilated United 4–0 in the fourth round of the League Cup. It was a night more famous for a devastating injury to Colin Bell. Tony had to change things around in the following weeks and Tommy Booth and Ged Keegan had spells in the number eight shirt. Life was tough without Bell.

'We were constantly looking for Colin's replacement,' explains Tony, 'trying all sorts of things, but of course we never found the answer.'

Without Colin, Tony's side still won the League Cup in 1976 and the following season were runners-up to Liverpool in the League. 'With Colin in the side we would have won the League in '77,' maintains Tony. 'We came within a game of winning the League. Even though there were a few of these disappointments, it was still a great time for us. We had replaced the old favourites and I took City into Europe three times running, so there wasn't too much wrong.'

Difficult Days

Chairman Peter Swales brought Malcolm Allison back as a 'coaching overlord' in 1979 and although Tony was still officially the team manager Allison was given the authority to control the destiny of the Blues on the pitch. It became a difficult time for Tony and in 1980, as it became clear the plan was failing, the two men were dismissed.

In the years that followed Tony returned to Maine Road to help a succession of managers and, on numerous occasions, he found himself fulfilling the role of caretaker manager. He later had a spell scouting for Sunderland. Tony is now retired but in recent years he has been a frequent and welcome visitor to Manchester City Supporters' Club branches and is a regular attender at City matches. He lives in Greater Manchester.

Tony's playing career brought him phenomenal success at a time of his life when many would have given up all prospect of playing League football. In addition to his playing success, his managerial record is on a par with some of Maine Road's best managers and he remains one of the most important figures in Manchester City's history. He was a tremendous player, a great manager, an inspirational coach and a loyal club servant.

Tony Book
collecting the Hall of Fame award in January 2004.

' What an honour this is, because I played in maybe the greatest side Manchester City have ever had. Naturally, I've got to thank one gentleman in the audience tonight; he gave me the chance at 32 years of age – Malcolm Allison. I'm delighted to see him tonight along with his daughter Dawn, who I haven't seen for many a year. It's lovely to see you both here. As I said, I played in a great side and most of them are here tonight, and I thank them, and for backing me as skipper. I was lucky enough to take over from Johnny Crossan. Last, I'd like to say a big thank you to my family. I wasn't there for 30 odd years but you've always been there for me. I appreciate that. '

Eric Brook

Eric Brook was a tremendous and highly popular goalscorer with City and, along with his great friend Fred Tilson, he was a key presence in City's attack throughout the Club's wonderful FA Cup runs during the 1930s. An unorthodox outside left, Eric was loved by supporters throughout his time in Manchester, particularly those who stood on the Popular Side at Maine Road. They always felt he could deliver something out of the ordinary, and he often did.

Eric Brook
1928–1935 AWARD

Thursday's Child

Eric was born in Mexborough, about 8km (5 miles) from Rotherham in South Yorkshire, in 1907. Coal mining, together with the steel industry, provided most locals with employment and it was inevitable that Eric would start to work in the mines. At the same time his interest in sport developed throughout his early life and he joined local teams both as a cricketer and as a footballer, including the entertainingly named Mexborough Thursday. While playing for Thursday, Eric was spotted by scouts from Barnsley and, at the age of 18, he joined the Division Two side. Almost immediately other clubs started to notice the 1.65m (5ft 6in) dynamo and with City playing in the same division – the Blues had been relegated in 1926 – Eric's abilities were on view for Club officials.

Joining City

After two years with Barnsley, Eric joined City on 16 March 1928 and made his debut the following day against Grimsby Town. His first goal for the Club came two weeks later as the Blues defeated Clapton Orient 5–3 and by the end of the season he had made 12 appearances and scored twice as the Blues won the Division Two Championship.

Eric's arrival at City brought a lot of attention his way as his transfer had actually been part of a double purchase from Barnsley, with his left-wing partner Fred Tilson also joining City for a combined fee of £6,000. It was never made public as to which, if either, player was valued the more highly of the two but initially it was Eric who was given most opportunity at Maine Road. During 1928/29 Eric was the Club's only ever-present as City finished eighth in their first season back in Division One.

From a national perspective, Eric started to be talked about as a player of true quality. He was viewed as an unorthodox outside left, known for roaming around the attack looking for opportunities rather than positioning himself close to the touchline as more traditional outside lefts would. Through such roaming, Eric would often stun the opposition by appearing in the centre-forward position ready to score. As a relatively small player Eric seemed to free himself of opponents at will and was known as a truly energetic individual.

After City's 3–1 victory in the Manchester derby of February 1931, respected journalist Ivan Sharpe was firmly of the opinion that outside forwards, in particular Eric, were the most valuable men in football. Eric scored the opening goal, had another disallowed and set up both of City's other goals. Sharpe ended one section of his match report, in which he eulogised about Eric, by saying, 'In future, wing men are going to be "Bank of England" men – high-priced players in transfer transactions.' City fans already knew the value of Eric and, following the controversial transfer of favourite Tommy Johnson to Everton in 1930, it was clear the board of Manchester City would not risk a further high-profile departure. Eric's place in City's future was assured, as long as he continued to win matches and the headlines.

England Calling

As Eric's reputation grew it became inevitable that he would be selected for representative honours. In 1929 he appeared for the Football League against the Scottish League and on 19 October 1929 he made his England debut in the 3–0 victory over Ireland in Belfast. It wasn't a particularly impressive

'The tough little Brook had a head of iron, and Ceresoli never saw the ball shoot off the City winger's blond head.'

performance and Eric had to wait until 20 May 1933 for his next international match when England defeated Switzerland 4–0 in Berne. Although he didn't get on the scoresheet, Eric did create a more permanent role for himself and he played in the following ten internationals, scoring seven goals.

Eric's first England goal came in the 3–0 defeat of Ireland in Belfast on 14 October 1933 but his most memorable international game of this sequence was the infamous 'Battle of Highbury' against Italy in November 1934. The match entered history as seven of the eleven players selected came from Arsenal. The match was also perhaps the most controversial and contentious game of the decade. The Italians were determined to win at all costs – the Italian dictator Mussolini saw this match as an opportunity to spread a political message and he was determined his nation would win. Eric and the other England men had different ideas.

Stanley Matthews, playing for England that day, gave his view of the opening minutes and of Eric's performance several years later. 'The bombastic Mussolini promised his footballers handsome bonuses if England were beaten. The match blew up after England made a flying start. In the first minute we were awarded a penalty. Eric Brook, usually a deadly shot, took the kick, which looked a certain winner to me, but I had not bargained for the agility of Ceresoli, the Italian goalkeeper, who made the daring young man on the flying trapeze look like an old man with rheumatism with the ease with which he dived across the goal to stop Eric's pile-driver.

'Ten minutes later Brook more than made up for this miss, heading in my spinning centre after I had run around Allemandi, Italy's left back. The tough little Brook had a head of iron, and Ceresoli never saw the ball shoot off the City winger's blond head.'

Player Career Statistics
Appearances

ERIC BROOK

Position
Outside left 1928–39

Typical Height and Weight
1.68m (5ft 6in)
79kg (12st 6lb)

Born
Mexborough, 27 November 1907

Deceased
Manchester, 29 March 1965

League Debut
Grimsby Town (home)
17 March 1928

	LEAGUE		FA CUP		TOTAL	
	App	Gls	App	Gls	App	Gls
1927/28	12	2	0	0	12	2
1928/29	42	14	1	0	43	14
1929/30	40	16	5	1	45	17
1930/31	42	16	1	0	43	16
1931/32	42	10	5	3	47	13
1932/33	42	15	7	6	49	21
1933/34	38	8	8	3	46	11
1934/35	40	17	1	0	41	17
1935/36	40	13	3	3	43	16
1936/37	42	20	4	2	46	22
1937/38	36	16	4	1	40	17
1938/39	34	11	2	0	36	11
TOTAL	450	158	41	19	491	177

WILLS'S CIGARETTES

E. F. BROOK (MANCHESTER CITY)

NOTE: The 1939/40 League campaign was abandoned, then expunged from records due to the Second World War. Eric Brook made three appearances and scored one goal during these games.

[Brook] 'left Ceresoli dumb-founded,

and he did not have a chance against the best free kick I have ever seen. The Italians went crazy.'

Pure Perfection

Shortly afterwards England were awarded a free kick, which Eric was determined to take. He grabbed the ball, placed it, took a few steps back then fired it goalwards. Matthews described how Brook 'left Ceresoli dumb-founded, and he did not have a chance against the best free kick I have ever seen. The Italians went crazy. It was then that Hapgood's nose was broken – the result of a blow from the elbow of one of Italy's forwards. Our boys were rattled. It was fortunate for England that Brook and Wilf Copping, the Arsenal left half, were playing. Eric and Wilf enjoyed themselves that day as never before and after they themselves had been handled roughly. Brook, with his shoulder strapped, gave the Italians something to think about – not by foul

tactics but by real honest to goodness English shoulder charging. They did their duty that day for England, and if ever it could be said two men won a match, it was Copping and Brook on this famous occasion.'

For Eric to have scored twice that day within the opening 11 minutes, especially after the opening minute penalty save (the first England penalty to be saved in the opening minute) and considering the circumstances, says a great deal about his attitude and spirit. After the match Eric, together with captain Hapgood, was sent to hospital for further treatment for his injuries.

Journalist Ivan Sharpe believed Eric was by far the star of this match and was particularly impressed with the free kick. 'A free kick from 20 yards [18m] which shook the premises, and the cameras showed the scorer to be 20 inches [51cm] off the ground as the ball entered the net.'

Bubbly Brook

Sharpe was always a fan. Years later, looking back on football in the 1930s, Sharpe claimed, 'Brook had enthusiasm so abounding that he was ready to play in any position, any time, and, not surprisingly, broke records for a quick return to first class football after an appendix operation. Brook had a spectacular way of leaping off his feet after shooting at goal.'

In total Eric made 18 international appearances and scored 10 goals. He also appeared in one wartime international, seven games for an FA XI, five international trial games and seven inter-League games.

FA Cup Glory

In club football Eric was always a star, particularly during City's great cup runs of the 1930s. The Blues were unlucky to lose the 1932 semi-final against a strong Arsenal side who scored the only goal in the

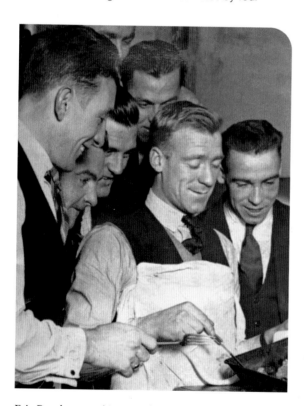

Eric Brook proves his versatility with a pre-training breakfast treat.

Eric Brook (fifth from right) watches on as the Duke of York is introduced to Matt Busby by captain Sam Cowan prior to the 1933 FA Cup final. The City side that day was Langford, Cann, Dale, Busby, Cowan, Bray, Toseland, Marshall, Herd, McMullan and Brook.

final minute of the match; then in 1933 they were defeated in the final by Everton; and in 1934, goals from Eric's former Barnsley team-mate, Fred Tilson, gave City a 2–1 victory over Portsmouth in the final.

Eric had played his part throughout each of those cup runs with his most memorable goal coming in the sixth round tie with Stoke in 1934. He also set up Tilson for City's first in the final.

At the whistle to signal the end of the final, Eric stood on the left wing beaming. He was delighted with the achievement and, as the team prepared to climb the steps to collect the Cup, Eric made sure he would be second in the queue, immediately behind captain Sam Cowan, for the presentation. He stood proudly watching as Cowan received the Cup from the king, George V.

Eric's Prime Time

Manchester City 1 Stoke City 0. FA Cup sixth round – 3 March 1934

Goalscorer Brook

City Team Swift, Barnett, Dale, Busby, Cowan, Bray, Toseland, Marshall, Tilson, Herd, Brook

Attendance 84,569

This game has entered the record books as attracting not only Maine Road's record crowd but also the largest-ever crowd in the provinces, a record that remains to this day. Everybody seemed to want to see this match and, as a result, the Maine Road terracing was uncomfortably packed.

The visitors were first to excite the crowd, with a youthful Stanley Matthews having several opportunities. The *Manchester Guardian* believed that the tension of the day affected him. 'Another chance fell to Matthews and, after Swift had beaten away the ball, it rolled the full width of the goal, not two feet [60cm] from the line, with no one able to master this excitement sufficiently to be able to kick it one way or the other.'

Eric Brook, always a man to thrive on the big game atmosphere, seemed rather calm and composed. Playing out on the left he could witness at first hand the problems of crushing being experienced by the large crowd, some of whom had now positioned themselves virtually on the touchline. Although it's difficult to prove, it seems his generally good rapport with the fans made him determined to give them something to celebrate. He received a wide pass out on the Kippax wing and raced for the Platt Lane corner flag. He then made a speculative lob from the wing. The Stoke goalkeeper Roy John appeared to have it covered and jumped up but just as he went to take the ball it seemed to change direction in mid-flight. It curled past the goalkeeper and into the goal.

In the days that followed the media were uncertain as to whether Eric's shot had been intentional or not but supporter Fran Parker was convinced it was carefully planned by the outside left. A big fan of Eric's, Fran remembers the day and the player well. 'He was a great player. He played for England and was one of our biggest stars. He knew what he was doing. From where I sat on the edge of the pitch it was as clear as day that he had shot at goal. He may have been on the touchline himself, but goalscorers like that look for openings all the time. Most players probably wouldn't have been able to score it, but Brooky was different.'

Other fans talked about Eric's planning in other games and, even if the media were uncertain, the supporters seemed convinced it was Eric's expertise that had made the goal.

MCFC statistics

	1928/29	1929/30	1930/31	1931/32	1932/33	1933/34	1934/35	Honours
League Position	8	3	8	14	16	5	4	FA Cup finalists 1933; FA Cup 1934
FA Cup Round Reached	3	5	3	Semi-final	Final	Winners	3	
Average Attendance	31,716	33,339	26,849	24,173	24,254	30,058	34,824	

One Eric fan who missed the goal was Harry Bramble. 'We had a business by then and my father went to the match and I had to look after the business. It was a real shame because Brooky was my hero. He was such a major star that they used to say he would put ten or even twenty thousand on the gate at away matches. He always seemed to have the ball, and if the opposition had it he'd rush and take it off them. It was unknown at the time for a forward to take the ball off opponents. Most forwards waited for it to be passed to them.'

After Eric's wonder goal the game remained very close right up to the final whistle, but the Blues won through and Eric was once again City's great hero.

The Blues entered the FA Cup semi-final for the third consecutive season.

Stoke had obviously played their part in the encounter although dedicated City fan Fran Parker felt there had only ever been one side in the game. 'None of the Stoke players could play! Not even Matthews. City were too good for them and Brooky was the outright star.'

The day belonged to Eric and just a few weeks later he would help City to win the FA Cup with victory over Portsmouth, but it was this meeting with Stoke that really demonstrated what a wonderful, popular player Eric was. Eric was a true hero in a team packed with stars.

Eric's amazing shot was captured by the Daily Dispatch. Incredibly Eric (player close to the touchline, immediately left of the 'keeper) scored from the edge of the pitch. Note the large number of spectators crowded on the touchline.

THE WAY TO WEMBLEY
BROOK'S AMAZING SHOT BEAT STOKE

Crazy Golf

From a personal point of view Eric loved this period of his life. Naturally he enjoyed City's success but he also enjoyed the team spirit prevalent at the Club. There was a large amount of humour and good-natured ribbing at the Club and, according to some of the other players, Eric was often at the centre of the frivolity. Talking of the preparations for the 1934 FA Cup success, the goalkeeper Frank Swift said, 'Some of the lads, particularly Cowan and Brook, were "crazy". Frequently, during the golf matches

which were played as part of our training, Sammy and Eric used to play "Cowboys and Indians" in the bunkers. Then there was a golf match between Cowan and Brook, over which it is best to draw a veil. Never before, or since, have I seen the rule book so often, and so obviously, disregarded. I wonder if the loser ever realised that the shot which won the match was actually a beautifully directed throw out of a bunker?

'Little Eric Brook was perhaps one of the most amazing characters I have ever played with. There

Eric's Finest Fellow Citizens

Throughout the period 1928–1935, as City developed into a successful side, the Blues possessed many star players.

JACKIE BRAY Wing-half Jackie Bray made 280 League and Cup appearances while with the Blues and also appeared six times for England. He joined City for a fee of £1,000 in October 1929 from Manchester Central and made his debut the following February in a Manchester derby match. Bray played in all of City's major successes during his career, including two FA Cup finals and the League Championship success of 1937. He made 177 wartime appearances for the Club and when League football resumed in 1946 he was still a useful squad member, although he never actually made a first-team postwar appearance. He eventually moved to Watford as manager in 1947.

JIMMY MCMULLAN Another tremendous captain, left-half Jimmy McMullan was also a great Scottish international player. He arrived at City in February 1926 from Partick Thistle after already having attained a Scottish Cup winners' medal. Arguably the greatest

Scottish half back, he captained Scotland to a famous 5–1 victory over England at Wembley. That victory, in March 1928, was one of Scotland's greatest achievements, and a remarkable moment in McMullan's career.

With City, McMullan appeared in two FA Cup finals (1926 and 1933) and won a Division Two Championship medal in 1928. In 1931 he was diagnosed as suffering from pneumonia and, for a time, it looked as if that would have a serious impact on his ability, but he continued to appear for the Blues once he had recovered. Then in 1933, after 242 appearances for the Blues, he became the Oldham player-manager and later managed Aston Villa, Sheffield Wednesday and Notts County.

McMullan was a tremendous hero to thousands of Scottish footballers and, as an uncle to future Blue Matt Busby, he was clearly a major influence on the British game. Even today, approximately 80 years after he hit his peak, he is still remembered as one of the most significant Scottish international stars of all time.

City prepare for Wembley 1934. From left to right (back row): Tilson, Dale, Busby, Swift, Barnett, Bray, McLuckie, (front row) Toseland, Marshall, Cowan, Herd, Brook and Bell (trainer).

ERNIE TOSELAND A sensational winger, Ernie Toseland arrived in Manchester in 1929 and, over the following ten years, he was one of the Blues' most dependable players. A favourite with the fans, he developed a good rapport with those who stood on the Popular Side (latter-day Kippax) when he was playing on that side of the ground. A member of City's 1937 Championship team and of the teams that reached the 1933 and 1934 FA Cup finals – his 1934 kit is on display at City's museum – Toseland made 409 appearances in League and FA Cup football for City. He left City in 1939, joining Sheffield Wednesday, but came back to guest for the Blues in wartime games.

ALEC HERD Within 15 months of his arrival in Manchester from Hamilton Academical on 1 February 1933, Alec Herd had played in two FA Cup finals. He also played in the 1936/37 Championship season, and proved to be a very entertaining player. For a while he lived in one of the Club houses on Maine Road itself – fans would often arrive on non-matchdays simply to try to spot the star player.

As an inside forward, Herd's speciality was the way he would always use the ball wisely to set up his colleagues in goalscoring positions, although he did also score 107 League goals himself. He made 260 League appearances but his total would have been much greater had war not intervened.

FRED TILSON Fred Tilson forged an exciting left-wing partnership with Eric Brook. The two men had played together at Barnsley and joined the Blues simultaneously in 1928. Tilson took longer to settle, but by the start of the 1930s he was one of the side's most important players.

He played in City's major successes of the 1930s and it's fair to say that the Blues' 1934 FA Cup triumph owed a great deal to Tilson's determination and skill. He netted four goals in the semi-final against Aston Villa and then in the final itself he scored two second-half goals to give the Blues a 2–1 victory. After his playing career ended, he returned to Maine Road to serve as coach, assistant manager and chief scout.

wasn't very much of him but what there was, was all dynamite. I really believe Brookie used to pray for me to be knocked out, for he was the chosen deputy, should such an accident happen during a game.'

Eric actually went in nets on at least three occasions while with City and on each occasion, perhaps because of his size, he received a great deal of attention from the media. It was a situation on which he thrived and, according to Swift, there was one particular game when Eric couldn't wait to take Swift's place. 'I was carried off on a stretcher. But before helping to tuck the blankets over me, Brookie had pulled my jersey off – about two sizes too big for him – and was ready to keep goal. I wasn't long off the field and little Eric was very annoyed because he had had no shots to save!

League Champions

After the 1934 FA Cup success, much was expected of the Blues and in 1935 they finished fourth in the League – Eric scored 17 goals in 40 appearances. City were one of football's best supported clubs at this point and on 23 February 1935 their meeting with Arsenal attracted a crowd of 79,491 – the League's highest crowd at the time. Eric, always a player for the biggest stage, was inevitably the only City goalscorer that day.

Two years later Eric was an ever-present as he netted 20 League goals when the Blues became League champions for the first time in their history.

Injury Strikes

City shocked the football world by being relegated the year after winning the Championship. It was a puzzling time, as many of the first team were still international players while the rest were of good quality. To many it seemed to be one of those 'typical City' periods when fans and players alike come to expect the unexpected, and for Eric the change in League status was seen as only a minor inconvenience. He certainly didn't view it as the major tragedy that players of the 21st century would. He continued to play for the Blues but the outbreak of war in 1939 led to major changes for football as well as ordinary life. League football was cancelled and regional Leagues set up. Eric's formal League career was over. He had scored a total of 158 League goals – equalling Tommy Johnson's record – by the time the 1938/39 season ended but had also scored in the opening match of 1939/40. This game was eventually expunged from the records, which means that Eric would share the record. Eric does still hold the record for the total number of first-team goals scored in his City career – 177. This figure excludes those goals scored during wartime football.

On 18 November 1939 Eric played in a wartime international against Wales. These games were aimed at boosting morale and were certainly appreciated by the public. England won 3–2 and then two weeks later Eric was scheduled to play against Scotland at St James' Park, Newcastle. Sadly, on his way to the match Eric and fellow City and England player Sam Barkas were involved in a car crash.

After missing the train at Leeds, the two men were travelling by car to Newcastle when they were involved in the accident near Ripon. Brook, now 32 years old, received a fractured skull and was later told by doctors that he would never be able to head the ball again. It was the premature end of his playing career.

After the Game
After the accident Eric tried to rebuild his life and he went on to take a variety of jobs. These included a time as a coach driver in his native Mexborough, then for two years he became the landlord of the Albion Inn in Halifax. Eventually he returned to Manchester, where he was still remembered with great affection by City fans and he became a crane driver for Metrovicks.

Sadly, he passed away at home in Minsterley Parade, Wythenshawe, on 31 March 1965. He was only 57. Eric Brook remains the highest City goalscorer of all time and will always be remembered as one of City's greatest, most exciting players. He was a true hero throughout the 1930s, proved himself a player of quality on the international stage and produced magnificent entertainment for supporters that helped to see them through some tough times.

Kevin Parker
from the Official Supporters' Club, collecting the Hall of Fame award in January 2004.

' There have been many great names associated with Manchester City Football Club. Some of them are deservedly being honoured tonight, but 65 years on, Eric Brook remains the record goalscorer of all time for the Blues. In addition, he was the only goalscorer in the Cup game with Stoke when the attendance record of 84,500 was set. It's a great honour for me to collect this award on behalf of such a wonderful player. '

Francis Lee

A World Cup international for England, Francis Lee remains one of Manchester City's most famous former players and one of the Club's greatest heroes. Supporters loved Francis for his determination and passion for success as he hustled and bustled his way to victory for the Blues. Always popular as a player, Francis was often described by manager Joe Mercer as the final piece in the 1968 championship winning team.

Francis Lee
PANEL AWARD

Clocking On

Born in Westhoughton, on the edge of Bolton, Francis remembers that sport played a big part in his early life. His father used to play a lot of football with him and encouraged him to develop his skills. The young Francis would play any other sporting activity but it was football that brought him to the attention of the local scouts. While training at Horwich Technical College an offer came from Bolton Wanderers. 'I went to college in Horwich but left to sign for Bolton. The principal said I was stupid but my father, who had spent 40 years working in a cotton mill doing something he didn't like, said why not give it a crack. He said I could always go back to college if I didn't make the grade and the idea was to give myself a year. Within six months I thought I had a chance of making it.'

Francis' new footballing career was about to develop at an incredible pace. On Bonfire Night 1960, he made his debut at the age of 16 after appearing in only eight Central League matches. The game was, coincidentally, against Manchester City and Bolton won 3–1, with Francis marking a superb debut with a goal. 'I scored at exactly 3.15. I know because there was a photo of me the next day, heading past Bert Trautmann with the time on the stand clock in the background.'

To score a debut goal against such a legendary goalkeeping figure was clearly something Francis could hardly have dreamed of six months earlier and inevitably it was enough to keep the Westhoughton youngster in the side for the following five League games. A further five games followed in 1961/62 and then the next season Francis found himself having a sustained run in the side, making 23 League appearances and scoring 12 goals. Four of those goals came from the penalty spot, including two in a game at West Bromwich Albion in September, and it's fair to say Francis' success from the penalty spot throughout his career helped to develop his name.

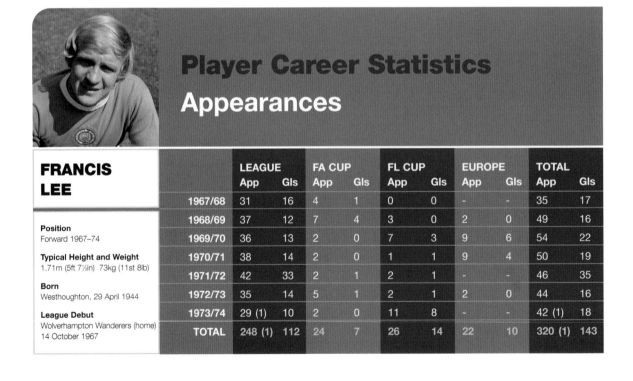

Player Career Statistics
Appearances

FRANCIS LEE

Position
Forward 1967–74

Typical Height and Weight
1.71m (5ft 7½in) 73kg (11st 8lb)

Born
Westhoughton, 29 April 1944

League Debut
Wolverhampton Wanderers (home)
14 October 1967

	LEAGUE		FA CUP		FL CUP		EUROPE		TOTAL	
	App	Gls	App	Gls	App	Gls	App	Gls	App	Gls
1967/68	31	16	4	1	0	0	-	-	35	17
1968/69	37	12	7	4	3	0	2	0	49	16
1969/70	36	13	2	0	7	3	9	6	54	22
1970/71	38	14	2	0	1	1	9	4	50	19
1971/72	42	33	2	1	2	1	-	-	46	35
1972/73	35	14	5	1	2	1	2	0	44	16
1973/74	29 (1)	10	2	0	11	8	-	-	42 (1)	18
TOTAL	248 (1)	112	24	7	26	14	22	10	320 (1)	143

Top Technique

During January 1964 Francis played against Malcolm Allison's Bath City in the FA Cup. On a miserable and difficult pitch at non-League Bath, Bolton were awarded a penalty. Francis prepared to take the kick but as he did so he heard his own captain whisper to another Bolton player, 'He's due to miss one, you know.' Whether it was the conditions or the vote of 'no confidence' is unclear but the penalty was not one of Francis' best. It did, however, go into the net off the inside of the post. It may not have been the perfect penalty but it certainly made Bath's Malcolm Allison notice the player and it saved Bolton from an embarrassing defeat.

The match went to a replay and the Trotters won the return 3–0 with Francis once again scoring from the penalty spot. Francis' approach to penalty taking is clear. 'You've got to want to take penalties to be good at it. You've got to enjoy it. The kick itself is the easy part. Any player who can't hit the corner of the goal from 12 yards shouldn't be playing. Nerve is the key. Everyone said I blasted the ball, but I used to aim for the stanchion and hit the ball at three-quarter speed, pretending I was passing the ball 50 or 60 yards. I would take a long run up to give the 'keeper longer to think about it – it gave him less of an idea which side I was going to hit it.'

Time to Leave

Francis' career at Bolton continued until October 1967. By that time he had made a total of 210 League and Cup appearances, had netted 106 goals and was clearly a man in whom other sides were interested. Unfortunately, his final year had become a difficult one as far as his relationship with the club was concerned. 'It was enjoyable at Bolton but frustrating. I really wanted to get away from the age of 18 or 19 because I could see they were going nowhere. The wages were poor and the club just wasn't changing with the times on or off the field. My contract was up in the June [1967] and they didn't want to sell me, so I signed a monthly contract. Bolton said they would never sell me and offered £150 a week to stay. I was only on £30 at

The exterior of Maine Road may appear drab, but Francis epitomised the style and the glamour fans came to expect from their players.

the time but I knew the only chance to further my ambition was to leave. By October I had served my contract, and the option and virtually retired! I hadn't played football for about three weeks. I just did a bit of training on my own. Eventually, Bolton realised they had a rapidly depreciating asset.'

Manchester City were interested in signing up Francis from the start. Malcolm Allison remembered Francis from the Bath-Bolton match and, of course, he had played in the Bolton-City Division Two game in November 1965 but the Blues were not the only interested party. Stoke made an offer; Wolves were very keen; and Bill Shankly at Liverpool had also been very interested. In the end it was Joe Mercer and Malcolm Allison who got their man.

Francis in action during the April 1973 meeting with United at Old Trafford. Only two of the fifteen derbies he played in ended in defeat.

A Vital Signing

At one point Mercer turned to the player and said, 'I hope you will sign. We feel we've got the start of a good side. We are just one player short, and we think you are that player. The odd goal or two will turn us into a great team.'

But even after the main negotiations had been agreed the transfer still stuttered – the League refused to accept the registration at first. Eventually Francis did sign and his transfer did help turn City into a great side, as Mercer had predicted. Within seven months of his arrival the Blues had become League champions for the first time since 1937.

Playing on the right Francis scored 16 League goals in 31 games and ended that Championship season as second highest goalscorer – only three short of Neil Young. There had been many memorable performances, with famous victories over Tottenham, Manchester United and the last-day

tussle with Newcastle all grabbing the headlines. Francis was a key player in each of these games and he excelled throughout the season. Prior to his arrival, City had lost five of the eleven games they had played. With Francis in the side, that record improved considerably and they were worthy champions.

Cup Success

Much was expected of the Blues at the start of the following season but injury to Tony Book affected City more than anyone could have anticipated. In addition, every side seemed to raise its game when it faced City, making average opposition appear like world beaters. Francis was moved into the number nine shirt for the second half of the season and, although League form remained mixed, City started to compete well in the FA Cup. 'Having murdered everybody in my first season,' says Francis, 'we floundered as soon as the next season started.

We thought we had a divine right to go out and thrash people. Mike [Summerbee] didn't start very well at centre forward because opponents got wise to his style. So they changed us. I was perfectly happy; it didn't matter where I played. But I don't think centre forward was my best position. I was happiest when I was supporting a big striker.

'When I played for England, Geoff Hurst was the striker up front, and when City bought big Wyn Davies I scored 33 goals one season. In my time at Maine Road there was talk of buying Joe Royle or John Toshack and I think if we had, my record would have been better.'

The 33 goals mentioned by Francis came in 1971/72 and that remains the second-highest total of goals scored in a League season by a Blue, but before that Francis played in three major finals for City. The first, the FA Cup in 1969, saw City defeat Leicester 1–0 with a goal from Neil Young. 'I was delighted to beat Leicester and win the cup but I didn't have the best preparation for the final. I'd been out since the semi with a leg strain and though I was fit, I had missed a couple of weeks' training. I don't think I played outstandingly. I just had an average game, which was a shame.'

A Euro Prize

Less than a year later Francis did play a major part in the League Cup success over West Bromwich Albion, and the European Cup Winners' Cup win

Francis Lee challenges Bobby Ferguson during City's 3–0 victory over West Ham on 13 August 1968.

A determined Francis in control during a goalless draw at Arsenal on 28 October 1972.

over Polish side Gornik Zabrze. Writing in his autobiography in 1970 Francis felt the Gornik match had been tough at times. 'The result was better than we dared hope. Secretly, I thought beforehand that Gornik were going to be really difficult and that with Mike Summerbee out we could easily struggle unless we hit absolutely peak form. After 11 minutes Neil Young snapped up a chance presented to him by a lapse on the part of Poland's international 'keeper Kostka and two minutes from half time I hit a penalty in via the 'keeper's legs.

'Our rhythm was disturbed for a while when Doyle was carried off in the first half with a leg injury, but we seemed to be cantering to victory when the Poles surprisingly pulled back the score to 2–1 in the 69th minute. The rain had started to bucket down and even when they scored I felt our only chance of losing the game was if it was called off. There was a real fear of this at one time, but Gornik obviously sensed they were back in with a chance because they tried to put the pressure on us. Even their goal was diverted off George Heslop and I think Joe Corrigan would have saved but for this.

'In the last few minutes I think Gornik got the message that we had been on top throughout the game and intended staying on top. We certainly felt we were good winners.'

Moving On

After Gornik, City were seen as one of football's most glamorous sides and Francis, with his never say die, bustling style, was a firm favourite. His goals in 1971/72 brought City within a point of the title and then in 1974 the Blues reached Wembley again when they got to the League Cup final. Sadly, the game ended in defeat, and at the end of that season Francis was sold to Derby County. 'I didn't want to leave. I felt I had a couple more good seasons in me but Tony Book [the manager] said he thought it would be better if I went.'

Francis moved to Derby County and, as if to prove City wrong, the forward helped his new club to the League title. 'I think City would have won the League that season if I'd stayed. The season before I signed for Derby, they won four away games. We won seven after I arrived and won the League.'

Francis' Prime Time

Manchester City 2 West Bromwich Albion 1. League Cup final – 7 March 1970

Goalscorers Doyle, Pardoe

City Team Corrigan, Book, Mann, Doyle, Booth, Oakes, Heslop, Bell, Summerbee (Bowyer), Lee, Pardoe

Attendance 97,963

There were so many brilliant performances by Francis Lee during his City career that it's difficult to highlight one above the others. This game, though, was viewed by neutrals at the time as the one that ensured Francis would be picked by England manager Alf Ramsey for the Mexico World Cup squad. Whether that's true or not is open to debate but his performance was certainly a major talking point of the match.

Albion's Jeff Astle scored after only five minutes and his goal was a major shock as City had opened brightly. The conditions were extremely poor: snow was piled up on the edge of the pitch, while the surface was appalling. Manager Joe Mercer described it as a 'cabbage patch' and it certainly was a difficult surface on which to play. Francis, though, seemed to enjoy the conditions. After 20 minutes, he crossed to Mike Summerbee for what looked like a certain goal. Sadly, John Talbut cleared.

A few moments later a corner from Glyn Pardoe was missed by Albion's goalkeeper, John Osborne, and Francis sent a tumbling header narrowly wide. The equaliser seemed close but each City attempt was either kept out or veered slightly off target.

On the hour an injured Mike Summerbee managed to hook the ball goalwards and Colin Bell headed to Mike Doyle, who slid home the equaliser. Summerbee left the field shortly afterwards with a hairline fracture of the leg – he had helped the Blues considerably in this match and, sadly, injury was ultimately to cost him a place in the European Cup Winners' Cup final.

Francis had several attempts to give City the lead, but the match went into extra time before the winner could be netted. In the 102nd minute Francis chipped a ball to Colin Bell who, despite pressure from two Albion defenders, backheeled to Glyn Pardoe. Pardoe flicked the ball over the goal-line to give City a 2–1 win.

Although he didn't make it on to the scoresheet, Francis' contribution was regarded by many as the best of the match. David Meek, the Manchester United journalist for the Manchester Evening News, felt compelled to write about Francis' role. 'The ex-Bolton man is still only 25 and it looks as if his career could reach its peak in Mexico this summer. He could play as big a part in England's fortunes as he did for City at Wembley. Certainly Albion had no answer except a great display by goalkeeper John Osborne.'

Another journalist singing Francis' praises was Meek's colleague, Peter Gardner. 'Francis Lee stood out head and shoulders as a Colossus whose insatiable appetite for work saw him emerge as a virtually unstoppable black and red streak of lightning, constantly carving up the opposition, harassing them into innumerable mistakes.

'Lee, playing like some big heart on a couple of legs that just refused to stop running, took some, at times, terrible physical punishment from the uncompromising Albion defence. Never can one man have put so much into a match as Lee did in the League Cup final.'

The League Cup success was the first of two major trophies for City in 1970, with the other, the European Cup Winners' Cup, coming six weeks later. By playing such a major part in both successes Francis Lee's status as one of England's leading players was confirmed.

Club football was not the only sphere in which Francis found success. He was also a wonderful England forward, scoring ten goals in twenty seven international appearances between December 1968 and April 1972. There are many who felt his international career should have continued for at least another year but it is worth stressing that he appeared for England at a time when there were many quality attackers desperate to make an impression. The England side of 1970, for example, is believed to have been one of the strongest national sides of all time. Francis himself believes the 1970 side was one of quality. 'I played three games in the 1970 World Cup finals and I felt we had a better side than in '66. The players who had won the Cup were more experienced [by 1970] and I think the fringe players were better. If we hadn't gone out to West Germany in extra-time in the quarters, I think we would have gone on to win it. Brazil certainly didn't fancy playing us.'

Business Sense

Francis' final game came on 24 April 1976, when he scored twice for Derby against Ipswich in the final two minutes – a perfect way to end a great career.

After football, Francis spent most of his time developing his business interests, most notably his toilet paper manufacturing, and race horse training. His business interests had started while he was still a Bolton player and helped to make Francis a multi-millionaire. Inevitably, there was often talk during the 1980s and early 1990s that Francis would one day turn his attention back to City. During 1993/94 the fans backed a campaign to help him take over the Club and he went on to replace Peter Swales as Chairman. Off the pitch, the structure of the Blues improved considerably after this change of leader, although on the pitch activities struggled.

In 1998 Francis stepped down as Chairman. Since that time Francis has continued to be a major shareholder and regular attendee at City. It's fair to say that his time as Chairman did not bring the level of success everybody anticipated but his time as a player certainly brought more rewards than any neutral could have predicted on the day he signed in October 1967.

Francis will always be remembered as one of Manchester City's greatest international players and a firm favourite with supporters.

Francis Lee
collecting the Hall of Fame award in January 2004.

'Thanks for this award. What a great era we played in. Most importantly, I'd like to thank the guys I played with. We had some wonderful players. We had a wonderful manager in Joe Mercer; a great coach in Malcolm. We had wonderful men like Ken Barnes, Johnny Hart and the rest of the team. That's the great thing about this period – we were all part of the team and it's great to see so many of them here tonight because we were a team. That's the most important thing. It's not the individual that counts; it's the team.'

Paul Lake

Paul Lake is remembered with great affection by City supporters. He was a member of City's entertaining FA Youth Cup-winning side of 1986 and was an inspirational player during the late-1980s resurgence under Mel Machin and Howard Kendall.

Paul Lake
1984–1991 AWARD

A Boy Wonder

At the age of eight, Denton youngster Paul was already proving to be a good footballer and playing in competitions designed for older boys. He was a member of the Denton Youth Under-12s side and he also played for St Mary's Primary School when they won the Smiths Crisps six-a-side tournament in London. More than 7,000 primary schools entered the competition and the overall standard was very high but Paul was the only member of his team who progressed to play at the highest domestic level. It wasn't long before League clubs started to notice Paul's qualities. 'I was spotted as a ten-year-old by City's chief scout Ken Barnes. He decided to keep an eye on me. A year later I had started playing for Tameside Boys and it was at this time that a Spurs scout came to watch me in one particular game against Oldham Boys. We beat them 8–0, I scored five, yet apparently he still didn't rate me! What more could a player have done? Despite this snub, I went on to get picked for Greater Manchester Boys.'

Ken Barnes, himself an outstanding City player during the 1950s, remembers seeing Paul for the first time. 'You look for talent for months and months. You attend lots of games... watching... waiting... hoping someone would appear that's a little bit special. You get used to seeing nothing, then suddenly it happens. You see a player with more talent than the rest of the team put together. That's what happened with Paul. I knew he was something special from the beginning. It was so clear. I remember seeing the way he took a ball that fell over his shoulder and then the way he controlled it on the run. He made it look so easy. He had flair beyond his years.'

Blue Star

It was around this time that the links with Manchester City developed. Paul, a City fan from birth, was invited to play for a side called Blue Star, a club that had strong links with City and was, basically, one of the Club's junior sides. Steve Redmond, Andy Hinchcliffe, Ian Brightwell, David

Player Career Statistics
Appearances

PAUL LAKE

Position
Defender/Midfielder 1985–96

Typical Height and Weight
1.83m (6ft 0in) 77kg (12st 2lb)

Born
Manchester, 25 October 1968

League Debut
Wimbledon (A) 24 January 1987

	LEAGUE		FA CUP		FL CUP		FM CUP		TOTAL	
	App	Gls	App	Gls	App	Gls	App	Gls	App	Gls
1986/87	3	1	0	0	0	0	1	0	4	1
1987/88	30 (3)	3	4	1	4	0	2	1	40 (3)	5
1988/89	37 (1)	3	2	0	2	1	1	0	42 (1)	4
1989/90	31	0	3	1	4	0	1	0	39	1
1990/91	3	0	0	0	0	0	0	0	3	0
1992/93	2	0	0	0	0	0	0	0	2	0
TOTAL	106 (4)	7	9	2	10	1	5	1	130 (4)	11

White, Paul Warhurst and Jason Beckford were all to play for Blue Star around this time and each one was to progress to League football. Paul's talent was cultivated carefully there and the encouragement he received gave him greater self-belief. 'I began to realise that I had a bit of talent as a player. At the time I was quite a shy, nervous kid, off the pitch, but I was very aware that I could hold my own in every game of football that I played in. I never got complacent, though, and never let the accolades go to my head. I was always aware that I still had a lot to learn and was always prepared to listen to advice about how to improve my game.'

As Paul's development continued so did the interest from other League clubs. Naturally, City were determined to sign him but a month before he was due to sign, a United scout invited the Dentonian on a tour of Spain with the Reds. United were very keen to sign the youngster and, at this time, it has to be said that the Old Trafford side may have looked the better proposition, particularly as City had been relegated in 1983 and, at the time of Paul's signing, were trying to find a way back to Division One. For Paul, though, there was no choice. 'I was flattered to be approached by United but there was never any chance of me going there when I had the chance to make it at City. I had been brought up as a City fan and my ultimate dream was to play for the Blues.'

On 1 July 1985 Paul's dream came a step closer when he signed apprenticeship forms through the Government-backed Youth Training Scheme and within a year he had made ten appearances in the Central League, twenty-three in the Lancashire League and had been an important member of the side that had won the FA Youth Cup final. The two-legged final saw City beat Manchester United 3–1 on aggregate, with Paul scoring in the first leg at Old Trafford. It was a major triumph and signalled new hope for the Blues.

First-Team Opportunity

By the middle of August 1987 seven of the FA Youth Cup-winning side had appeared in the first team, with Paul making his debut on 24 January 1987

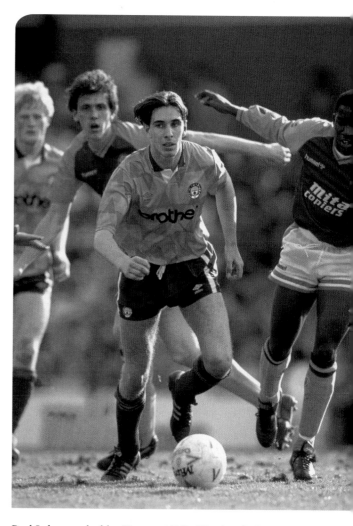

Paul Lake, watched by City man Colin Hendry, during City's 2–1 win at Aston Villa on 1 April 1990.

against Wimbledon. He featured in three League games and one Full Members' Cup match that season and managed to score in the 1–1 draw with Luton on 21 February. This was Paul's first League match at Maine Road. 'I felt a hell of a lot of pressure on me and when I walked down the tunnel and heard the roar I thought I was going to boil over. But as soon as I got on to the pitch that feeling evaporated. Although I only played about 65 minutes of the game against Luton, it's an experience that I'll never forget. I actually scored my first-ever goal for City in that match but apart from that I had a terrible game. I was really nervous and was trying things that just weren't coming off at all.'

Viv Anderson and the rest of Alex Ferguson's multi-million-pound side were no match for homegrown Paul and the other Blues in September 1989.

City were relegated to Division Two at the end of the 1986/87 season and, with finances extremely tight, the Blues needed Paul and the other youngsters to develop quickly. Steve Redmond, David White, Ian Brightwell, Andy Hinchcliffe, Paul Moulden and, of course, Paul Lake himself had to form the backbone of new manager Mel Machin's side. Paul overcame the nerves he felt had affected him against Luton and proved to be one of City's most accomplished players over the following seasons.

Paul's initial year in the City first team included City's 10–1 demolition of Huddersfield Town. 'The match seemed to pass by those of us who didn't score,' recalls Paul. 'We felt like spectators; just there to make up the numbers. I don't think I broke sweat during the whole game.'

That victory ensured the football world became much more aware of Paul and the other young City players but the Blues were never able to mount a serious promotion challenge that 1987/88 season and finished ninth in Division Two. For Paul, however, it had been a good season. He had made 33 League appearances and had been voted City's Young Player of the Year. His reputation was growing all the time and in September 1988 he played for the England Under-21s against Denmark. He had previously been selected for the Under-21 European Championships but on that occasion had had to pull out through injury. 'I'd missed the last nine or ten games of the 1987/88 season but, luckily, managed to get fit over the summer break. The Club were a bit concerned about a recurrence of the injury and

'Every run, cross and tackle that I made went my way and it was one of the best England performances I ever put in.'

told me to take it easy against Denmark, advising me to come off the pitch if I felt any pain or soreness at all. Anyway, the first half went like a dream for me. Every run, cross and tackle that I made went my way and it was one of the best England performances I ever put in.

'The senior England squad had been watching the match and after the game I spoke with the likes of Peter Beardsley and Bryan Robson, who gave me a lot of encouragement and told me that I was head and shoulders above the rest on the day. For the seasoned pros to take the time out to tell me that made me so pleased. I was on top of the world. I felt so proud and it was definitely one of the pinnacles of my career.'

Paul went on to make six Under-21 appearances and an appearance for the England B team. He seemed destined for full England honours but a knee injury would later intervene to cut short his budding international career.

Rising Stars

Paul had clearly become a major City star and one of the Club's biggest assets by the late 1980s, so much so that transfer speculation began to circulate,

suggesting that Liverpool, among others, were keen to sign the 20 year old. Chairman Peter Swales announced in February 1989 that Paul would be going nowhere. Within a month, potential disaster had struck when Paul swallowed his tongue in the League match with Leicester. Paul doesn't remember too much about the actual incident but a few weeks later he told reporters that he had watched it on video several times. 'It's horrible watching it. I can talk about it light-heartedly and crack jokes about doing an acid house dance on the floor but I realise how lucky I was. I have got over it without any problems but seeing myself spontaneously shuddering – it's a bit perturbing.'

It was a nightmare situation and only the actions of Club physio Roy Bailey saved Paul from death. Paul missed the following match but returned to the side to help with the final push towards promotion, although, in typical City style, promotion depended on a final-day match at Bradford City. The day proved to be an extremely tense one with Bradford in the lead for much of the game. Fortunately, Trevor Morley netted a late equaliser to guarantee promotion. 'As soon as the whistle went it was mayhem,' says Paul, as he casts his mind back to

MCFC statistics

	1984/85	1985/86	1986/87	1987/88	1988/89	1989/90	1990/91	Honours
League Position	3 (in Div 2)	15 (in Div 1)	21	9 (in Div 2)	2	14 (in Div 1)	5	Full Members' Cup finalists 1986; promotion from Division Two 1985 and 1989
FA Cup Round Reached	3	4	3	6	4	3	5	
League Cup Round Reached	4	3	3	5	4	4	3	
Average Attendance	24,220	24,229	21,922	19,471	23,500	27,975	27,874	

Paul's Prime Time

Manchester City 5 Manchester United 1. Football League Division One – 23 September 1989

Goalscorers Oldfield (2), Morley, Bishop, Hinchcliffe

City Team Cooper, Fleming, Hinchcliffe, Bishop, Gayle, Redmond, White, Morley, Oldfield, Brightwell, Lake (Beckford)

Attendance 43,246

'We had spent years preparing for this day. I've been a City fan all my life, and all my life I'd worked to beat United. We all had. This was the day we'd dreamed of and this was a truly great day to be a Blue,' are the stirring words Paul uses when looking back on this wonderful victory over Alex Ferguson's expensively assembled United.

City had been promoted the previous May after spending four of the previous six seasons in Division Two. During this same period United had appointed Alex Ferguson manager and, although they had yet to win a trophy under the Scotsman, he had already spent more on players than any other club in the League. The individual amounts may seem small in comparison with modern-day transfer fees but at the time these were astronomical figures for any manager to spend. Ferguson's signings included Gary Pallister

Fleming, Bishop (number four), Oldfield and Lake (number eleven) celebrate during the Maine Road Massacre.

(£2.3 million), Paul Ince (£1.7 million), Danny Wallace (£1.2 million) and Neil Webb (£1.5 million), while City's team had cost £1.9 million in its entirety.

Early in the match neither side dominated. Then crowd disturbances, caused as a result of United fans obtaining tickets for the North Stand, forced referee Neil Midgley to take the players off for a few minutes. When they returned, City took control almost immediately. David Oldfield scored and less than a minute later Paul Lake dodged past Viv Anderson to set Trevor Morley up for the Blues' second goal. The two City men had been able to rip United to shreds with ease.

After 36 minutes Ian Bishop headed past Jim Leighton to make it 3–0. From that point onwards, Paul Lake and the others seemed to completely overawe United but shortly into the second half Mark Hughes netted an impressive volley to make it 3–1.

In other years the Blues might have become hesitant after a goal like that but any fears the fans may have had soon evaporated as the City men dominated again. In the 58th minute Paul pushed down the right flank, sneaked past Anderson and headed forwards. He teed up the ball for David Oldfield, who scored at the Platt Lane end of the ground. Many of the United fans who had been sitting behind that goal left immediately, while City fans chanted 'Easy, Easy!'

Four minutes later Andy Hinchcliffe headed home City's fifth and immediately held up his hand with five raised fingers. 'When Andy did that he was saying what we all felt,' says Paul. 'He was showing the United fans what this game meant to us and, as a team, we'd been groomed for that day. All our lives

The 1989 derby was commemorated in a variety of ways. This postal cover, by Dawn Covers, was hugely popular.

we'd waited and hoped for that moment and then it came. There couldn't have been a better result.'

The Platt Lane Stand now emptied of almost all away supporters. The scene was captured by Granada TV and since 2004 the film of that moment has formed part of the Manchester City Experience, the Blues' museum and tour.

Shortly afterwards Paul went off injured. 'My knee got stamped on by one of the United players,' he says. 'Although it wasn't a serious injury I looked to the bench and saw my best mate Jason Beckford sat there and I decided to come off so he could sample some of the atmosphere too. As I came off, the ovation I got from the City supporters was incredible, and I was really delighted that the fans had witnessed such a great derby performance.'

The following week City's home programme for the meeting with Luton proclaimed 'Paul Lake – the Derby Day Goalmaker', and included a couple of photographs of Paul's role in the match.

This was one of the best Manchester derby results of all time, and for loyal Blue Paul it capped an amazing spell that saw him win the FA Youth Cup, achieve promotion, and win England Under-21 honours. City fans felt certain that this would be one of many successes for both the player and the Club.

that eventful day. 'The feeling of elation was so strong that the hairs went up on the back of my neck and a shiver went down my spine.'

The following September Paul played superbly as the Blues defeated Manchester United 5–1 at Maine Road and in January 1990 he travelled to Lilleshall for a pre-World Cup get-together with the full England squad. He never actually made it to the World Cup but it was clear he was on the verge of an England career. At Maine Road Howard Kendall, who had replaced Mel Machin as manager in December 1989, was very impressed with Paul. 'As soon as I saw him in action I knew I'd got a real gem,' states Kendall. 'Paul was very quick, great in the air, and also had fantastic technical ability and I knew that he would be an essential part of my plans for the City side.

'When I first took over, Paul played on the right side for me. I played the team with a sweeper system at first because the defence had been conceding far too many goals and it badly needed to be tightened. Whilst I knew at the time that Paul had far too much ability to play this role, I had to bide my time and play him in a position that would benefit the team most.

'During the pre-season build up for the 1990/91 campaign I decided that I would now be able to use Paul exactly how I wanted – as a centre back. We went on tour and he played brilliantly.'

Captain of the Blues

Kendall took the decision to appoint Paul captain at the same time. 'He was a local lad and a big, big City fan who simply adored the club. It was so obvious that he would have killed for that blue shirt and I thought he would be the right man to instil this feeling into everyone else. Paul had this special feeling for the club and the fans that I felt had to be used to the best possible advantage. Once he had that blue shirt on, Lakey battled 100 per cent and ran himself into the ground.'

With the future looking immensely positive, Paul took on the captain's role. Tottenham, with a very powerful side, defeated the Blues 3–1 at White Hart

Paul's Finest Fellow Citizens

The period 1984–1991 saw the Blues enjoy two promotions and several entertaining victories. The period started with Billy McNeill as manager and ended with Peter Reid in control and, in between, Jimmy Frizzell, Mel Machin and Howard Kendall had spells in charge. As for players, each manager had to rely on a mixture of youth and experience.

STEVE REDMOND A member of City's youth development programme, Steve Redmond made his League debut in February 1986 and a little over a month later he appeared at Wembley in the 1986 Full Members' Cup final against Chelsea. By the time he captained City to the FA Youth Cup final success in May that year he had appeared in eight Division One games, twenty-one Central League games and fifteen Lancashire League matches, plus the Wembley appearance.

In subsequent years he won the supporters' Player of the Year award and succeeded Kenny Clements as captain, making him City's youngest captain of all time. He captained the Blues to promotion in 1989 before moving to Oldham in 1992 after 283 starts and four substitute appearances for City.

NEIL MCNAB In a City career lasting almost seven years, Neil McNab was a committed presence in midfield. He joined the Blues in 1983, shortly after relegation, and immediately helped manager Billy McNeill inject some control into the side. A key member of the side during two promotion campaigns, McNab is fondly remembered by supporters for his never-say-die attitude and for the way he helped the youth-team players of the mid-1980s to develop. He should also be remembered for scoring the opening goal in City's 10–1 defeat of Huddersfield in 1987 – prior to his goal Huddersfield had actually been the more impressive side!

McNab played in the 1986 Full Members' Cup final and, after leaving City, he made further trips to Wembley with Tranmere Rovers in the Leyland-Daf Trophy. He also had a spell as a youth-team coach at Maine Road.

PAUL MOULDEN 'Goalden' Moulden's debut in the side was eagerly anticipated by the City faithful. They had already heard about his goalscoring abilities – his record-breaking achievements for Bolton Lads Club, for whom he had netted 289 goals in 40 games – and during late 1985 rumours circulated that the player was on the verge of his first League appearance. Eventually he made his City debut at Aston Villa on New Year's Day 1986 and over the following three years Moulden's performances ensured he remained a fans' favourite. Sadly, Mel Machin transferred Moulden to Bournemouth in 1989 – the fans were far from happy – after 48 League appearances (plus 16 as substitute) and 18 League goals.

DAVID WHITE Another popular member of City's 1986 FA Youth Cup side, David White made his debut in September 1986 and went on to become one of City's finest attackers. He scored a hat-trick in the 10–1 defeat of Huddersfield in 1987 and he scored four goals against Aston Villa in April 1991. That same month he won his first England B cap and then in 1992 he made his first appearance for the full England side. He was a shade unfortunate when his first kick of the match proved to be a great goalscoring opportunity. He didn't score and his confidence seemed to drop. Had the opportunity arrived later in the match, who knows how his England career may have developed. City fans prefer to remember his powerful, surging runs down the wing and the excitement generated by him over the eight seasons he played at Maine Road before he moved on to Leeds United.

MICK MCCARTHY As with Neil McNab, centre-half Mick McCarthy arrived at City to help the Blues recover after relegation in 1983. He was another steadying influence in McNeill's side and while with the Blues he was regularly selected to play for the Republic of Ireland. He later became Ireland's manager, taking them to the 2002 World Cup.

The 1986 youth team stars Ian Brightwell (back far left), Paul Lake (third from left), Ian Scott and David White (holding the cup) all went on to play for the first team.

McCarthy was one of City's more determined players. At the start of the 1984/85 season he was given the captaincy but soon handed it back to Paul Power. McCarthy felt his contribution reduced during that time and wanted to focus on improving his own performance. That said much about McCarthy's dedication and both City and the player improved as a result of the decision. After leaving City, McCarthy enjoyed a successful spell at Celtic. He remains a popular figure in Manchester.

ANDY HINCHCLIFFE Of all the youth-team players who represented City in the 1986 FA Youth Cup final, Andy Hinchcliffe is the one who has achieved most on the international scene. Although injury reduced his opportunities, Hinchcliffe made a total of seven appearances for England and won an FA Cup winner's medal with Everton. At City he made his debut in 1987 and went on to make 42 (out of 44) League appearances in his first season. His finest individual moment came on 23 September 1989 when his wonderful header gave him the fifth goal in City's 5–1 Maine Road Massacre of a multi-million-pound United side. In recent years Hinchcliffe has worked for local radio station Greater Manchester Radio commentating on City's matches. His honest assessment of City's abilities has proved hugely popular with fans.

Lane in the opening match of the 1990/91 season but that was followed by victories for City over Everton and Aston Villa at Maine Road. Paul's career should have reached enormous heights, particularly as England call-ups were once again starting to come his way, but a knee injury sustained in a rather innocuous challenge with Aston Villa's Tony Cascarino brought an early end to Paul's season. Eventually the diagnosis came through to say that Paul had suffered a serious cruciate ligament injury.

For the following couple of seasons Paul bravely pushed himself forwards, determined to return to first-team action. As with Colin Bell during the mid-1970s it was a tough period for the player. 'Paul worked so hard in rehabilitation it was unbelievable,' remembers Howard Kendall.

Paul did manage to return to action at the start of the 1992/93 season, but in only his second match he collapsed after just eight minutes at Middlesbrough. The battle to return to first-team action started again but, sadly, Paul never managed to resurrect his City career.

A touching moment as Paul Lake takes the applause from the fans at his testimonial match.

In 1996 he announced his retirement and, almost immediately, the Blues granted him a testimonial match against Manchester United. More than 20,000 fans turned out to pay tribute.

Since then, Paul has put most of his energy into forging a new career looking into sports injuries and sports physiotherapy. Paul sees this role as an opportunity to help prevent others from suffering the same fate as him.

Another City man who was later to suffer cruciate ligament damage is Niall Quinn. At the 2004 Hall of Fame Awards, Niall paid tribute to Paul. 'Tony Book speaks with affection about the great team he played in. Well, in the City team I played in there was one smashing player who never fulfilled his potential. I think he should never be forgotten and I know he doesn't like me saying this but Paul Lake was the best footballer I ever played with; no question."

Such testimony from a distinguished former team-mate reflects the esteem in which Paul Lake is held in football. Seeing such a wonderful player cut down in his prime almost seemed like a crime. Blues fans, though, prefer to focus more on their memories of Paul at his best. He was an amazing player and a huge talent.

Paul Lake

collecting the Hall of Fame award in January 2004.

' I owe this to quite a few people, actually. There are three gentlemen in the room tonight that I owe a lot to both as a player and as a person – Ken Barnes, Tony Book and Glyn Pardoe. These guys helped to nurture a side that basically saved the Club an absolute fortune but most importantly they gave the City fans the history of beating Manchester United 5–1, which I will never ever forget. I've been fortunate to play with some great players... made some friends that I have had now since ten years of age: Andy Hinchcliffe, David White, Steve Redmond... known them all my life. I love these guys dearly. But I want to say a special word to the person who basically brought me into the world. He died a long time ago but I owe this to the person who salvaged everything, scraped every penny together he could to give me some sort of career – that's my Dad. Thank you. '

Frank Swift

Frank Swift was one of football's biggest stars.

He was a tremendous goalkeeper for City and England and was also a firm favourite with the fans. He enjoyed life and his enthusiasm was always abundantly clear. During the late 1930s and 1940s fans would be desperate to find the best place behind his goal as they knew that their hero would laugh and joke with them while the action was taking place at the opposite end. Frank's rapport with supporters was legendary.

Frank Swift

Frank demonstrates his skills for the camera in his favourite goal at the Scoreboard End of Maine Road.

The Boots Scamp

From his earliest memories, Blackpool-born Frank was always obsessed with the game of football. He played at every opportunity with his brothers, one of whom, Fred, became Blackpool's first-team goalkeeper, and started to develop a good reputation locally. After leaving school he went to work for the Blackpool Gasworks and each Saturday he played for his employers' football team. During the summer months football took a back seat as Frank and his brothers operated a boat for sailing trips along the Blackpool coast. It was while carrying out that activity that he met his future wife.

After a while Frank started to consider that his goalkeeping talents were progressing and after one of his best performances for the Gasworks he wrote to Lancashire Combination side Fleetwood for a trial. The following Saturday he received a letter from them asking him to report that afternoon for a trial. Throughout his life Frank used to enjoy telling the tale of what happened next. 'I rushed home, picked up a neatly-studded pair of boots, all trim and ready for the afternoon. Not until I got to the Fleetwood ground did I realise they weren't my boots, but those of Fred, who was also due for a game that afternoon. It was too late to take them home, I reasoned, and anyway mine was the more important match. Fred was only keeping goal for Blackpool first-team in the opening public trial of the season!'

Frank's trial went well and he went on to keep goal for Fleetwood for the rest of the season.

Moving to Manchester

With Fred Swift already established at Division Two Blackpool, Frank was keen to progress into League football himself. Blackpool, Blackburn and Bradford all showed interest in him before the opportunity to move to Maine Road occurred. Frank played in the City A team and continued to work for the Blackpool Gasworks but by November 1932 he had impressed enough to be offered professional terms with a wage of ten shillings (50p) a week.

In 1933 Frank paid to watch City play Everton in the FA Cup final and vowed that he would be City's first choice if the Blues were ever to play in the final again. Little did he realise that his opportunity would come just 12 months later.

After a couple of months of the 1933/34 season Frank had progressed to the reserve side and then, after only three reserve games, he made his League debut against Derby County on Christmas Day 1933. The game ended in a 4–1 defeat and Frank was seriously concerned that he had blown his chance.

However, City's previous game had ended in an 8–0 defeat, so Frank was seen as an improvement. The next day the return fixture with Derby ended 2–0 to the Blues and Frank was to become a permanent fixture in goal – he only missed one match from his debut through to the outbreak of war in 1939.

Sad Scenes

Frank's arrival in the first team did help the Blues tighten up and, despite his age – he made his debut at the age of 19 – he seemed relatively at ease in the City goal.

One of the key features of Frank's first season was City's progress in the FA Cup. Under manager Wilf Wild, the Blues had developed into a good cup side and were a very exciting team to watch. As a result, huge crowds rolled up for most of City's cup games. Not only was the Maine Road attendance record of 84,569 set for a sixth-round tie with Stoke but the attendance record for Hillsborough was set for City's meeting with Sheffield Wednesday.

For 19-year-old Frank this day was one of tremendous excitement but also great sadness. 'It was one of the most amazing games I have ever played in. The 72,841 crowd brought all the sights, scenes, sounds that are only provided by a cup crazy mob.

'After we had changed and were ready for the field, we found that the narrow tunnel from the dressing room to the pitch was blocked by ambulancemen tending groaning casualties. After forcing my way through with the other players, I had to stand aside to let pass a stretcher bearing a man crushed to death against the railings on the Spion Kop.'

It was a terrible scene but the authorities decided the game had to be played. The Cup run progressed and, ultimately, the Blues went on to win the trophy with a 2–1 victory over Portsmouth.

Life During Wartime

After the FA Cup win, Frank's reputation continued to grow and critics started to suggest he would play for England. This was a particularly strong period

Player Career Statistics
Appearances

FRANK SWIFT

Position
Goalkeeper 1932–49

Typical Height and Weight
1.88m (6ft 2in)
89kg (14st)

Born
Blackpool, 26 December 1913

Deceased
Munich, 6 February 1958

League Debut
Derby County (home)
25 December 1933

	LEAGUE		FA CUP		TOTAL	
	App	Gls	App	Gls	App	Gls
1933/34	22	0	8	0	30	0
1934/35	42	0	1	0	43	0
1935/36	42	0	3	0	45	0
1936/37	42	0	4	0	46	0
1937/38	42	0	5	0	47	0
1938/39	41	0	2	0	43	0
1946/47	35	0	4	0	39	0
1947/48	33	0	3	0	36	0
1948/49	35	0	1	0	36	0
1949/50	4	0	0	0	4	0
TOTAL	338	0	31	0	369	0

NOTE: The 1939/40 League campaign was abandoned, then expunged from records, due to the Second World War. Frank Swift made three appearances during that season.

Swift takes a goal kick during 1948. Notice the church occupying the site that later housed the Club shop and social club.

although, officially, wartime internationals were not recognised as full internationals by the Football Association. Opportunities were few and far between during the following years through a lack of regular internationals – only two were played in 1940 – and the instabilities caused through war. Frank still managed to make a total of 15 wartime and victory international appearances.

Postwar, Frank made 19 full international appearances, keeping 9 clean sheets. This run included two games as captain, making Frank the first goalkeeper to captain England in the 20th century. His first match as captain was against Italy in May 1948, a game that was played in Turin and one that was viewed as a major test since Italy had been such a powerful force prewar. Frank felt immensely proud to captain his country and was determined he would lead by example. The general view was that Italy would bombard the England goal and so it was vital that Frank played at his best.

The game commenced as expected, with the Italians laying siege to England's goal. Frank's team-mate Tom Finney, who was to have a tremendous game himself, scoring twice, remembers, 'Frank was at his brilliant best in his first outing as skipper.' England eventually managed to get the ball into the other half and Stan Mortensen scored a surprise goal. By the 25th minute England had taken a two-goal lead.

The Italians seized control again and for the rest of the first half and the opening minutes of the second they placed significant pressure on Frank and his defence. A brilliant performance by the City goalkeeper kept Italy at bay, while every England attack was made to count as two further goals by the visitors ensured a 4–0 England win.

England's Zenith

At the final whistle, Frank was carried shoulder high by his team-mates after a tremendous performance. Tom Finney rates this match as one of England's finest. 'Only those who played for England in Turin or the few supporters who were there, will ever

for the national side with several extremely good goalkeepers playing League football. Frank, mainly because of his youthfulness, was discounted for some time as a succession of goalkeepers, such as Birmingham's Harry Hibbs, Everton's Ted Sagar and Chelsea's Vic Woodley were given spells. Then, with City having won the League Championship in 1937 and with Frank being taken more seriously, disaster struck for the Blues. The relegation that followed only 12 months after the Championship success was a major blow to the Club and to the ambitions of their young goalkeeper. Frank seemed unlikely to dislodge Woodley while City were in Division Two despite the City man generally being more highly regarded.

Worse was to follow. War broke out in 1939, causing all League football to be cancelled. Fortunately for Frank, a decision was taken to continue with internationals, as a morale-boosting exercise. On 18 November 1939, Frank made his

'Frank was a wonderful character

with a huge heart. He believed in getting fun out of life.'

properly appreciate the true merit of the performance. It was what today's pundits might call "the ultimate professional display" and, aside from the 1966 World Cup victory, it has a very good claim to be the highpoint of the English game.'

Finney reckons Frank was a major influence that day, not only because of his determination to see England succeed but also because of his general humour and love for life. 'Frank was a wonderful character with a huge heart. He believed in getting fun out of life. He took the business of goalkeeping very seriously and was damned good at it, too, but he was also a great companion who was rarely without a smile on his face. With his laugh-a-minute personality, he was popular with colleagues and opponents and he had an unofficial fan club the world over. The

continentals loved him. During one game in Switzerland, while we were attacking, he nipped behind the goal to accept a toffee from an admirer.'

Another great England player, Tommy Lawton, talked of Frank's role in the Italian game in an interview during the late 1990s. 'We won that day in Turin thanks to our wonderful understanding. Probably on sheer football alone the Italians had the edge, but there was something about our teamwork, inspired by that great character in goal, that won us the day.'

The Italian game was often described by Frank as his greatest day although he had so many during a wonderful career that his judgement must have been based mainly on his selection as captain – a major honour at the time as captains took on many of the duties managers and coaches do today.

Frank has total control during England's 3–0 demolition of France at Highbury on 3 May 1947.

Frank's Prime Time

Manchester City 2 Portsmouth 1. FA Cup final – 28 April 1934

Goalscorer Tilson (2)

City Team Swift, Barnett, Dale, Busby, Cowan, Bray, Toseland, Marshall, Tilson, Herd, Brook

Attendance 93,258

Following City's defeat in the 1933 FA Cup final, captain Sam Cowan vowed the Blues would be victorious the following year. For most of the players the experience of 1933 would help them but for young Frank it was a nervous time. He couldn't afford to let the side down and this thought preyed on his mind. At one stage he was even convinced that Len Langford, his predecessor, would be brought back. He wasn't, and a nervous Frank was selected to play.

Sam Cowan and the other players tried to calm Frank but the combination of nerves and inexperience continued to play a little on his mind. On the day itself the weather was not particularly great. It had been a miserable, wet morning, and at kick-off the surface of the pitch was still a little damp. Frank watched to see if his opposite number in the Portsmouth goal was wearing gloves or not. As he wasn't, Frank decided to follow his lead, reasoning that the more experienced goalkeeper must have a better understanding of the conditions. It was a mistake and before half-time Portsmouth scored.

Frank was bitterly disappointed with his own performance. 'The ball slithered through into the net off my fingers. I was desolate and as I picked the ball out of the net, thought, "Just another Wembley goalkeeper!" In the dressing room at half-time, I must have looked so disconsolate that Fred Tilson came over to me and said, "What's up with thee?" I answered, "I thought I should have stopped their goal." Fred replied, "Tha doesn't need to worry. I'll plonk two in next half." Which, of course, he did.'

Tilson's two second-half goals gave City a 2–1 win but the emotion of the day was too much for Frank and as the final whistle blew, he fainted. He recovered well enough to make his way up the steps to the Royal Box for the presentations, where the king, George V, asked him how he was feeling. The following Monday a telegram arrived on behalf of the King expressing similar sentiments while the young goalkeeper found he was now the toast of Manchester. His overall performance during the Cup run and the sight of him fainting at the final whistle made Frank a cult figure. No matter how great his performances would be over the following seasons Frank had already achieved enough to enter Manchester folklore.

Shortly after the final, the *Topical Times Sporting Annual* claimed that Frank was one of the 12 best discoveries of the season. They wrote in his praise: "Few players can have risen to the heights so quickly as Manchester City's 'keeper, Frank Swift. Within four months of entering League football Swift appeared at Wembley and collected a Cup winners' medal. His own ability and courage helped to put him there. He was but a raw kid from minor football when he came into the City team. But the improvement was noticeable in every game he played, until at the end of the season he was the cool and finished 'keeper one associates with a First Division club. He is very tall and strong. He is daring to a degree. He times a dive to a nicety. Has saved many a bad situation by this. He is keen eyed, alert, and agile, and, now that he has cured a tendency to run out, there seems a bright future for this lad from Fleetwood.'

The 1934 final gave Frank the opportunity to be recognised as a great goalkeeper nationally but after the final the youngster was more concerned with the fact that he had fainted at the whistle. An embarrassed Frank later said, 'Fancy a great strapping fellow like me fainting in front of all those people and the King.'

Frank punches clear while watched by City's Billy Dale
(dark shirt in centre) during the 1934 FA Cup final.

The captain was the one expected to make most tactical decisions and he was certainly the man responsible for morale, team talks and team building.

Fun in the 1940s

The immediate postwar period saw the Blues return to Division One at the end of the 1946/47 season. Frank made only 35 appearances that season but the games he missed were as a direct result of his international appearances: England matches were often played on the same days as League football. He was still very much City and England's first choice and fans would often travel to Maine Road simply to watch the great goalkeeper. A favourite place to stand would be immediately behind Frank's goal. In those days, supporters were able to walk from one end of the ground to the other during a match and, traditionally, City fans liked to stand at

the end the Blues were attacking. However, by the 1940s Frank's reputation and rapport with the crowd were so high that supporters would follow him around instead. If he was defending the Platt Lane end of the ground, many would try to be near him, particularly the younger fans.

During games Frank liked to talk to fans and would often share a joke. Stories of Frank leaning against the post, chatting away, while play was taking place at the other end seemed to follow almost every City match and some supporters claim the great goalkeeper was often handed sweets, sandwiches and even a share of a hot drink from a fan's flask. Frank was certainly the player with the greatest rapport with the fans.

Despite performing superbly, Frank felt he wanted to retire at the top and he decided that the 1948/49 season would be his last. He was still

Frank's Finest Fellow Citizens

At the start of the period 1936–1950 the Blues were one of football's most successful sides. They had won the FA Cup in 1934 and had developed a great reputation as a cup side. The general view of neutrals was that City were on the verge of major success in the League. As Manchester's best supported side, that success came in 1937.

BERT SPROSTON England international full-back Bert Sproston joined City in 1938 and made his debut against his former club Tottenham on Bonfire Night that year. Incredibly, he had actually travelled up to the game with his former colleagues.

At the time of his transfer he was one of the hottest properties in League football and City had to pay a near-record fee of £10,000 for him. After only one season, though, war broke out and the player's career had to be put on hold. By the time League football resumed in 1946, Sproston had been robbed of his peak years. Nevertheless, he was still impressive. He formed part of City's promotion side in 1947 and remained a steadying influence until he moved to Ashton United in 1950.

SAM BARKAS Stylish left-back Sam Barkas was City's inspirational captain during the 1936/37 Championship season. He joined the Blues in April 1934 and made his debut on 2 May against Liverpool but couldn't play in the FA Cup final as he was cup tied. As with Bert Sproston,

he lost six seasons to the war but in 1946/47 he managed to captain the Blues to the Division Two title. He was 38 years of age and at the end of that season he moved on to Workington as manager. He later returned to City as a scout.

GEORGE SMITH The story of George Smith's life is an amazing one. War broke out when Smith was on the verge of a great career. He made many wartime appearances for the Blues but while serving with the forces in Africa he was a victim of 'friendly fire' from the South African Air Force. A bullet travelled almost the full length of his left arm, internally, and, as a result, his arm was more or less entirely paralysed. It was a terrible blow and, when he returned to Manchester, City insisted he underwent a series of trials to ensure he was able to play. Both the Club and the Forces tried to ensure he kept the truth about his injury quiet, and for the next 50 years he barely told anyone exactly what had happened in Africa. Supporters assumed he had lost part of his hand –

England's number one and still a major international figure but he believed the time had come to step aside. The City directors were far from happy and they did all they could to persuade him to stay.

On 9 April 1949 Frank played his final international match – against Scotland at Wembley. Eighteen days later he appeared in what was supposed to be his final game at Maine Road – a surprise 3–0 defeat by Arsenal. At the final whistle, fans ran on to the pitch as Frank was chaired off the field by team-mates. He was cheered and clapped off the field by fans of all ages and by both sides. The same happened in the final game, at Huddersfield, 11 days later and, as far as everyone was concerned, particularly Frank, that was the end

of his career. There was even a celebratory procession back over the moors to Manchester.

Sadly, Alec Thurlow, Frank's replacement, became ill and the Blues were without a goalkeeper of any standing. Frank was finally convinced by the Club to fill the void and he stipulated that he would only keep goal for a few games, while City found a replacement. He went on to make four final appearances, with his very last City match being a goalless game at home to Everton in September 1949.

Tragedy Strikes

Frank's retirement at the age of 35 came too soon. He could have played for both City and England for a further couple of seasons but his desire to go out

he usually had it strapped up and hidden during matches and public appearances – while others speculated on the extent of his injuries.

When League football resumed he proved to be a tremendous goalscorer and, at one point, he was watched by senior figures within the FA. They were planning to pick him for the national side but they chose not to do so, believing – incorrectly – that his damaged arm would have an impact on his all-round performance.

Smith went on to make 179 League and Cup appearances and scored 80 goals after the war. Had England's selectors been a little braver then Smith would have had the chance to perform exceptionally well for the national side as well.

BOBBY MARSHALL Nottinghamshire-born Bobby Marshall appeared in each of City's 1930s successes and was noted for his excellent ball control. He joined City in 1928 and at the start of his career he performed superbly as an inside forward. On being asked to fill the centre-half position in an emergency Marshall was so outstanding that he embarked on what could almost be called another City career. In total he played 355 League and Cup games for the Blues during an 11-year career before moving to Stockport County in March 1939.

BILLY DALE Full-back Billy Dale joined City from Manchester United in 1931 and went on to make 269 League and Cup appearances while with the Blues. He featured in the two FA Cup finals of the 1930s and in the 1936/37 League Championship season and was regarded by most Mancunians as the best full back in the country during his early years with City. Sadly, he was never selected to play for England but he did remain a popular Blue throughout his career. In 1938 he was transferred to Ipswich.

ERIC WESTWOOD Like Dale, Eric Westwood was both a Mancunian and a player for City and United, although he was an amateur in his days at Old Trafford. He joined City in 1937 and made his debut on the same day as Bert Sproston. During the war, Westwood guested for Chelsea and appeared in the 1944 wartime-Cup final but resumed his career in Manchester once League football had resumed.

A skilful left back, Westwood won a Division Two Championship medal in 1947 and was City captain at the time of Bert Trautmann's arrival in 1949. Westwood, who had served in Normandy, ensured that the former prisoner-of-war was welcomed to Maine Road in the same way any new player would be.

MCFC statistics

	1936/37	1937/38	1938/39	1945/46	1946/47	1947/48	1948/49	1949/50
League Position	Champs	21	5 (in Div 2)	-	Champs (in Div 2)	10 (in Div 1)	7	21
FA Cup Round Reached	6	6	4	4	5	5	3	3
Average Attendance	35,872	32,670	31,291	-	39,283	42,725	38,699	39,381

Honours

League Championship 1937; Charity Shield 1937; Division Two League Championship 1947

at the top probably helped his reputation develop further. Fans loved meeting him and the media were keen to hear his views on a variety of issues. He began to write a column for the *News of the World* and gave his opinion on issues such as World Cup football, refereeing, European competition and all the other major developments in 1950s football.

This role led to Frank becoming the *News of the World's* most popular sporting columnist. People would often buy the paper simply to read his views. Often his stories were serious, sometimes they were humorous, but they were always interesting. The *News of the World* would send Frank to all the major games and by 1957 he was being sent by the paper to follow Manchester United in European Cup action. He was one of the first footballing men to see the opportunities afforded by European competition and because of his rapport with fans, he called for the authorities to subsidise travel to help supporters to go abroad for games.

Sadly, it was while fulfilling his role with the newspaper that Frank was killed. He was flying with United back from their February 1958 match in Belgrade when their plane crashed while trying to take off at Munich. It was a major tragedy and

Mancunians of both the Blue and the Red persuasion were devastated by the blow. Frank, who by this stage was president of the City Supporters' Club, was sorely missed. The sports editor of the *News of the World* wrote a touching obituary. He revealed how the newspaper had received calls, letters and telegrams from thousands of people around the world, expressing their sorrow. These calls came from ordinary supporters and from significant international figures; even Santiago Bernabéu, the president of Real Madrid, called. Frank's humour, courage and general humility had touched everyone in the game.

The interest in Frank can best be demonstrated by an event from the final months of his life. Journalist John Hepburn recalls a telling incident that occurred after a match between Northern Ireland and England that Frank attended in November 1957. As the players and media representatives were leaving the ground, local schoolboys and other fans wanted to get autographs. 'Frank was being pressed for his signature in the midst of more than 50 schoolboys,' recalls Hepburn. 'Twenty yards away the England players were allowed to file into their bus unmolested – and unnoticed!'

'A few years back I interviewed Sir Tom Finney, the great England star, and he told me that Frank Swift was the greatest goalkeeper he had played against and with. Not only that, he told me, but Swift was a great entertainer. As a supporter, I believe football is all about entertaining. I'm delighted Frank has won this award and I hope City can keep on entertaining. That's what it's all about.'

Gary James
Manchester City Experience
museum manager,
collecting the Hall of Fame
award in January 2004.

Colin Bell MBE

A considerable number of supporters believe that Colin Bell is without doubt the greatest City player of all. He is a player remembered for many superb performances and also for his remarkable stamina and determination. He is also the Manchester City player to have been capped most by England, while with the Club. In addition to these significant attributes he is also the only footballer ever to have had a stand named after him at either of Manchester's clubs.

Colin Bell MBE
1972–1977 AWARD

Sad Beginnings

Colin was born in Hesleden, a small mining village in Durham, in 1946 and, as for many footballers from working-class backgrounds, his early life was difficult. His was also tinged with sadness. 'My mother died when I was born and, because my dad was a miner, working shifts, my sister had to look after me.' In those days there were few nurseries and child minding services were non-existent, so Colin's sister had to spend most of her time thinking of ways to keep him occupied while she was at school. In the end she had no option but to take him to school with her and as a two-year-old Colin used to keep himself occupied by playing football in the school yard. 'I used to play in the yard while my sister had lessons. She says that half the pupils would be looking out of the window watching me with the ball!'

Football was one of the family's main preoccupations. Colin's father was a noted local player who attracted attention from Nottingham Forest, while his mother had played for a pioneering ladies' side in the North East, as did his sister.

As Colin grew, his interest in the sport increased and he inevitably moved up the grades. He played for East Durham Boys and for the Horden Colliery Welfare junior side. League sides started to show interest, especially the local giants, Newcastle United. 'I had a trial at Newcastle when I was about 15 or 16 but they weren't interested, so I then had a trial with Arsenal.'

Turning Down Newcastle

The Arsenal opportunity fizzled out but two other sides, Huddersfield and Bury, were very keen to sign the youngster. Colin's father suggested that time should be spent at both clubs so that they could gauge properly which one it would be in Colin's best interests to join. They also agreed that the final decision would not be made until father and son were back home in the North East. After two reserve games for Bury, a couple of Bury directors tried to get Colin to sign immediately but, wisely, the player chose to hold off until he had spent a similar amount of time at Huddersfield. In the end both sides were desperate to sign him and both offered a wage of £12 a week.

Colin knew he wanted to sign for Bury – they appeared a much more homely and friendly club – but before he agreed terms, Newcastle renewed their interest. At the time Newcastle, Bury and Huddersfield were all Division Two sides but clearly Newcastle were significantly larger than either of the others. Nevertheless, the young Colin told them he was not interested in any offer: they'd had their chance and had missed it.

True to his instincts, Colin became a Bury man, in July 1963. Seven months later, he made his League debut against Manchester City. It was a rather unusual match and came at a time when City were at an extremely low point in their history. A pitiful Maine Road crowd of 14,698 watched the game but on the pitch Colin made it a memorable debut by scoring. 'I side-footed the ball in from six yards [5.5m] while City were appealing for offside. All I could think about were the headlines I would get in the next day's 'papers. The City 'keeper Harry Dowd got injured – these were the days before substitutes – so Harry went up front with his arm in a sling and he was City's most dangerous attacker! The inevitable happened and Harry scored the equaliser, which ruined my debut a bit.'

'The legion of City supporters roared ceaselessly in the last 15 minutes, "We're back in Division One", and Bell was cheered off the field.'

Despite the headlines going elsewhere, Colin's Bury career was off to a great start and by the time he left in March 1966 he had scored 25 goals in 82 League matches and had become team captain. He had also been noticed by a great number of clubs, in particular City and Blackpool. City were struggling financially and although new manager Joe Mercer and assistant Malcolm Allison had already started to turn things around at Maine Road, City could not afford to embark on an auction. Allison decided on a plan. 'I knew everybody was interested and I remember sitting in the directors' box at Gigg Lane. They all seemed to know I'd come to watch Colin but City were so strapped for cash that we couldn't really make a move until they'd raised enough. When the match started I kept saying that Colin was out of position... that he couldn't pass... he couldn't kick...

couldn't head the ball... he couldn't do anything right. They all started to agree with me! I said I'd wasted my time and they agreed!

'Behind the scenes the directors were getting the money together and on the eve of the transfer deadline we got him for about £45,000.'

Dodging the Deadline

Blackpool had been very interested, despite Allison's best efforts, and the transfer almost didn't make it in time. According to journalist Len Noad, writing in 1966, 'City paid £45,000 last night for Bury's Colin Bell. But the next-biggest deal since City paid Huddersfield £53,000 for Denis Law, had to wait for a pit shift to finish at Hesleden in Durham before it was completed. City manager Joe Mercer and chairman Albert Alexander arrived at Gigg Lane at

Player Career Statistics
Appearances

COLIN BELL

Position
Midfielder 1966–79

Typical Height and Weight
1.80m (5ft 11in)
72kg (11st 4lb)

Born
Hesleden, 26 February 1946

League Debut
Derby County (away)
19 March 1966
(scored one)

	LEAGUE		FA CUP		FL CUP		EUROPE		TOTAL	
	App	Gls	App	Gls	App	Gls	App	Gls	App	Gls
1965/66	11	4	0	0	0	0	-	-	11	4
1966/67	42	12	6	1	2	1	-	-	50	14
1967/68	35	14	4	2	4	1	-	-	43	17
1968/69	39	14	5	0	3	1	2	0	49	15
1969/70	31	11	2	0	6	5	9	5	48	21
1970/71	34	13	3	4	1	0	7	2	45	19
1971/72	33	12	2	0	1	2	-	-	36	14
1972/73	39	7	5	2	2	1	2	0	48	10
1973/74	41	7	2	0	11	3	-	-	54	10
1974/75	42	15	1	0	2	3	-	-	45	18
1975/76	20	6	0	0	5	1	-	-	25	7
1976/77	0	0	0	0	0	0	0	0	0	0
1977/78	16 (1)	2	2	0	2	0	0	0	20 (1)	2
1978/79	10	0	1 (1)	0	1	0	3 (1)	1	15 (2)	1
TOTAL	**393 (1)**	**117**	**33 (1)**	**9**	**40**	**18**	**23 (1)**	**8**	**489 (3)**	**152**

lunchtime and put their offer to Bell. The young player, who had already been approached by Blackpool, asked for time to think things over and to talk to his coalminer father when he came off his shift at 5pm.'

Once Colin did sign for City, Joe Mercer told reporters, 'It's the biggest fee I've ever paid, but I think he'll prove to be worth every penny of it.' The youngster immediately started to show it had been money well spent, with a goal on his League debut on 19 March 1966. The Blues beat Derby 2–1 and Colin's goal had proved vital but it was a rather unusual first goal, according to the *Manchester Evening Chronicle*. 'Bell received the ball from the brilliant Summerbee and drove it towards the goal. Saxton cleared rather vaguely and the ball bounced back into the net off Bell. An odd but acceptable way of celebrating a first appearance with a new club. To show that he was capable of better things, Bell developed the best shot of the game just before half time. Matthews did well to tip it over the bar.'

Approximately six weeks later Colin netted the goal that brought City promotion at Rotherham. Journalist Alec Johnson wrote at the time, 'City's fair-haired inside right, Colin Bell, rose high into the air in the 47th minute to head the ball into the back of the Rotherham net and send City back into the First Division after a three-year absence. It was a

golden goal – one that means a big cash bonus for the City players and the chance of really big-time soccer at Maine Road next season. The legion of City supporters roared ceaselessly in the last 15 minutes, "We're back in Division One", and Bell was cheered off the field.' Immediately after the game Colin told reporters, 'This is the most exciting goal I've ever scored.'

That goal in itself guaranteed that Colin would be remembered for a long time at City, but the events of the next few years helped to create a special relationship with City fans that survives to this day. Once promotion had been achieved, the Blues developed swiftly as a team and Colin started to become recognised across the country as a major talent, although he is the first to admit he was still learning. 'We beat Liverpool at the start of 1966/67 at Maine Road and Tommy Smith crocked me on the halfway line. As a youngster I didn't know what it was all about, though in later years you learned not to get too close to certain players if you could help it!'

Top Dogs

In 1967/68 City won the League Championship with Colin contributing 14 goals in 35 appearances. This was a period of great success for City as they won the FA Cup in 1969, the League Cup in 1970 and the European Cup Winners' Cup, also in 1970.

MCFC statistics

	1972/3	1973/74	1974/75	1975/76	1976/77	Honours
League Position	11	14	8	8	2	Charity Shield 1972; League Cup 1974 finalists; League Cup 1976
FA Cup Round Reached	5	4	3	4	5	
League Cup Round Reached	3	Final	3	Winners	2	
UEFA Cup Round Reached	1	-	-	-	1	
Average Attendance	32,351	30,756	32,898	34,281	40,056	

Colin Bell, watched by Leeds' Allan Clarke and City's Alan Oakes, has control at Maine Road on 31 August 1974.

Colin figured prominently in these triumphs and he was now widely regarded as one of England's greatest talents – a fact recognised by his inclusion in the England squad for the 1970 World Cup finals in Mexico.

Colin's England career had commenced with an appearance in the May 1968 friendly with Sweden and by the time of the 1970 World Cup he had appeared in 11 internationals and had scored 2 goals, although Colin believes those first few years of his international career were tough. 'It was hard getting my international career off the ground. I seemed to be injured whenever I was called up in the early days. After playing in the First Division, playing for my country had always been my greatest dream. No matter how many times I played, I still got a lump in my throat every time the letter with the FA stamp dropped through the letter box.'

The last England appearance made by Colin came on 30 October 1975 in the 2–1 defeat by Czechoslovakia in Bratislava. Colin had become a regular for England by then but a devastating injury was to prevent any further appearances.

Before the injury, however, Colin's City career continued to bring much praise his way. Johnny Hart, City's manager for a spell during 1973 and a member of City's great 1950s side, felt Colin was one of the best players he had ever worked with or seen. Talking in the early 1970s, Hart told Peter Gardner of the *Manchester Evening News*, 'Bell is an example of the complete professional footballer. City are indeed lucky to have a fella like this on their staff. His stamina is fantastic and his ball control is a delight to watch. He also sees situations like lightning and there are many opponents who have felt the full fury of his scoring potential. Bell is a

Colin's Finest Fellow Citizens

City were famous during Colin's era for being one of England's most entertaining sides. Attacking, stylish play was the order of the day as the Blues challenged for the title and had success with a League Cup victory in 1976.

DENNIS TUEART As goalscorer in the 1976 League Cup final, Dennis Tueart guaranteed that his name would be remembered for a very long time. His amazing, match-winning, overhead kick has been recognised as one of City's greatest-ever goals. Tueart, though, offered considerably more to football than simply that goal. Prior to joining the Blues, he had been a member of Sunderland's FA Cup-winning side of 1973 and in 1981 he appeared for City in the replay of the 100th FA Cup final. In between, he had become an England international and a popular City player. During the 1990s he became a City director, and remains a popular presence at the City of Manchester Stadium.

TOMMY BOOTH Often described by manager Joe Mercer as 'the best centre half since Stan Cullis and Tommy Jones', Tommy Booth first hit the headlines when he netted the only goal of the 1969 FA Cup semi-final against Everton. He went on to play a part in each of City's major successes, making his last appearance for the Blues in September 1981. All together he made 476 appearances, plus 2 as substitute, in the League, FA Cup, League Cup and in European competition while with the Blues. Supporters loved the fact that he was a Mancunian and a product of City's scouting system.

WILLIE DONACHIE Glasgow-born Willie Donachie proved to be one of City's best full backs during the 1970s. An ever-present in 1973/74 and 1976/77, Donachie also appeared in 35 internationals for Scotland, and was a member of Scotland's 1978 World Cup squad. He also appeared in two League Cup finals with City and went on to make over 420 appearances for the Blues. During the 1990s he returned to Maine Road as assistant to Joe Royle and the two men guided City to successive promotions.

PETER BARNES Popular winger Peter Barnes was voted PFA Young Player of the Year in 1976 and in that same season he netted the opening goal of the League Cup final. As the son of 1950s great Ken Barnes, Peter was expected to make a good impression when he made his debut in 1974 and he didn't disappoint. He scored his first League goal in only his third match, at Carlisle on 19 March 1975, and went on to become a fine City entertainer, with some dazzling runs down the wing. He became an England international in 1977 and made a total of 22 international appearances, 14 of which came while he was with City.

MIKE DOYLE Renowned for his dislike of Manchester United, locally born Mike Doyle was one of City's great success stories. A member of the struggling pre-Mercer side of 1965, Doyle enjoyed the transformation he witnessed over the following decade or so at Maine Road. A key player in every success between 1965 and 1978, Doyle was captain when the Blues lifted the League Cup in 1976 with victory over Newcastle United, and he remained with City until June 1978.

GARY OWEN After joining City from Manchester Boys in August 1974, Gary Owen made his debut in March 1976. Always popular with supporters, the midfielder made a total of 122 appearances, plus 2 as substitute, for City and netted 23 goals before his controversial move to West Bromwich Albion in 1979. Neither the player nor the supporters wanted the transfer but the move came at a time when Malcolm Allison was determined to create a new team. Owen was one of several high-profile departures at the time. Despite the move, Owen remained very much a Blue at heart and in recent years he has worked for the local media commentating on City's matches. He remains hugely popular with supporters.

Hall of Fame inductees Colin Bell, Francis Lee and
Mike Summerbee pause during training.

midfield dynamo but he can also be a marksman
supreme, given half the chance. He has an explosive
shot and he is, too, a brilliant header of the ball,
making him extremely dangerous anywhere within
sight of goal. He is, in fact, a modern Peter Doherty.'

Moral Victories

In 1974 Colin scored City's only goal of the League
Cup-final meeting with Wolves. Sadly, Wolves won,
but many felt that City had been the dominant side.
Colin agrees with that assessment. 'In my career I've
played in two games of this kind. One was when
England drew with Poland at Wembley and missed
qualifying for the '74 World Cup. Wolves was the
other. If either of those games had been boxing
matches, the opposition would have thrown the
towel in! We were 1–0 down to Wolves at half time
but I always felt if we pulled one back we would win.
I got the equaliser and we were never out of their
half after that. Then, late on, a ball was played

across our area, Rodney Marsh just got a toe to it
and helped it in the direction of John Richards who
scored the Wolves' winner.'

The disappointment hung over City for a while
and, in truth, that League Cup final saw the end of
the great Bell-Lee-Summerbee combination, as over
the following months first Lee, then Summerbee
were to move on. Of the 1968 Championship side
only Colin, Mike Doyle and Alan Oakes were still
regulars by the start of the 1975/76 season, but the
mid-1970s side was still packed with internationals
and top-quality players. The side had finished eighth
in 1975 and as the new season opened there was
great optimism around Maine Road. Everything
seemed perfect and when the Blues drew recently
promoted Manchester United in the fourth round of
the League Cup, in November 1975, City couldn't
wait for the opportunity to prove which side was
the dominant force. Colin, who felt he had struggled
at times during the previous year, was feeling very

Colin's Prime Time

Manchester City 4 Newcastle United 0. Football League Division One – 26 December 1977

Goalscorers Tueart (3), Kidd

City Team Corrigan, Clements, Donachie, Booth, Watson, Power (Bell), Barnes, Owen, Kidd, Hartford, Tueart

Attendance 45,811

This match has entered Manchester folklore as one of those games you just had to experience to fully appreciate it. All of those present that night, from players to fans to club officials to newspaper reporters, talk of it as one of football's most emotional nights.

The story of Colin Bell and his injury had become one of football's most discussed issues. The tea-time BBC television news show *Nationwide* had profiled Colin's tragic story and as a result the player received thousands of good luck messages from neutrals and ordinary non-footballing members of the public. They had been touched by his long, hard training schedules; his lonely runs through the streets of Moss Side and Rusholme; and by his absolute determination to return to full fitness. To them Colin's story was incredible, to City and England supporters it was a deeply disappointing and tragic story.

Colin's gruelling training regime ensured he had forced his way into manager Tony Book's thinking by December 1977 and on Boxing Day he was named as substitute for the visit of Newcastle. Anticipation was high as supporters believed this would be the day they would see their hero return to action.

Chairman Peter Swales rated Colin highly and shortly before his death in 1996 Swales explained, 'The supporters loved him. You can never kid supporters. They know great players. It's no good a manager saying, "This is the best player we've ever had." The supporters will know after a few weeks whether he really is the best. Bell was the best; no question.'

On the night itself Tony Book had planned to send Colin on as substitute for the final 20 minutes but an injury to Paul Power meant the manager had to take decisive action. The supporters didn't realise it but as the players were making their way into the dressing room for the interval, it was decided that Colin would play the second half. During the interval fans started to speculate as to when they would see their hero, with the majority believing he would come on for the final flourish, but as the players came back out on to the pitch it was clear that Paul Power was missing and that Colin was coming on.

The stadium erupted and the fans on the Kippax terracing began to chant his name. It was a truly marvellous sight and a tremendous feeling of anticipation and excitement that had never been felt midway through a match for any player before. It was the most amazing individual moment witnessed at the old ground. Dennis Tueart, a player that day, remembers, 'He came on at half time, and it was like World War Three. I've never known a noise like it in all my life! The crowd gave him a standing ovation and he hadn't even touched the ball. I've never seen a guy work as hard to get back. The hours and hours he put in. The pain he went through... it was a phenomenal amount of work and he definitely deserved that ovation.'

For the player himself the day remains one of the most significant memories of his life. 'As I came down the tunnel I could hear a whisper go right round the ground. I knew that reception was for me alone. I was never an emotional player but I got a big lump in my throat. I've been lucky to win cups and medals and play internationals, but of all my great football memories, that is the one that sticks in my mind.

'The City crowd and I had this mutual respect really, and that standing ovation from over 40,000 people brought a lump to my throat for the only time in my career.'

The substitution totally transformed the atmosphere and the result. The game had been goalless, but the Blues tore into Newcastle as if they were playing in the most important game of all time. Dennis Tueart played superbly and scored a hat-trick, with Brian Kidd also scoring, to make it a convincing 4–0 win for the Blues. At one point Colin had a header that just sneaked over the bar but the fairytale goal on his return did not arrive.

A modest Colin feels he didn't contribute a great deal. 'I don't think I touched the ball. It was ten men versus eleven but the atmosphere got to our team and we ran away with it.'

Normally, this game would be a footnote in history, but for many it remains the most emotional of all time.

Classic Bell – Colin seen at Maine Road during 1968/69.

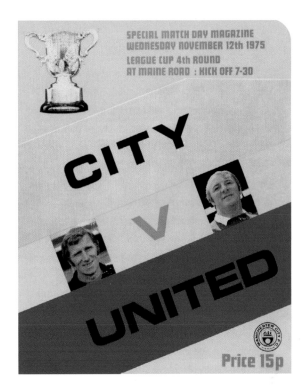

The programme from Colin's career-threatening game with Manchester United.

positive about the future. 'Two or three games before we played United I suddenly felt everything had come right. I couldn't do a thing wrong. I thought, "Terrific".'

A Melancholy Moment

The League Cup tie with United proved to be one of City's most mesmerising performances but it also contained the saddest moment of the decade as far as many fans were concerned. The game opened brightly with Dennis Tueart scoring after only 35 seconds. United struggled to match the Blues and resorted to a physical approach. After only five minutes, a calamity occurred, when Colin Bell remained on the ground after a tackle by Martin Buchan. 'I remember Dennis Tueart knocking me through on the inside right position,' says Colin, 'and I had three options. The first was I was going to have a shot if the ball would sit right, from about 25 to 30 yards out. Or I could even quicken up and go for goal first thing. The third option was to drag the ball inside a defender – and it was Martin Buchan, as it happens. I was weight bearing on my right leg as I dragged the ball to let him go past at speed and he caught my knee... bent the knee backwards, burst a couple of blood vessels, did the ligaments, did the cartilage and off I went. That was the beginning of the end of my career.'

Although Colin does not blame Martin Buchan, the supporters did – and still do. On the night they chanted 'Animal' at Buchan as Colin was stretchered from the field. City went on to win the match 4–0 as they swept United aside and eventually the Blues were victorious at Wembley in the 1976 League Cup final, but the meeting with United damaged not only Colin's career but also City's chance of major success in the League. Dennis Tueart believes the side was disrupted too much by the injury. 'It left a major hole in our side – a major hole! He would have been a major loss to any side but ours in particular because we had such a balanced side; such a settled team. Although we went on to win the League Cup, that was the biggest setback and I don't think we were ever really as good after Colin's injury.'

Over the following seasons Colin tried hard to resurrect his career. He did return briefly at the end of the 1975/76 season but it was clear he was far from fully fit and, potentially, the early return caused more damage. Eventually, he returned to action on Boxing Day 1977 and went on to make a further 27 League appearances before finally calling it a day in 1979. During his recovery period he was a key member of the City reserve side that won the Central League in 1978 – a triumph of which he feels immensely proud.

The previous season a Colin-less City side had missed the League Championship by a point and many believe a fit Colin would have made the crucial difference.

A Major Honour

In retirement Colin concentrated on the restaurant business that he had opened midway through his City career and then in 1990 he returned to Maine Road to assist with reserve and youth-team coaching. Seven years later that City career ended but in recent years Colin has been a member of City's matchday corporate hospitality team. Then in 2004 he received the honour of having the West Stand at the City of Manchester Stadium named after him, and was awarded an MBE by the Queen. These are major honours and both recognise the achievements of an incredible talent and a tremendously popular City player.

‘ This is very special to me. I'd like to say a big thank you to the people who have backed me for 34 years now; that's the supporters of Manchester City. Thank you. ’

Colin Bell MBE
collecting the Hall of Fame
award in January 2004.

Billy Meredith

Billy Meredith was football's first true superstar.

He was an immensely popular figure, appearing in all the sporting press of the day, but he was also a highly controversial player. For years he campaigned for the rights of footballers and was always one of the first to air his views on the issues of the day. He was a very patriotic Welshman but as far as Mancunians were concerned, Billy was a true Blue. His attitude to life was typical of many City fans and his commitment to the causes in which he believed was total.

Billy Meredith
PRE-1910 AWARD

A Rich Seam of Talent

Billy grew up during the 1870s and 1880s in Chirk, at that time part of an important coal-mining area of Denbighshire, Wales. At the age of 12 Billy started to work in the mines, helping to move the tubs of coal along as they came through the tunnels. Sometimes he would guide ponies through the mines; at other times he would push the tubs himself. Life was tough but football was the chief release. During his City career Billy talked of his family's interest in the game. 'All my brothers were players. Elias, the eldest, was fond of football but he didn't play as much as Jim, a right full back, and Sam, a left full back, who went on to play for Stoke.' Sam actually left Chirk for football some years before Billy but it was the younger man who would eventually become one of the most famous names in Britain. Billy, a winger, played for the local Chirk side and even appeared for them in two Welsh FA Cup finals. He also appeared in games against English sides, usually the reserve sides of League clubs, and one of these games was against one of Manchester City's earliest local rivals, Gorton Villa. Chirk defeated Gorton Villa 10–1 in October 1892 with Billy in outstanding form.

The following season Billy played some games for Northwich Victoria, as well as Chirk, before officials from several League clubs came with offers.

A Mother's Advice

Billy's transfer became one of early football's best stories and gave some indication of the lengths clubs would go to sign players. The story, as told by witnesses during the early years of the 20th century, is that two officials from City, probably two of the Club's founding fathers, Lawrence Furniss and Joshua Parlby, arrived in Wales looking for the player that Furniss had spotted while refereeing a Northwich match. The two men were chased by locals and thrown into a duck pond. They then sought disguises and had to buy drinks for all of Billy's co-workers at the mine before they were allowed to speak to him.

Furniss and Parlby also had to face Billy's mother, who, according to her son, said: "It is all very well for you gentlemen to leave your big cities and come to our villages to steal our boys away. You offer good money, I know, and I suppose it pays you to do so, or you would not come. But a mother thinks of other things besides money. Our boys are happy and healthy, satisfied with their work and their innocent amusements. You gentlemen come and put all kinds of ideas into their heads. Tell them they can get more money for play than they can for hard but honest work... if Billy takes my advice he will stick to his work and play football for his own amusement when his work is finished.'

Whether Billy listened to his mother is not clear but the player did sign for City in October 1894. He also continued to commute to Chirk and work in the mine for at least a year, possibly four, after his transfer. Perhaps he needed to prove to his mother that he wasn't off to the big city simply to enjoy himself.

Within two weeks of signing he made his League debut at Newcastle on 3 November 1894 he played his first home game at City's Hyde Road ground. The match was the very first League meeting between Manchester City and Newton Heath, who were later to become Manchester United. The Heathens won the game 5–2 but Billy scored both of City's goals, causing the *Umpire* newspaper to state, 'The play of the young Welsh player, Meredith, was far superior to that of any other.'

The First Superstar

As Billy's career in England developed, so too did the fortunes of City. In 1894 the Blues had re-formed as City out of the ashes of an insolvent Ardwick AFC and the ambitions of the new club were to achieve Division One football and parity with the great clubs of the period, such as Everton and Aston Villa.

In 1896 City finished second in Division Two but promotion was not guaranteed for any side and the Blues failed in the end of season test matches.

In 1899, however, the Blues became the first Manchester side to gain promotion, when they won the Division Two title for the first time. Billy scored 29 goals in 33 games – he only missed one match – and was City's most important player by far. He had also been a Welsh international since 1895 and the national media were already aware of his immense talent. So much so that when he married his childhood sweetheart in 1901, one national sporting newspaper covered the story – something that was unheard of at the time. The article noted that, 'William Meredith, City's crack outside right and probably the cleverest man in his position throughout the United Kingdom, was married to Miss Negus in the early part of last week.'

Billy's fame was to grow during the early years of the century and by the time of City's great Cup run of 1904 he was football's most famous star. Rightly acclaimed as the greatest winger of the period by the *Umpire* newspaper in 1903, Billy's stature in the game grew after every match. He was made City's captain and after a Cup tie with Sunderland in 1904 the *Athletic News* reported, 'The City captain was the raider in chief and undoubtedly the most dazzling forward on the field. Assiduously supplied, the famous Welshman hardly ever failed to respond to the calls made upon him. His command of the ball as he threaded his way through the maze of his adversaries commanded admiration. Against a team of such class Meredith has not often given a more dazzling display. I have no wish to be guilty of exaggeration, but Meredith was the King of the Realm.'

Player Career Statistics
Appearances

BILLY MEREDITH

Position
Wing forward 1894–1906,
1921–24

Typical Height and Weight
1.72m (5ft 8in)
67kg (10st 7lb)

Born
Chirk, 30 July 1874

Deceased
Manchester, 19 April 1958

League Debut
Newcastle United (away)
27 October 1894

	LEAGUE		FA CUP		Test Matches		TOTAL	
	App	Gls	App	Gls	App	Gls	App	Gls
1894/95	18	12	0	0			18	12
1895/96	29	12	0	0	4	1	33	13
1896/97	27	10	1	0			28	10
1897/98	30	12	2	0			32	12
1898/99	33	29	1	1			34	30
1899/00	33	14	2	0			35	14
1900/01	34	7	1	0			35	7
1901/02	33	8	4	0			37	8
1902/03	34	22	1	0			35	22
1903/04	34	11	6	2			40	13
1904/05	33	8	2	1			35	9
1921/22	25	0	0	0			25	0
1922/23	1	0	0	0			1	0
1923/24	2	0	4	1			6	1
TOTAL	366	145	24	5	4	1	394	151

Success and Scandal

Under Billy's direction, the Blues won the FA Cup for the first time and finished second in the League in 1904. It was a fantastic achievement and the most successful season ever recorded by either of the Manchester clubs up until that time. Billy became Manchester's leading personality and, again, his national fame continued to grow. Every newspaper started to feature the player, while poems were sent in stressing his skills and his importance to Manchester. There were even songs written about him. According to Billy's biographer John Harding, the following was a very popular song sung by the fans on the Hyde Road terraces during 1904:

'Oh I wish I was you Billy Meredith
I wish I was you, I envy you, indeed I do!
It ain't that you're tricky with your feet,
But it's those centres that you send in
Which Turnbull then heads in,
Oh I wish I was you,
Indeed I do,
Indeed I do...'

The Cup success saw Billy become an even more prominent figure off the field. Railway Companies and products such as OXO started to use him in their publicity, while local politicians encouraged him to support their campaigns. Sadly, this higher profile also caused many footballing establishment figures to question what was going on

MCFC statistics

	1892/3	1893/4	1894/95	1895/96	1896/97	1897/8	1898/99	1899/00	1900/01
League Position	5 (in Div 2)	13	9	2	6	3	Champs (in Div 2)	7 (in Div 1)	11
FA Cup Round Reached	Q1	Q1	-	Q1	1	2	1	1	1
Average Attendance	3,000	4,000	6,000	10,000	8,000	8,000	10,000	16,000	18,300

	1901/02	1902/03	1903/04	1904/05	1905/06	1906/07	1907/08	1908/09	1909/10
League Position	18	Champs (in Div 2)	2 (in Div 1)	3	5	17	3	19	Champs (in Div 2)
FA Cup Round Reached	2	1	Winners	2	1	1	3	1	4
Average Attendance	17,000	16,000	20,000	20,000	18,000	22,150	23,000	20,000	18,275

Honours

FA Cup 1904; Division Two League Championship 1899, 1903 and 1910

Other Significant Events

Founder members of Division Two as Ardwick AFC in 1892; re-formed as Manchester City FC in 1894; failed in promotion test matches (similar to modern day play-offs) in 1896

'City was always his team and meant more to him than United ever could.'

behind the scenes at Hyde Road. The transformation of City from being a lower than average Division Two side into FA Cup winners within ten seasons had caused some to question the general organisation of the Club.

The southern-based Football Association were desperate to find an excuse for investigating the Club and, City being City, the Blues handed them that excuse on a plate. As with the Cup success in 1904, Billy was at the centre of the story.

Second-placed City needed to beat Aston Villa and rely on Newcastle dropping a point at Middlesbrough on the last day of the 1904/05 season to bring the Blues their first League title. It was not going to be easy but, according to Billy, the City officials offered their players a £100 bonus if they won at Villa Park. The bonus was enormous at the time and Billy and his team were determined to succeed. However, the game became extremely confrontational, with City's Sandy Turnbull and Villa's Alec Leake the key protagonists. According to the Bolton *Football Field*, 'Leake found [Turnbull] a real hard opponent and, becoming annoyed at the rough impact, gathered up a handful of dirt and hurled it at the City man. Turnbull was not hurt and responded with an acknowledgement favoured by the bourgeoisie – thrusting two fingers in a figurative manner at the Villa man.'

Amazing Allegations

Leake then, stated the report, gave Turnbull 'a backhander' and then a fight broke out. As the players left the pitch at full time, the report claimed, Turnbull was dragged into the Villa dressing room and then thrown out seconds later with cuts and bruises to his body.

The FA started their investigations almost immediately and at the start of August they announced their findings. The news caused an

outcry and northern football was absolutely amazed when the announcement was made that Billy – and nobody else – was to be banned from football until April 1906. According to the FA, the City captain had attempted to bribe Alec Leake to throw the match.

Billy was devastated. 'I am entirely innocent,' he said. 'Such an allegation as that of bribery is preposterous! I could never risk my reputation and future by such an action and I repeat that I never made such an offer. It is totally unjustified and grossly unfair. This sort of thing will demoralise Association Football. Manchester has not many

City became the first Manchester side to win a major trophy with their FA Cup success in 1904.

Billy's Prime Time

Manchester City 1 Bolton Wanderers 0. FA Cup Final – 23 April 1904

Goalscorer Meredith

City Team Hillman, McMahon, Burgess, Frost, Hynds, Ashworth, Meredith, Livingstone, Gillespie, Turnbull, Booth

Attendance 61,374

The 1904 FA Cup final was undoubtedly the moment when Manchester City established themselves as a footballing power. For captain Billy Meredith, this had to be one of the proudest moments of his career. Not only was he the Blues' influential leader, he was also the sole goalscorer on the day when Lancashire took over the capital city.

Billy had taken a good look at the pitch during the late morning. He was confident of victory but not complacent. A journalist from the Daily Dispatch asked him what he thought of City's chances and he replied, 'Good. We ought to win. You never know, but if we play anything like our normal game, the Cup is ours. All the boys are going for all they are worth.'

Later, shortly before kick-off, Billy led the City team out, chewing on his trademark toothpick.

Meredith surges towards the Bolton goal prior to scoring in the 1904 final.

He proceeded to win the toss and, once the match kicked off, both sides seemed well matched. Then an opportunity came City's way. Journalist Jimmy Catton from the Athletic News witnessed the action. 'At the end of 20 minutes Livingstone made a long, swinging pass out to the right for Meredith, who forged ahead and scored practically without opposition. Struthers was left, and with only Davies to beat, the deed was done quietly but effectively. Bolton seemed to lag behind as Manchester played even better still, and when the interval arrived they were certainly entitled to their lead of one goal – if not more, on the play.'

Boltonians claimed the goal was offside but Mancunians felt otherwise, as did the referee. Billy was adamant for the rest of his life that the goal had been perfectly legitimate. Maybe the Bolton fans and players were particularly upset because for most of the second half Billy had seemed determined to waste time and, not only that, had done so by moving frequently into offside positions.

The game ended with the 1–0 victory and Billy received the trophy on behalf of the Blues. This was the first major trophy won by either of the Manchester sides and as such was a major moment in the history of Manchester sport. Journalist Eric Thornton interviewed Billy during the 1940s about this day and, based on what Billy said, Thornton later wrote about City's homecoming, 'It was the very first time the trophy had been brought back to Manchester and I'm told the town went mad, with Meredith the big hero. He took most of the cheers while holding the Cup aloft on Manchester's first triumphal soccer tour. It was a terrific night. The townsfolk let their hair down.'

friends among the Association officials. The FA was too influenced by Aston Villa. Manchester City is becoming too popular to suit some other clubs.'

The controversy raged on for some time and the FA started investigating City's finances as well as player conduct. In May 1906 they announced that the Blues had been making illegal payments to their players for years. The maximum wage stood at £4 per week and the FA identified that Billy had been paid £6 and that others had been paid similar amounts. As a result the FA imposed their most severe penalty ever on one of football's largest clubs. They decreed that 17 players were to be suspended until January 1907 and that the manager Tom Maley and former Chairman W. Forrest were to be banned sine die. They also suspended two directors. Inevitably, there were also fines for the players – Billy was fined £100 – and for the Club.

After the Scandal

No club in the history of football has ever suffered to such an extent and all Mancunians were united in their disgust at the Club's treatment. Worse was to follow as the FA made it clear that the banned players had to be transferred by the Club and pressure was placed on the Blues to transfer some of the players to the then poor relations of local football, Manchester United. Billy, as the most important member of the side, should have been worth a small fortune but his transfer to the Reds brought the Blues no fee. Ironically, United paid Billy an amount of £600, which was, in effect, equivalent to his transfer fee.

Most Mancunians were delighted that football's first true star was to remain in Manchester, although it's fair to say the rivalry between the Reds and the Blues was not particularly intense at this point in history. For Billy the move was a good one, especially as several other 1904 Cup winners joined the Reds at the same time.

Billy remained with United until the outbreak of the First World War, by which time he and the other City men had helped United to their first honours. Again the Welshman was the inspirational figure and

Five months short of his 50th birthday, Meredith is the star of Brighton v City on 23 February 1924.

his fame continued to develop. His fight for players' rights also increased during this time as he became one of the leading figures behind the formation of the Players' Union, the forerunner of the PFA. The Union was often described as 'Meredith's Union' as he was usually seen as the inspirational figure behind it. He was certainly the most public player.

During the First World War Billy returned as a player and as a coach to Hyde Road, despite still officially being a United man, and in July 1921 he returned to City on a formal basis. According to his daughter Winifred, speaking in 2004, his heart had always been with the Blues. 'He felt at home at City. I know he had great success at United but I don't think they ever really appreciated him in the way City did. I think United were not paying him properly after the war and, because of his age, they probably didn't value him. But City did and it's clear they still love him today. City was always his team and meant more to him than United ever could.'

Middle-Aged Maestro

Billy made 25 League appearances in 1921/22, and one in 1922/23 – the last season at Hyde Road. The

Billy's Finest Fellow Citizens

After joining Division Two in 1892 as Ardwick, the Blues' development was rapid. They re-formed as Manchester City in 1894 – the name represented their desire to create a team to represent all Mancunians – and they narrowly missed out on promotion in 1896. In 1899 they became the first Manchester side to be promoted and then a mere five years later they won the FA Cup and finished second in the League. They became recognised throughout football as a leading force and by 1910 were one of football's most popular sides.

BILLY LOT JONES Welsh international forward Billy Lot Jones joined the Blues in 1903 and made his debut in April 1904. He went on to serve the Club with distinction until 1919. A member of the Division Two Championship side of 1910 – he scored 12 goals in 37 appearances that season – Jones was well liked by supporters and in 1908 his benefit match with Middlesbrough raised the significant amount of £835. He netted 69 goals in 281 League appearances, but although this is a decent ratio, journalists of the period felt Jones missed rather too many chances. They did recognise, however, that his all-round play was significantly better than most players of his generation. Jones made 20 Welsh international appearances, 19 of which came during his time with City.

WALTER SMITH At 5ft 7in (1.68m) tall, Walter Smith was an unlikely goalkeeper but during a 14-year career with City he was immensely popular and, like the brilliant Swift and Trautmann in later years, he made many truly great performances. In 1914 he won representative honours when he played for an England XI against a Scotland XI and in 1915 he played for the Football League against the Scottish League. Inevitably, the First World War limited his opportunities but he did manage to make a total of 256 League and Cup appearances during his City career.

BILLY GILLESPIE After Meredith, Billy Gillespie was the most popular player in Manchester's first FA Cup-winning side. Although his style was significantly different to Meredith's – one of his favourite activities seemed to be barging or bundling the opposition goalkeeper over the line to ensure a City goal – he was loved by fans. When his City career was prematurely cut short by the FA investigations into the bribery and illegal payments scandal of 1905, Gillespie decided that he wouldn't pay the £50 fine. Instead he emigrated, and for the following 40 years or more, stories of his exploits regularly did the rounds in Manchester. Some said he had gone prospecting for diamonds in South Africa; others said he was living in Montreal. Each year a new version of the story seemed to emerge as the Gillespie legend developed. In truth, Gillespie had emigrated to the United States and had become noted locally as a terrific sportsman. At one point he and the legendary baseball player Babe Ruth held centre stage at a sporting event in Gillespie's home state of Massachusetts.

SANDY TURNBULL A 1902 signing for City from Hurlford, a Scottish club, 5ft 5in (1.62m) Turnbull was an impressive inside forward for the Blues until the illegal payments scandal investigations rocked the Club. He eventually signed for United – City supporters were determined their heroes would remain in Manchester and actively encouraged the likes of Meredith and Turnbull to join the Reds – in December 1906.

During his City career he netted 60 goals in 119 League and FA Cup appearances and was a key member of the 1904 Cup-winning side. Sadly, on 3 May 1917 he was killed in action at Arras. Some historians claim he participated in the famous Christmas Day battlefield match against the Germans during the First World War.

GEORGE DORSETT From a famous footballing family – his brother Joe also played for City and another relative, Dickie, played for Wolves – George Dorsett joined the

Future Prime Minister Arthur Balfour – a Club patron – meets Meredith prior to the 2–0
victory over Stoke in September 1900 at Hyde Road. Note the referee's clothing on the left.

Blues as an outside left in 1905 but was soon switched to wing half. Dorsett made 211 League and FA Cup appearances and scored 65 goals while at Hyde Road and participated in City's first overseas tour in May 1910 when the Blues travelled by ship to Germany and Denmark. Dorsett never managed to appear for England but he was selected to play for the Football League against the Irish League in October 1905 – a game staged at Hyde Road.

JIMMY ROSS When Jimmy Ross arrived at City in February 1899 he was already a major star. Ross was probably the first recognisably great player to join the Blues. Clearly, Meredith and others became major stars while at Hyde Road but Ross was the first already to be

a national figure. Ross had been a member of the great Preston side that had won the League and Cup double in 1888/89, the first season of League football, and was already well known around the Manchester area for his goalscoring feats against Hyde in the FA Cup. Ross had scored seven (sometimes quoted as eight) of Preston's goals when they had defeated Hyde 26–0.

At City he helped the Blues to win the Division Two Championship in 1899 – he arrived for the final weeks of the season and scored seven goals in nine games – but, sadly, he passed away during the 1902 close season after a short illness. Journalists reported that he had been afflicted by 'an acute skin disease and a raging fever'. It was a devastating blow to the Club and to football.

Blues moved to Maine Road at the start of the 1923/24 season and, incredibly, Billy went on to play in two League games at the new venue. But that wasn't all he achieved that season because, at the age of 49, he played a key role in City's FA Cup run, scoring at Brighton in the third round. One match – the fourth-round tie against Cardiff – was watched by an incredible 76,166, which, at the time, was the largest football crowd in Manchester for any fixture, including two Cup finals and numerous semi-finals. Most people had come to see the legendary Welshman's quest for a Cup medal and for a few weeks it looked as if Billy might just make an appearance at the newly opened Wembley Stadium. Sadly, it wasn't to be as City lost 2–0 to Newcastle in the FA Cup semi-final. It was to be Billy's last match.

An Iconic Figure

For the next few years Billy's fame continued to grow. He was the star of a film, *The Ball of Fortune*, and became a popular presence at major events around Manchester and Wales. He had several years as a licensee – he'd been the licensee of the Church Hotel in Longsight while still a City player during the early 1920s – and he also enjoyed a series of benefit matches played in his honour in his home country of Wales and in Manchester.

His footballing life continued for some time when he became a founder member of Manchester Central FC, playing at the Belle Vue Athletics Stadium. Central hoped to fill the void left by City when they moved to Maine Road from east Manchester but by the mid-1930s this enterprise had collapsed. The great man continued to follow the Welsh international team and was also present at many significant footballing events until his death in April 1958 at the age of 83. He was buried at Southern Cemetery.

At the time when he passed away, football and Manchester residents were mourning the loss of Frank Swift and the Busby Babes and as a result Billy's death received considerably less coverage than it would normally have warranted.

Proving that interest in the player never dies, in 1997 a television programme was made about his life. Today, over 100 years after Manchester's first trophy success, Billy's name stands clear as football's first true superstar and a man idolised by all Mancunians. He remains a truly iconic figure.

Kevin Keegan
prior to a standing ovation
for Meredith's daughter at
the Hall of Fame Awards
in 2004.

' I can't understand why I was asked to present the pre-1910 category – there's other members of my staff, Peter Bonetti and Arthur Cox, who have played against these guys! Having said that, I'm very honoured to be presenting this award to Billy Meredith. Now understandably Billy can't be here tonight but I'm delighted to ask Billy Meredith's 98-year-old daughter Winifred to collect the award on his behalf. '

Peter Doherty

There are many truly great players featured in Manchester City's Hall of Fame but there is one man whose name and reputation is so great that, even today, 70 years after his arrival at City, Peter Doherty is still regarded by many as the greatest of them all.

Peter Doherty
PANEL AWARD

Self-Taught Skills

Born in Magharafelt in Ireland in 1913, Peter Doherty, like many of the players featured in this book, was devoted to football from the beginning. In his autobiography, published in 1947, he remembered that the sport was always in his thoughts. 'I practised at every opportunity. My life seemed to be dedicated to the game and I was never happier than when I had a ball at my feet.' Opportunities to play football on a formal basis at school were limited. 'I went to St. Malachi's in Coleraine. It was just an ordinary elementary school. We never had a school team. The small teaching staff was far too busy trying to cope with ordinary lessons to ever bother about sport. A properly organised game with 11 on each side didn't come my way until I was in my teens – and even then I hadn't a pair of football boots to call my own. They were far too expensive a luxury for me.'

Today it is hard to imagine a world where even the most gifted of sportsmen were unable to afford simple items, such as boots, but for many youngsters footballing skills had to be learned using ordinary footwear, regular clothing and makeshift balls. Sometimes these balls would simply be rags or newspaper tied up with string, and games would take place in the street or any open space they could find. As a result, Peter and the players of his generation developed skills that would help them play in whatever conditions would be thrown at them.

Peter's footballing skills eventually led him to begin playing for a local junior team called Station United. Shortly after leaving school he received an invitation to join local side Coleraine as an amateur. Although most youngsters would be thrilled with this offer, it seems Peter remained level-headed. He felt that every decent player in the area had received a similar offer. It wasn't long, however, before Peter began to believe that his offer was a little different and that Coleraine were keen to see exactly what

the boy could do. He was asked to report to the Coleraine ground as a reserve – the idea was to give him the opportunity to participate in the regular match routine. Peter became excited by this prospect and started to realise that this could be his big chance. 'When Saturday came I could hardly contain my excitement. I raced to the ground, and then prowled about outside the dressing rooms, too nervous to even poke my nose in. Suppose someone doesn't turn up, I thought – I'll be playing, actually playing for Coleraine! And then as I toyed with my hopes, I suddenly found myself being hustled into the dressing room, and told to change. Someone actually hadn't turned up. By the time I'd donned a jersey and rummaged amongst the pile of boots in the middle of the floor to find a pair to fit me, the game had started. But once outside, the air and shorts and jersey gave me that free, fresh feeling you always get at the beginning of a game.'

Bitter Disappointment

Despite his hopes, the game was not a positive experience for Peter. He hardly had an opportunity to impress and at half time he was largely ignored. Then the player he had replaced arrived and Peter was asked to hand him his football shirt. It was a bitter blow. 'I struggled out if it [the shirt], fighting hard to keep back the tears, and vowing bitterly that Coleraine would never get another chance to treat me so badly.'

Peter continued to play for Station United and also managed to find a job as an apprentice to a local builder. He was earning seven shillings (35p) a week but, understandably, he still wanted to progress as a footballer. The brother of a Glentoran full back owned a local business and he urged the Belfast-based club to give Peter a trial. One thing led to another and, within a short period of time, Peter was offered a trial. 'I realised that a trial with Glentoran might be the gateway to money and

'I was gaining experience rapidly.

In many respects, a small club like Glentoran is the best training ground for a young player on the threshold of his career, and when a good coach is also available, the set-up is ideal.'

independence, but I didn't feel very keen about it at first. Belfast is 60 miles [96km] from Coleraine, and to play there meant staying overnight. I'd never been away from home before.'

Fortunately, Peter went to the trial and it proved very successful. He was offered a contract and promises were made to find him a trade to support his footballing income. Those promises soon vanished. That experience, together with the game for Coleraine, helped to shape Peter's views of football as a business. He became aware that players were often treated appallingly by clubs and that the management always had the upper hand. Throughout his career, he sought justice and was keen to ensure that players were treated in a professional manner.

Small is Beautiful

At Glentoran Peter's career developed. 'I was gaining experience rapidly. In many respects, a small club like Glentoran is the best training ground for a young player on the threshold of his career, and when a good coach is also available, the set-up is ideal.'

After a couple of seasons the opportunity arose for Peter to move to an English club. Blackpool made a formal approach and in 1933, after only ten minutes' worth of discussion, Peter decided to make the move to England.

Peter settled quickly at Blackpool and soon developed into an international player. 'I soon felt completely at home, and after making several spasmodic appearances with the first team,

Player Career Statistics
Appearances

PETER DOHERTY

Position
Inside forward 1936–45

Typical Height and Weight
1.78m (5ft 10in) 73kg (11st 6lb)

Born
Magharafelt, 5 June 1913

Deceased
Blackpool, 5 April 1990

League Debut
Preston North End (home)
22 February 1936

| | LEAGUE | | FA CUP | | TOTAL | |
	App	Gls	App	Gls	App	Gls
1935/36	9	4	0	0	9	4
1936/37	41	30	4	2	45	32
1937/38	41	23	5	2	46	25
1938/39	28	17	2	1	30	18
TOTAL	119	74	11	5	130	79

NOTE: Peter Doherty also made three League appearances and scored two goals during the 1939/40 season. Due to the Second World War, the League season was suspended and these games were subsequently expunged from the records.

Irishman Peter Doherty was a supremely talented player throughout his City career.

I eventually gained a regular place in the side. I kept it until the beginning of my second season with the club, when I was dropped for a public practice match. Later on in the season, I not only regained my place, but was chosen to represent Ireland against England – a proud moment indeed for me.'

Sadly, while Peter was en route to that match, his international debut, a telegram was sent before kick-off telling him that his brother, Joe, had had a leg amputated. The authorities held back the news until after the game and, with support from the Blackpool chairman, Sir Lindsay Parkinson, arrangements were then made for Peter to travel back to Ireland. He seemed very positive about the support of Blackpool during this period and it seems likely he would have

liked to have stayed at Bloomfield Road for several years. However, Sir Lindsay Parkinson passed away and Blackpool started to struggle financially. They had to sell players and Peter was one of their most valuable properties. 'I had no wish to leave and was dreading the prospect of being transferred to another club, perhaps many miles away.'

City Boy

Peter joined City for a club-record £10,000 in February 1936. It was a good time to join the Blues. Only two years earlier, record crowds had been thrilled by their great Cup-fighting side and in 1935 they had finished fourth in the League. There had been high hopes that the 1935/36 season would see them win the coveted League Championship for the first time but a series of five successive defeats only a month before Peter arrived had effectively killed off that ambition. It may also have prompted the transfer, as the Blues clearly needed to strengthen their attack.

After a fairly unimpressive debut, Peter had heard a fan criticising the fee, 'Ten thousand pound? You mean ten thousand cigarette cards!' Soon, though, Peter proved his worth to the Blues and two weeks after his debut he scored the first of 76 League goals for City as Middlesbrough were defeated 6–0. By the end of the season he had scored four goals in nine games and City finished in ninth place.

In the following season, 1936/37, season both Peter and City were in terrific form. The opening weeks were rather mixed, with superb victories, such as the 6–2 defeat of West Bromwich Albion, followed by draws. Nevertheless, by Christmas the Blues had started to progress and then they embarked on an unbeaten run of 22 games. Those games guaranteed them the Championship but it was far from easy, especially as Arsenal had been the dominant force for some time and had taken some shifting. A thrilling 2–0 victory in April over the Gunners had allowed City to leap above them into pole position. Four days later, Peter scored twice as the Blues won 3–1 at Sunderland.

City's next match, against Preston, saw Preston take a two-goal lead early in the first half. It was a match City had to win and, early in the second half, Peter tried to foil Preston's defence by regularly swapping places with inside-forward Alec Herd. The move had failed in the first half but, in the

The Championship-winning side at West Bromwich Albion on 2 January 1937, prior to a 2–2 draw.

Peter's Prime Time

Manchester City 2 Arsenal 0. Football League Division One – 10 April 1937

Goalscorers Doherty, Toseland

City Team Swift, Dale, Barkas, Percival, Marshall, Bray, Toseland, Herd, Tilson, Doherty, Brook

Attendance 76,000

This game was played on the same day as the FA Cup semi-finals and, in those days, FA Cup ties were normally the major crowd-pulling fixtures. The importance of this meeting between the two most significant sides of the decade, though, made it the nation's biggest draw. A crowd of 74,918 paid on the day – the Club claimed season-ticket holders took the figure to 76,000 – and although this was around 4,000 short of the record League crowd at the time (coincidentally, City v Arsenal on 23 February 1935), it was a significant attendance.

Arsenal had been the team of the decade. They had won the Championship in four of the previous six seasons and were, prior to this match, League leaders. The general view in football was that the Gunners were unstoppable. City lay in second place and knew that a victory would send them above Arsenal and, it was hoped, set the Blues up for a successful finish to the season.

Peter Doherty had been City's main goalscorer – he would end the season on 30 goals from 41 games – and it was evident that Arsenal viewed him as a major threat. They closely marked the Irishman and, in the early stages, the Gunners dominated play. It was difficult for City to challenge but as the first half progressed the Blues started to match Arsenal. 'We were outplayed in the opening stages,' admitted Peter, 'but gradually we hit back, and the all-important first goal fell to us before half time. Bernard Joy sliced one of his clearances to Tilson, who had wandered out on to the left wing. Freddie steered a long pass through to me and with Eddie Hapgood in close attendance I hooked the ball into the roof of the net from a very narrow angle. Boulton, the Arsenal 'keeper, looked amazed, as well he

might, for I was very nearly on the goal-line when I shot.'

The goal came in the 35th minute and, according to journalist Arthur Simmons, the goal owed a great deal to Peter's skill. 'Tilson caught a badly placed ball from Joy inches inside the touchline; centred cleverly; Doherty got on. Boulton was drawn out. Doherty had to make his close-in shot from an awkward position. He judged it perfectly. That's where ball control comes in. Doherty could spare some, and still be an artist. A nice goal.'

In the second half a penalty appeal was turned down – the Blues were convinced Arsenal's Hapgood had handled in the area – and then after about 24 minutes of the half Ernie Toseland scored a second. From that point on, the Blues were destined to win.

Frank Swift, City's goalkeeper during this match, was able to lean against the goal post for much of the second half, watching play. Like most people at Maine Road, he enjoyed watching Peter attack the Arsenal goal at the other end. In his autobiography Frank talked of Peter's qualities. 'Peter is such a delight to watch, for it is obvious to all that he loves to play football. I, like almost everybody who has seen him play, think he is one of the greatest forwards of our generation.'

The Arsenal match ended in a 2–0 City win and was followed by exciting victories at Sunderland (3–1), at Preston (5–2) and at home to Sheffield Wednesday (4–1) to bring the League Championship to City for the first time. A 2–2 draw at Birmingham ended the season, but those final weeks had seen Peter in outstanding form as he scored seven in the final four games. To many fans he was the linchpin of that great side.

second period, as Peter recalled, it was different. 'This time it worked, and I went through to rub one of the arrears off. A minute later, I got a second, and immediately afterwards Alec cracked in one of Toseland's centres to give us the lead. The game had taken a sensational turn.' Preston were eventually defeated 5–2, with Peter scoring a hat-trick. A week later Sheffield Wednesday were beaten 4–1 at Maine Road and that victory guaranteed that City would be crowned League champions for the first time.

'We were champions at last!' said Peter of that day. 'There were amazing scenes at the end of the game; thousands of people rushing on to the playing pitch.'

Hard Times

Two years after that tremendous success, war was declared and professional football, understandably, had to take a back seat. The Football League was suspended and footballers, no matter how successful or famous they had been, were left with no guarantee of work. 'Contracts were automatically torn up,' stated Peter, 'and for those players who had families to support and no savings to fall back on, the immediate prospect was grave. It was a grim lesson for the professionals, and one that some of us took to heart very seriously. Without a scrap of consideration or sentiment, our means of livelihood were simply jettisoned, and we were left to find fresh ones as best we could. Obviously, the first thing to do was to find a job.'

For Peter the war years caused a serious strain on his relationship with Manchester City. The club argued with him over job offers he received and over guest appearances he made for various clubs. It seems City wanted to either guarantee his availability for the Blues or to make him appear as a guest player for teams they had chosen. Peter wanted to work and play where he chose, and for those clubs within a reasonable distance of where he was based on wartime duties. 'I was naturally keen to play whenever the opportunity arose; but I resented dictation from my club. In view of the scrapped contracts I didn't consider it justified.'

The first of two Irishmen in City's Hall of Fame, Doherty is also in the National Football Museum's Hall of Fame.

These disputes, which, on the face of it, may seem petty, were an indication of how the big clubs viewed their best assets. Peter was one of football's biggest stars and City did not want to lose him, or to see him make a move that might jeopardise their investment. However, their attitude was typical of the period and actually did significant damage to the relationship between Club and player. Inevitably, Peter moved on once the war was over and an FA Cup-winners' medal with Derby in 1946 was followed by spells at Huddersfield and Doncaster.

While at Derby, Peter played in an FA Cup semi-final against Birmingham at Maine Road. The tie ended in a 4–0 Derby win but the remarkable feature of this match as far as City fans are concerned is that the crowd was an incredible 80,480. Reports from the period suggest that thousands of Mancunians had attended the game simply to see Peter play. They hoped he would be on the winning side and his two goals that day received significant cheers from both the Derby fans and Mancunians in attendance.

The Complete Footballer

City fans idolised Peter. To them he was a complete footballer who put in many breathtaking performances. As an inside forward he seemed perfect. He created chances, continually challenged the opposition and scored with regularity. He also possessed a great tactical brain and was clearly more gifted than most of his contemporaries.

More than 20 years after Peter had stopped playing, City's great manager Joe Mercer described him as the greatest player ever produced by Ireland. Mercer knew his comment would raise a few eyebrows in the media since another Irishman, George Best, was already being talked of as a great player. Interestingly, no one appeared to disagree with Mercer's comments at the time. In fact, in 1974

– when George Best had already achieved most, if not all, of his best playing performances – the *Rothmans Football Yearbook* recorded that Peter was 'regarded by many judges as the greatest player Ireland has ever produced'.

Peter moved into management at Doncaster and went on to guide Northern Ireland to the 1958 World Cup quarter-finals. It's also a little-known fact that during the mid-1960s Peter very nearly became City's manager. Peter's son, Paul Doherty, was a local journalist with close involvement with the Club: he later edited the City match programme and went on to become head of sport at Granada TV. Directors at Manchester City were known to have asked him about the availability of his father but the move failed and City eventually appointed Joe Mercer.

In April 1990 Peter passed away after a lifetime of sporting achievement. He was the sort of player everybody respected and idolised and he was also an inspirational influence in Manchester and in Ireland. Danny Blanchflower, the captain of Tottenham's 1961 Double-winning side, once admitted, 'As a small boy I cherished the name of Manchester City... my dreams each night were full of the sky-blue shirts. I waved the flag for no better reason than that Peter Doherty played for them.'

Stephen Doherty

grandson of Peter, collecting the Hall of Fame award in January 2004.

' Thanks very much for this. Peter truly loved the game of football. And of all the clubs he played for and that he had the privilege to manage, there was always a special place in his heart for Manchester City, and that's what makes it so special for all the family tonight. If Peter was still alive today and able to collect this himself he would be very proud. I know I certainly am. This just leaves me to say on behalf of myself and my sister Sue, and my father, who unfortunately couldn't be with us today, and the rest of the Doherty family... Thank you. '

Niall Quinn

Niall Quinn was a player idolised by fans during a six-year spell in Manchester.

First impressions were of a tall, gangling sort of striker but supporters quickly realised he had much more to offer than just height. He had a tremendous first touch and great skill and within a year of arriving he was a true fans' favourite, earning the Player of the Year tag during his second season. It was a thoroughly deserved award and proved that the fans appreciated his enthusiasm and passion for his club. Despite moving to Sunderland in 1996, Niall has remained a true hero in Manchester.

Niall Quinn
1992-2002 AWARD

A Born Sportsman

Niall was born in Dublin on 6 October 1966 and, inevitably for someone who was to have such a wonderful career as a professional footballer, sport was a major part of his childhood. 'As kids, we played everything, and in the excited commentary that ran through our heads as we played we could be anybody we wanted to be. Sport links all my childhood memories together. My family were immersed in sport. School was one long celebration of it. All week we played school games. At one stage, I played on just about every team that my school Drimnagh Castle had.' Niall played a variety of sports. He enjoyed soccer but he also played

Gaelic football for Dublin Schoolboys and at one point went on a tour to Australia. The idea was to test the Gaelic footballers at Australian Rules. Niall recalls, 'I had a chance to stay in Australia because a couple of sides asked me to turn professional. I was also doing a bit of hurling – I played for Dublin Minors in the 1983 All-Ireland Hurling Minors final after I came back from Australia.'

Niall's father, Billy, had been a great hurling star and the sport meant a considerable amount to the young Niall. 'Although reared in Dublin, I was brought up mainly as a Tipperary person. This is important. When it comes to sport, Tipperary people believe hurling to be the greatest game in the world. When it comes to hurling, Tipperary people believe themselves to be the chosen tribe.'

Despite the opportunities to excel at hurling, Niall was destined to play football, and at 16 he was given a trial at Fulham. However, after a couple of reserve games, manager Malcolm Macdonald took the young player to one side to tell him, 'Son, you've no future in football. Go home; get yourself a good education. Forget about this life.'

Role Models

Fortunately, the Fulham manager was in the minority and it wasn't long before Arsenal came to Dublin to offer Niall a chance. 'For a Dublin kid,' says Niall, 'it seemed that if you could make it anywhere, you could make it at Highbury. We'd all seen photos of Stapleton, Brady and O'Leary in their young days at Arsenal. They were Dubliners who'd made it as we watched. When Arsenal sold the dream to me, those pictures of the lads floated into my head."

At Arsenal Niall impressed and after only a week of a two-week trial period he was offered a contract. On 14 December 1985, at the age of 19, he made his League debut and scored in the 2–0 victory over eventual champions Liverpool. It was a dream start and Niall retained his place for the following five

Niall Quinn in action against Leeds at Maine Road during his final season with the Blues on 21 October 1995.

matches, before going on to make 12 League appearances that year. The following season he played in Arsenal's League Cup final victory over Liverpool and scored eight goals in thirty-five League outings. However, by the time Arsenal won the League in 1989 he was on the fringes of the side.

In Manchester at the start of 1990, manager Howard Kendall urgently needed to increase City's firepower and Niall became the manager's target. 'If City hadn't been struggling in the bottom half of the table, I don't think that I would have got him,' explains Kendall, 'because George Graham [the then Arsenal manager] rated him highly and would have been loath to sell him to a club which was in with even half a chance of winning the Championship. I say that with some assurance because Aston Villa had tried, but failed, to sign him, probably because they were enjoying a very successful League campaign.'

A Head Start

Niall joined City in March 1990 and made his debut against Chelsea on the 21st of that month. It was as successful a start as his Arsenal debut. Chelsea were leading 1–0 when David White sent a great cross in Niall's direction. The big Irishman headed home for a great goal. 'It felt like such a release,' he says. 'I was a footballer again. I didn't know Maine Road, so I ran towards the Chelsea fans and celebrated in front of them. The City fans thought I was one cocky so and so and it was a bit of a love story from then on.'

Another three goals were scored by Niall before the end of the season and the Irishman was definitely one of the contributory factors in City avoiding relegation. Manager Kendall felt that Niall's time on the fringes at Arsenal had dented his confidence. 'He already had the skill and the enthusiasm; all I did was add a dash of confidence. Once Niall realised that he was a regular, first-choice player, all his inhibitions disappeared and he began to flourish. Niall is one of the best one-touch finishers I have seen in a very long time.'

At the end of his first full season – 1990/91 – Niall was the Club's highest goalscorer, with 20 League goals, and became only the second Blues player since 1977 to break the 20 League-goal barrier. He was also the fans' Player of the Year and said at the time, 'I was thrilled that they had taken to

Player Career Statistics
Appearances

NIALL QUINN

Position
Forward 1990–96

Typical Height and Weight
1.92m (6ft 4in) 80kg (12st 8lb)

Born
Dublin, 6 October 1966

League Debut
Chelsea (home)
21 March 1990 (scored one)

		LEAGUE		FA CUP		FL CUP		FM Cup		TOTAL	
		App	Gls	App	Gls	App	Gls	App	Gls	App	Gls
	1989/90	9	4	0	0	0	0	0	0	9	4
	1990/91	38	20	2	1	3	0	3	1	46	22
	1991/92	35	12	1	0	4	2	0	0	40	14
	1992/93	39	9	5	1	3	0	-	-	47	10
	1993/94	14 (1)	5	0	0	3	1	-	-	17 (1)	6
	1994/95	24 (11)	8	1 (3)	0	4 (2)	2	-	-	29 (16)	10
	1995/96	24 (8)	8	4	2	3	1	-	-	31 (8)	11
	TOTAL	183 (20)	66	13 (3)	4	20 (2)	6	3	1	219 (25)	77

Substitute Quinn was one of the goalscorers when City achieved a 2–0 victory over Ipswich on 22 February 1995 at Maine Road.

me so much but I have had tremendous support and help from them and my team-mates. The people of Manchester have always made me feel welcome and I have thoroughly enjoyed my stay. What I want to do now is help the team to win more honours. We have a very good squad and great faith in player-boss Peter Reid. This is a very big club and I am proud to be part of it.'

In April of that season he hit the headlines with two thrilling performances. The first saw him score a dream hat-trick – using left foot, right foot and head – against Crystal Palace on April Fool's Day. Against Derby County he not only scored one of City's two goals that day but also went in nets, following the dismissal of Tony Coton, and saved

a Dean Saunders penalty. The season ended with a thrilling 3–2 victory over Sunderland. That day the striker netted two goals, with David White scoring the other, to send his future club into Division Two.

A Worrying Time

A cruciate ligament injury suffered on 27 November 1993 against Sheffield Wednesday ended his part in the 1993/94 season. Niall remembers that drastic moment well. 'In the second half I go for a ball, chest it and go to turn, but my studs stick in the ground and I fall over. I get treatment and try to play on – I even hit the post with a header – but when I run, I fall over and remain in pain for maybe ten or twelve seconds before I try to get going again.'

'A move to Sporting Lisbon almost happened, and then Aston Villa and Sheffield United both showed interest, but each time the deals fell through. City fans did not want to see their hero sold, but it seemed his future lay elsewhere.'

The injury also prevented Niall from taking part in the 1994 World Cup for his beloved Ireland and for a while it looked as if his career was over. Niall remembers the thoughts running through his head on the day he heard it was cruciate ligament damage. 'Gazza is struggling with one. Paul Lake is struggling with one. A lot of people I know have had to quit. The word is that the taller you are, the harder it is to come back. Something to do with leverage. Thanks! I'm a beanpole and I'm gone. You do your cruciate and your friends are soon coming by to shake your hand and say how sorry they are for your troubles.'

Unlike City-playing colleague Paul Lake, however, Niall did manage to return to full fitness and went on to make 24 League starts and a further 11 appearances as substitute. Although the fans wanted to see him appear in every match, he was no longer an automatic choice. The reasons were unclear but according to Niall in his autobiography, published in 2002, City were determined to reduce the wage bill. A move to Sporting Lisbon almost happened and then Aston Villa and Sheffield United both showed interest, but each time the deals fell through. City fans did not want to see their hero sold but it seemed his future lay elsewhere.

Ball Games

The 1995/96 season commenced with Niall still a City man but the season was one of struggle. Alan Ball was by this time the manager and an air of despondency had started to spread. Some of the fans' favourite players had already been sold, while the rumours that Niall was on his way did little to encourage supporters that the future was bright.

City struggled through the season until the final day, when the Blues were to face Liverpool at Maine Road. It was a tense day as City needed to achieve a point more than either Southampton or Coventry to stay up. Sadly, the Merseysiders took the lead

Niall Quinn, seen here in his last season, was a true fans' favourite.

Niall's Prime Time

Manchester City 2 Derby County 1. Football League Division One – 20 April 1991

Goalscorers Quinn, White

City Team Coton, Hill, Pointon, Heath, Hendry, Redmond, White, Brennan, Quinn, Harper, Ward (Reid)

Attendance 24,037

The 1990/91 season was proving to be City's best in the League for almost 15 years and there was a general air of excitement around Maine Road. A 2–2 draw with Niall Quinn's former club, and eventual champions, Arsenal three days before the meeting with Derby had seen the Blues come from two goals down so confidence for the meeting with a struggling Derby County was high.

Niall remembers the match as one of his favourite performances. 'They were exciting times. We were fourth in the old First Division and we had only lost one of our previous seven matches. It was a really great time and everybody at the club was buzzing. I remember Peter Shilton [the Derby goalkeeper] pulled out just before the game with an injury. We were all delighted with this because he was obviously a world-class goalkeeper... We thought we might get something if we could test his young replacement early on.'

The game commenced with Derby trying desperately to find an opening but it was City who took control during the early stages. Midway through the

Niall follows Brennan, Heath and Reid off the field after his goalkeeping heroics.

first half, Niall saw his chance to give the Blues the lead. A cross from Mark Ward set the Irishman up on the edge of the penalty area. 'I scored with a volley from outside the area after about 22 minutes,' remembers Niall. 'I was quite pleased with that, but about ten minutes later, our 'keeper, Tony Coton, brought down Dean Saunders on his way to goal. Tony got a red card and for a while nobody was really sure what was going on.'

The watching supporters felt the game was about to turn Derby's way as they were awarded a penalty and the Blues were down to ten men. They also wondered who would fill the City goalkeeper's shirt. During the late 1980s and early 1990s the Blues had lost their goalkeeper through injury or dismissal on several occasions, with Nigel Gleghorn and Steve Redmond the two men who usually moved into the nets. Gleghorn had long since moved on and Redmond had never really been that successful in goal. 'Everyone started to look around and I said "I'll go in!" 'says Niall. 'As I was putting the jersey on, I got a bit nervous about the penalty. I remember Tony throwing his gloves in anger and I picked them up and went in goal.'

Nobody expected Niall to save the penalty but the Irishman was determined to give it a go. 'I decided before he [Dean Saunders] ran up to dive low to my left. That's where he hit it. What nobody mentioned, and nobody ever shows, is that from the resulting corner, I went out, bowled a few players over and made a Pat Jennings-style, one-handed catch. That pleased me more than anything.'

The penalty save and subsequent catch gave Niall tremendous confidence and it seemed that he could do no wrong. As goalscorer and penalty saver the

Quinn, supported by Michael Brown, fights valiantly against United during a controversial 3–2 defeat on 6 April 1996.

headlines had already been written. 'After the save it was all beer and skittles,' says Niall. 'I was spinning the ball from my kickouts, having a whale of a time. In the second half, after David White had put us two in front, I caught and cleared from a Derby attack and then clutched my upper thigh. Down the sideline I could see Peter Reid reach for his hair and start pulling it out. Our physio Roy Bailey came sprinting down the sideline like there was a fire, bawling at me, "What's wrong, Quinny?"' I contorted my face into a look of pain as if I was about to cry. "Got a bit of mud on my shorts, Roy."

Throughout the second half City remained the dominant force despite being a player down, with David White's goal coming about 14 minutes from time. In the final minute, Niall was eventually beaten when Derby's Mick Harford scored from a header.

The game ended 2–1 and Derby's fate was sealed. City ended the season in fifth place – their highest finish of the 1980s and 1990s – while Niall was deservedly voted Man of the Match.

through an own goal from Steve Lomas. Ian Rush later increased the lead to 2–0 and City looked dead and buried. Liverpool, though, seemed genuinely interested in seeing City survive and the Blues managed to pull a goal back from a penalty. Then Kit Symons scored an equaliser in the 78th minute.

By this time every supporter knew that results elsewhere were not going City's way. The Blues now needed to win the match to stay up. It was clear to everyone except, for some reason, Alan Ball. The manager had told the players to waste time and hold the ball in the corners. Niall had already been substituted and was not happy with City's approach. Liverpool tried to open up play but Ball's men were not interested. 'We needed to win to stay up,' says Niall. 'It was a shambles. A wrong message was sent on to the pitch with five minutes to go. I'd already come off. I had a radio and knew that Southampton were winning elsewhere, so we needed to score. Alan Ball had a conflicting

Niall's Finest Fellow Citizens

The 1990s was a mixed decade for City. In 1992 they were founder members of the Premier League, but six years later they dropped into the third tier of English football for the first time. Successive promotions, another relegation, and then promotion back to the Premier League followed, making this one of City's most eventful periods.

PETER REID joined City shortly after the arrival of Howard Kendall as manager. Reid signed on 15 November 1990 on a free transfer from Queen's Park Rangers and immediately made a positive impression. He helped to inspire the Blues on the pitch and his determination ensured that City tightened up as they battled to avoid relegation. When Kendall left the Blues, Reid became City's first player-manager and during his three seasons in charge the Blues twice finished fifth and once ninth in the Premier League.

A sign of Reid's importance as a player can best be illustrated by the Manchester derby of October 1990. City were leading 3–1 with only ten minutes remaining when Howard Kendall substituted Reid. Without the enthusiasm and grit of the former England player, City conceded two goals in those final minutes and the match was drawn at 3–3. Had Reid remained on the pitch it would have been a victory.

UWE ROSLER German-born Rosler was one of English football's greatest imports. He arrived at City for a trial in March 1994 and was immediately tested in a reserve match. He scored twice before being substituted, then made his League debut a few days later against Queen's Park Rangers. By the end of that season he had played 12 League games and had scored 5 goals, leaving him only 1 goal behind highest goalscorer Mike Sheron. Overnight he had become a cult figure at Maine Road and over the following four seasons he was a major figure as far as the fans were concerned.

Shortly before Maine Road's final game in 2003 it was announced that Rosler was fighting a battle against chest cancer and supporters sent thousands of goodwill messages to him. During the opening season at City's new stadium, Rosler made a surprise appearance prior to a game. It was a wonderful moment and the adulation he received that day was typical of the support and interest fans have always shown towards him.

IAN BRIGHTWELL As with Paul Lake, Ian Brightwell was one of City's 1986 FA Youth Cup-winning side. He made his League debut in August 1986 and remained with the Blues until June 1998, by which time he was the last of City's youth team to be playing for the Club.

During his 12-year career Brightwell was a popular and reassuring presence, making 285 League starts, plus 36 as a substitute, and scoring 18 goals. His most famous goal has to be the February 1990 Old Trafford derby equaliser. From about 25 yards (23m) out, Brightwell sent a stunning shot searing past United goalkeeper Jim Leighton and into the net. Afterwards the City youngster was asked to describe his goal and, in an extremely excited manner, he simply stated, 'I just wellied it!'

The comment became part of City folklore and Brightwell's place in the hearts of Mancunians was further strengthened.

TONY COTON £1 million-signing Tony Coton arrived at Maine Road from Watford in July 1990. He had already developed a great reputation as a goalkeeper but during his time in Manchester this reputation was enhanced as he became one of City's most consistent performers. Highly regarded by his fellow professionals as well as fans, Coton seemed a certainty to play for England. Sadly, that honour did not come, although he did manage an appearance for England B.

After 163 League appearances with City he joined Manchester United. It seems that City manager Alan Ball saw no future at Maine Road for the fans' favourite and so Coton was forced to move on.

message and he was telling the lads to hold the ball up. I had to run down the sideline and scream at Steve Lomas that we needed another goal. It made Alan Ball look bad, I suppose, but when you are bringing a great club down a division, you can't worry about vanity.'

True Blue

The sight of Niall running along the touchline has remained an enduring image of his determination and love of the Blues. That night on television his reputation as a true Blue was confirmed as he appeared on *Match of The Day* to apologise to the fans. He told the BBC, 'There's a huge cloud over the club. As a player – and on behalf of the rest of the players – I can only apologise. Not for today's performance, or for the last couple of performances, but for perhaps the way we started the year and the problems we placed upon the club. As one of the

team, I can just apologise to those who have travelled the length and breadth of the country following us. At the end of the day the buck stops with us.

'Our form in recent games counts for nothing now. The feeling amongst all the players, including myself, is that you look back to your careers, you look back when you started and you go to big clubs on trials. You think football is the greatest thing in the world. You get accepted at a club and you're the bee's knees. Everyone is happy for you. Nobody ever told me there'd be days like this. It's a bit hard to swallow.

'Without doubt the Club was let down badly by the players. I feel so sorry for the fans who have supported us so magnificently. My only wish now is to be part of a City side which bounces straight back into the Premiership – the only division Manchester City should be in.'

MCFC statistics

	1992/93	1993/94	1994/95	1995/96	1996/97	1997/98	1998/99	1999/2000	2000/01
League Position	9 (in FA Prem)	16	17	18	14 (in Div 1)	22	3 (in Div 2)	2 (in Div 1)	18 (in FA Prem)
FA Cup Round Reached	6	4	5	5	5	4	3	4	5
League Cup Round Reached	3	4	5	3	2	1	2	2	5
Average Attendance	24,698	26,709	22,725	27,869	26,753	28,196	28,261	32,088	34,058

	2001/02	Honours
League Position	Champs (of Div 1)	Promotion from Division Two 1999; promotion from Division One 2000; Division One League Championship 2002
FA Cup Round Reached	5	
League Cup Round Reached	4	Other Significant Events
Average Attendance	33,059	First season of the FA Premier League (1992/93). City were founder members; play-off final – City's last appearance at the old Wembley in 1999

Sadly, Niall never had that chance as, on 17 August, he was transferred to Sunderland. However, the player's future over the following seasons proved to be significantly more successful than City's, as in 1998 the Blues dropped down into the third tier of English football for the first time. For Niall, his time at Sunderland brought him tremendous support and he became as great a hero to his new fans as he still is to the Blue half of Manchester.

Irish Joy

Niall had already become a full Republic of Ireland international by the time he joined City in early 1990. His first international appearance had been while still with Arsenal and then, at the end of his first season at Maine Road, Niall was named as a member of Jack Charlton's exciting 1990 World Cup squad. The tournament helped the player to develop enormously and against Holland he scored his first World Cup-finals goal. 'On 71 minutes Packie Bonner hoofs a huge ball forward,' is how he remembers it. 'I go for it with Benny van Aerle, who turns and jabs a surprisingly-firm back-pass to Hans van Breukelen. It comes off the 'keeper's chest. I have chased in, optimistic as ever, so I stick out a long leg and deflect it home. A World Cup goal! Against the European champions! I can barely describe the feeling.'

Niall was to play in two World Cup tournaments altogether and make over 90 appearances for his country. On his 35th birthday in October 2001 he also became Ireland's then all-time leading goalscorer and remained so until Robbie Keane surpassed his record in October 2004.

Following his playing days, Niall returned home to live in Dublin and concentrate on media work, mainly for Sky TV, often acting as a summariser at games involving City and Arsenal.

Niall's time at City was a delight for the majority of fans. He will always be remembered for his willingness to support the Blue cause, while his role as target man provided much enjoyment. At the Hall of Fame dinner in 2004, Niall was deeply touched by the recognition and he explained that Manchester City was immensely important to his life and career. 'This football club took me on as a guy who couldn't get a game in another club's reserves and turned me into an international footballer. For that reason I will always be indebted to this wonderful Club.'

Niall Quinn
collecting the Hall of Fame award in January 2004.

'It's a tremendous honour for me and my wife to be here tonight to be inducted into the Hall of Fame. When I arrived here I was a kid who couldn't get into the Arsenal side, but by the time I left I'd had a wonderful time and had become a full international. When I left, myself and Francis [Lee] sought to differ that I was getting a little bit too old. I apologise for all that time, Francis, but we were both trying to do our best for the Club, and as long as everybody keeps doing that this Club will always remain special. I am very pleased with this award. Thank you.'

Roy Paul

Roy Paul was City's inspirational captain during the mid-1950s Cup successes. Often regarded as a tough, no-nonsense leader, he was loved by supporters for his clear determination and desire to see the Blues successful. The 1956 FA Cup final typified his approach to the game and cemented his name as one of the Club's greatest captains.

Roy Paul
1951-1957 AWARD

A Trial of Strength

As with City's 1904 FA Cup-winning captain Billy Meredith, Roy grew up in a coal-mining area of Wales. It was inevitable that most of the youngsters growing up in this area of the Rhondda Valley, South Wales, would find employment in the mines but young Roy wanted to escape this. He had an enormous desire to become a footballer, but it wasn't easy. At school he was deemed too small and too weak by his sports teacher. The criticism hurt. Roy, talking in 1956, remembered, 'Nothing I have ever suffered since was ever quite as bad as the bitter disappointments I had at school. "Not strong enough..." the unintended slight stung me like a whiplash. I'd show them! I'd build my body up by exercises and chest expanders. I'd show the world that little Roy Paul could become strong enough for this game.' Roy kept trying and vowed he would become a footballer but, at the age of 15, he took the inevitable route and went down the pit as a colliers' assistant. Others may have settled for this but Roy continued to tell everyone that it was only temporary, that he was heading for a career in football. 'The miners had heard all this before. They kidded me about it. They had seen lads leave the pits, and then come crawling back to the coal face football failures. I swore that would never happen to me.'

At that stage, Roy was combining coal mining with playing for the Ton Boys Club. He was convinced that a scout would appear at one of his games but no scout ever did. However, fate did play a hand when one day the youngster returned home from the mine to find a Swansea Town scout waiting for him. Apparently, Swansea had received a letter of recommendation from someone and the club had decided to give the boy a trial. Roy never did find out who put his name forward. 'I suspect some of my pals at the coal face were so fed up with my constant chatter about football that they must have taken steps to see I got my chance! Within the month, I signed as an amateur and later signed professional. Then I quit the pit for good; packed my football boots in a brown paper parcel and went off on the long trail in search of football fame.'

'In 1939, after serving my apprenticeship in the junior sides, I was picked to play in a wartime League game against Cardiff City.'

The war affected Roy's opportunities and did also mean that he had to spend a short time working in the mines again, but postwar his career came alive. He made 160 postwar League appearances as a half back for Swansea before joining Manchester City in 1950.

Time to Move

Roy's development at Swansea had been noticed by the larger clubs, particularly when the Swans faced Arsenal in the FA Cup in 1950. Arsenal won the match but Roy had been inspirational for Swansea in pushing his team-mates forwards. Even when Swansea were losing 2–0, Roy had been convinced the battle wasn't lost and he himself gave up defending and started to mount serious attacks on the Arsenal goal. Future City manager Joe Mercer was the Gunners' captain that day and 20 years later he described Roy as one of the best footballers he had ever seen, quoting this match as a prime example of Roy's tenacity, determination and never-say-die attitude.

'Football games were played with enormous barbed-wire fences separating the fans from the players.'

Arsenal won the match but immediately afterwards the Gunners made a substantial offer for Roy. They had tried to sign him 12 months earlier but Arsenal were to be frustrated for a second time, as Swansea refused to release their star man.

Around this time Roy, along with several British stars, received an offer to move to Bogota in Colombia to play for Millionarios FC. He was offered £3,000 simply to sign a contract, plus £150 a month together with other perks. This was substantial compared to potential earnings in Britain and the Welshman travelled with others to see what Bogota offered. Roy was not impressed with the contrast between rich and poor in the city and was shocked to see that football games were played with enormous barbed-wire fences separating the fans from the players. He returned to Wales determined he would continue to develop in Britain. Unfortunately, his trip to Bogota received so much negative press that Swansea felt they had to transfer the player.

City manager Les McDowall travelled to Swansea, met the player and Roy became a Blue, with the Swans receiving a £25,000 transfer fee – only £1,500 short of the British transfer record.

Captain Roy during the 1955 FA Cup final. Ten-man City came close to matching Cup favourites Newcastle.

Player Career Statistics
Appearances

ROY PAUL

Position
Wing half 1950–57

Typical Height and Weight
1.78m (5ft 10in) 81kg (12st 10lb)

Born
Gelli Pentre, 18 April 1920

Deceased
South Wales, 21 May 2002

League Debut
Preston North End (away)
19 August 1950

	LEAGUE		FA CUP		TOTAL	
	App	Gls	App	Gls	App	Gls
1950/51	41	3	1	0	42	3
1951/52	35	1	2	0	37	1
1952/53	38	0	3	0	41	0
1953/54	39	0	2	0	41	0
1954/55	41	1	6	0	47	1
1955/56	36	1	7	0	43	1
1956/57	40	3	2	0	42	3
TOTAL	270	9	23	0	293	9

City Lover

Roy arrived at Maine Road not fully aware of the stature of the Club. He knew that City had been a major side before the war but he also recognised that the Blues had struggled to re-establish themselves after the conflict. By the time Roy signed in July 1950, City were a Division Two side, just like his former club Swansea. Around six years after his arrival in Manchester, Roy admitted, 'I joined City almost on the spur of the moment. I had made up my mind to leave Swansea and when City came to sign me I said, 'Yes'. I did not realise at the time I was joining one of the most famous and spectacular clubs in the Football League. The City fans are among the most loyal and knowledgeable in the country and as a player I have now good reason to salute their loyalty and encouragement. We have had our successes – but sometimes there have been disappointments – but on all occasions we have been urged on by our supporters.'

Roy made his debut in the opening match of the 1950/51 season, when the Blues won 4–2 at Preston, and managed to appear in all but one of the Blues' League games that season. The one he missed was, ironically, the game with Swansea on 21 October and the reason he was absent was simply because he had been picked to play for Wales. City colleague Roy Clarke was also on international duty with Wales.

The arrival of Roy at Maine Road in the early 1950s helped the Blues to develop greatly during the decade and to many fans he was the key force behind City's transformation from relegated side in 1949/50 to pace setters in Division Two. The respected journalist 'Old International' believed City were now playing as a unit and he believed it was mostly down to the arrival of Roy. After a 1–0 victory against Coventry on 30 September he commented, 'Paul played beautifully and with that air of authority one is entitled to expect from a City captain.'

Revolutionary Tactics

At the end of Roy's first season he had captained the Blues to promotion but City hardly set the world alight over the next three seasons as Roy's side finished 15th, 20th and 17th. Some questioned whether manager Les McDowall's side would ever find true success, especially when the opening day of the 1954/55 season ended in a 5–0 defeat at Preston. McDowall had tried a revolutionary new tactic whereby the centre forward would play deeper than usual.

The approach, later dubbed the Revie Plan after Don Revie, City's centre forward, was criticised but in the second game of the season the Blues beat Sheffield United 5–2. The difference had been Roy Little and, significantly, Ken Barnes. Ken Barnes had made the tactic work in the reserves and his arrival made the tactic succeed.

Barnes was the man working in partnership with the centre forward (Revie or, in the reserves, Johnny Williamson). City's goalkeeper would get the ball out to the centre forward, who would be lying in a deep position (similar to right back or right midfield).

MCFC statistics

	1951/52	1952/53	1953/54	1954/55	1955/56	1956/57	Honours
League Position	15	20	17	7	4	18	FA Cup finalists 1955; FA Cup 1956
FA Cup Round Reached	3	4	4	Final	Winners	3	
Average Attendance	38,302	34,663	30,155	35,217	32,198	30,005	

Barnes would travel with him and the centre forward would pass to Barnes, who would hold the ball up until the centre forward was in the opposition half and ready. Then Barnes would release the ball, just at the right moment, to allow the centre forward to charge forward. Barnes' role was really to choose the right moment to launch the attack, or to confuse the opposition. While Barnes had the ball, the opposition didn't know whether to track him, or follow the centre forward. It sounds simple but at the time it baffled everyone.

Roy Paul loved the transformation. 'Instead of leaving the centre forward like a dummy standing dutifully beside the centre half – making that man's already easy task even easier – we actually had the audacity to play our centre forward with a number nine on his back behind the other four forwards! This apparently was not in the FA coaching manual. Instead of using normal common sense, many teams were beaten before they ever went out. All we did was give Revie the job of wandering about the field with a number nine on his back. He had to get into the open spaces and the rest of the team played to him. He would then link up and use his accurate, long passes to carve the opposing defence to ribbons. What a stir this created!'

The Revie Plan

Using the Revie Plan, the Blues moved up the table and ended the 1954/55 campaign in seventh place, only six points behind the champions, Chelsea. One of the first indications that City had developed into a quality side came in the Maine Road derby match of 25 September 1954. Matt Busby's Manchester United side, containing the likes of Roger Byrne, Tommy Taylor and Duncan Edwards, were defeated 3–2 but the most significant aspect was that under Roy's captaincy the Blues were a true team, not a disparate group of individuals, as, perhaps, United

were. Clearly, the Reds possessed some great talent but as a team City were the more composed. Roy was the key figure behind this. Les McDowall had selected the players and developed the tactics but Roy had been the driving force behind team morale, attitude and comradeship. He was the leader on the pitch and 'his' team worked superbly as a unit.

Roy Paul training at a muddy Maine Road, with the old Platt Lane Stand in the background.

Roy's Prime Time

Manchester City 3 Birmingham City 1. FA Cup final – 5 May 1956

Goalscorers Hayes, Dyson, Johnstone

City Team Trautmann, Leivers, Little, Barnes, Ewing, Paul, Johnstone, Hayes, Revie, Dyson, Clarke

Attendance 100,000

At the banquet following the 1955 FA Cup final, Roy Paul stood up to make a speech. He was totally deflated by the defeat and really did not want to say anything. However, as he rose to his feet he looked around the room. The Blues had invited every former City Cup-finalist to the banquet and Roy noticed Sam Cowan, the captain for the 1933 and 1934 finals, sitting close by. The sight of Cowan made Roy think. 'Then the little imp within me made me smile as I said as confidently as I could, "We'll be back again next year to win it. Sam Cowan knows how I feel. He captained City's losing Cup final team in 1933 and returned a year later to collect the Cup." People applauded politely. They did not believe it. Maybe I did not myself. But in that hour of disaster and despair was born the fierce determination that we would be back.'

City did, of course, return to Wembley and Roy was even more influential than he had been in 1955. In the dressing room he warned the other players of the potential dangers and watched them all prepare. Naturally, most of the side had featured at Wembley the previous year and so they knew what to expect but Roy still checked each player out. 'As captain it was my responsibility to put on the swashbuckling air of supreme confidence. As one who has worn the gloves in the boxing ring on occasions I know that it is no use going out with a defeatist attitude. Tell yourself you can win... that you must win.'

After two minutes and forty-seven seconds Joe Hayes put the Blues into the lead but Birmingham equalised. 'I could have wept,' said Roy. 'After that smash-hit opening, Birmingham were level and only 14 minutes gone. They threw everything at us.'

At half time the majority of people in the stadium were convinced that Birmingham now had the edge but Roy was not convinced. He felt that a determined effort by his side would sweep aside any potential Birmingham threat. Twenty minutes into the second half City took the lead again. This time Jack Dyson applied the finishing touch and the players celebrated wildly. Roy was the first to settle and he bellowed at the others to calm down. 'No relaxing. Keep it up. No shirking now!' They all listened to their tough captain and two minutes later Bobby Johnstone scored, becoming the first player to score in successive Wembley finals.

Roy instructed the other players to keep the ball in play as much as possible to try and tire Birmingham out. His plan worked but then, about 14 minutes from time, goalkeeper Bert Trautmann was injured in a collision with Birmingham's Murphy. 'To me, as captain, Trautmann's injury came as a shock,' said Roy. 'I was faced with the problem – should I tell him to go off and put Roy Little in goal? Or should he stay on the field? Trautmann made my mind up for me. "I'll stay," he said, although it was apparent that every move was torture.'

A further collision caused Trautmann to suffer further but the goalkeeper bravely played out the final minutes. It was later discovered that Trautmann had actually broken his neck.

The Blues won the match 3–1 and Roy collected the trophy. 'I was too overcome. I wiped a tear away. They say I am something of a tough character on the field but at that moment I didn't know whether to laugh... cry... or sing! Proudly the Cup was held aloft as the boys carried me shoulder-high to the far parts of the ground to show the trophy to our faithful supporters who had followed and encouraged us in so many difficult games.'

The 'Old International' journalist enjoyed City's team approach against United. 'It is a strategy which shows off to perfection the strength and maturity of Paul among his younger defenders and which gives full scope to the inspired wanderings of Revie. City have staked their all on pure football and they are proving that football pays. What is more, by one of those delicious strokes of irony which play round the uncertainties of sport, the City's forwards helped themselves to three goals and narrowly missed scoring as many more – without taking into account hot claims for an odd penalty or so – against a defence the three least masterful members of which were to be chosen later in the day as England's bulwark against Ireland.'

Roy's marshalling of the City team was highly successful and as the season progressed he guided the Blues through to the 1955 FA Cup final. Prior to taking to the field the England manager, Walter Winterbottom, spoke to the City men and warned them that the Duke of Edinburgh was in attendance and that, as a result, players were not allowed to kiss one another after they had scored. The players laughed and then Roy piped up, 'I'll try to remember but I'm the emotional type. If we score first, I may forget and kiss the nearest person... even if it is the referee!' The England manager didn't know how to react to City's captain and he left quickly, while Roy and the others continued to laugh at the stupidity of the request.

Sadly, the game ended in defeat to Newcastle but City had been desperately unlucky. A goal by Jackie Milburn in the opening minute put the Blues under pressure and then an injury to Jimmy Meadows meant they had to play most of the match with only ten men. They continued to try and make the Revie Plan work but it was a struggle. Roy said, 'Like certain generals I believe that in dire emergency it is often better to attack. I clapped my hands and yelled, "Let's show these Geordies the stuff that's taken us to Wembley." We gave 20 minutes of vintage football, then caved in. The Deep Revie Plan had failed... We had failed... Had I failed as captain?'

The driving force, Roy Paul, celebrates FA Cup success with his son.

In the weeks, months and even years since that final the story of Trautmann's injury, and also the role of the Revie Plan in City's victory have dominated the memories of that final. However, Roy's inspirational leadership was perhaps the main driving force throughout the FA Cup campaign. Roy, at Wembley in 1956, gave a performance that many people regarded as his best of all. His determination was infectious while his encouragement helped the other players to focus. This was his finest hour.

Roy's Finest Fellow Citizens

The 1950s proved to be a glorious period for the Blues, with their quality football culminating in them contesting successive FA Cup finals. There were many popular players during this period of great success and wonderful memories.

ROY LITTLE Full-back Roy Little joined City in August 1949 and made his debut in a superb FA Cup victory over Swindon on 10 January 1953. The Blues won 7–0 and the following week Little made his League debut in the 1–0 victory at Liverpool. He went on to make 186 League and Cup appearances for City and played in both the 1955 and 1956 FA Cup finals. Although he later moved to Brighton, then became player-manager of Dover, he eventually returned to Manchester and spent several years working for Manchester University's leisure department. During the 1990s he became a founder member of the City former players' association.

DON REVIE One of football's most controversial figures, Don Revie was idolised during his six seasons at Maine Road. The first City man to be awarded the Football Writers' Association Footballer of the Year trophy, in 1955, Revie was an immensely talented forward whose name will forever be linked with City's mid-1950s success. The Revie Plan was a revolutionary tactic that allowed the centre forward to be positioned deep, thus confusing the opposition. Although this sounds a relatively simple strategy, it's fair to say that opponents found it extremely difficult to cope with the new tactic. Revie played the role of the deep-lying centre forward but, interestingly, the plan had been developed in the reserves through Revie's great friend Johnny Williamson.

Revie made a total of 177 League and Cup appearances with the Blues, scoring 41 times. In later life he became the inspirational manager of Leeds United and also had a spell as England manager. City fans, however, prefer to remember the quality of his performances while playing in Manchester.

FIONAN FAGAN Republic of Ireland international Fionan 'Paddy' Fagan was a versatile winger who was loved by supporters for the excitement of his play. He joined the Blues from Hull City on Christmas Eve 1953, played for the reserves on Christmas Day, then made his League debut on Boxing Day in City's 2–1 victory at home to Sheffield United.

In total Fagan made 164 League and Cup appearances and netted 35 goals while with City. He also appeared in the 1955 FA Cup final. He moved to Derby in March 1960 and later moved back to the Manchester area for spells with Altrincham, Northwich Victoria and Ashton United. Together with Roy Little and Roy Clarke, Fagan was one of the key players behind the creation of the former players' association.

BOBBY JOHNSTONE The first man to score in successive Wembley FA Cup finals, Bobby Johnstone was an exciting forward for the Blues. He arrived in Manchester in March 1955 for a fee of £22,000 after a highly successful spell at Hibernian and he immediately proved popular with fans.

During his City career Johnstone scored 51 goals in 138 League and Cup appearances and his equalising header in the 1955 final is still regarded as one of Wembley's greatest goals. The following year he netted City's third as Birmingham were defeated in the final. Johnstone left the Blues in 1959 to return to Hibs but later came back to Manchester to play for Oldham, where he netted 35 goals in 143 League games. A painting of Johnstone is on display at the City of Manchester Stadium.

JOHNNY HART One of City's longest-serving figures of all, Johnny Hart joined the office staff at Maine Road as a boy in 1944. His duties at that time included helping out with wages and generally acting as a deputy to Club secretary-manager Wilf Wild. Inevitably, Hart pushed to establish himself as a player and on 10 April 1948 he was given a chance to impress in the League with a debut against Bolton. Gradually, over the following seasons, he started to appear more frequently and he went on to score 73 goals in 178 League and Cup appearances.

Once he retired he became a key member of City's backroom staff, and then in 1973 he had a brief spell as manager. It was a position he didn't really want, believing that he was much better as part of the coaching team. However, his six months in charge did have a few successful moments and he was responsible for the return to City of former hero Denis Law.

A typical 1950s line up shows, from left to right (back row) Roy Paul, Ken Barnes, Bert Trautmann, Bill Leivers, Roy Little, Dave Ewing, (front row) Billy Spurdle, Joe Hayes, Bobby Johnstone, Jack Dyson and Roy Clarke.

A Sombre Scene

Roy definitely blamed himself, although in truth he had done more than most to try to secure the Cup. City's determination after the Meadows injury kept them in the match – they equalised through a brilliant Bobby Johnstone header – but the simple fact of having one player short told in the end and gave Newcastle a 3–1 victory.

Manchester journalist Eric Thornton tried to talk to Roy after the match. 'He started tearing off his crumpled shirt while the others hauled their tired, naked bodies up the cold, concrete steps to the king-size bath on the raised floor. He halted in his labours, wiped away some of the sweat with the back of his hand, looked across to me, shook his head and said, "It's a devil!." He washed, changed, came back to his seat, pulled the medal out of his jacket pocket and had another look at it. He still

looked grim and said, "Do you want this medal, Eric, because it's no good to me. I've no time for a loser's medal. I want a winner's medal, that's what I want." It was no good giving him a sympathetic pat and murmuring the old woman's comment about there always being a next time. He knew all about that. But he also knew that all the Cup fighting he and his mates had done over the previous four months had proved just useless in the end.'

Contrary to popular opinion, it took Roy some time to get the Cup-final defeat out of his system. Immediately after the game, he vowed that City would return and supporters felt this showed that the great leader had already started to look forward in a positive manner. In truth, Roy found it hard to accept. Later he admitted, 'I wanted to say I was retiring. I had had a good run in the game, there seemed no prospect in carrying on. Why not go out while still on top even though we had lost the final?'

Brief Brilliance

Fortunately, Roy did not make any hasty decisions and 12 months later he guided City to an FA Cup-final victory over Birmingham City and fourth place in the League – City's best finish since their Championship-winning season of 1937. Sadly, the success wasn't to last and in the following season the Blues were knocked out of the FA Cup in a third-round replay – a thrilling 5–4 tie with Newcastle at Maine Road – and finished the league season in 18th place. Roy left Manchester City on a free transfer to become the Worcester City player-manager. The high point of his time at Worcester was probably the sensational 2–1 FA Cup third-round victory over Liverpool in January 1959.

Later, Roy returned to the Rhondda and joined Brecon Corinthians and Garw Athletic, both times as player-manager. He also sought employment outside of the game and became a lorry driver until retirement.

On 21 May 2002 Roy passed away at the age of 82. As with fellow countryman Billy Meredith, Roy Paul had proved himself to be one of City's most important captains. Always a determined figure, Roy ensured his team-mates offered the same level of commitment as he did and, as a result, the Blues succeeded. The team spirit encouraged by Roy helped City enormously, and as captain Roy was a major force in the game.

Writing in 1969, Eric Thornton summed up Paul's approach: 'He wasn't everybody's cup of tea, but I don't think he had an enemy. He lived a very full life.'

'I know this means a lot to Roy's family and I'm sure he will be looking down on us tonight and feeling very proud. He was a great player and a wonderful friend to my husband Roy and myself.'

Kath Clarke
collecting the Hall of Fame award on behalf of Roy Paul's family in January 2004.

Mike Summerbee

Mike Summerbee was the first member of City's great 1960s side to be considered by England manager Alf Ramsey for an international appearance, and throughout his ten-year City career the entertaining winger was an immensely popular player. He was idolised by supporters and he did so much to ensure they were entertained. To Mike, football wasn't simply about winning, it was also about enjoyment, and the supporters certainly enjoyed his time at Maine Road.

125

Mike Summerbee
PANEL AWARD

Football Family

Mike came from a footballing family. His father, George, had played for a variety of sides, including Winchester City, Aldershot and Preston North End and had gone on to manage Cheltenham Town. It was inevitable that the young Mike would fill his time with sporting activities. Sadly, Mike's father passed away while Mike was still at school and life became difficult, financially, for the family. Football remained Mike's main preoccupation and he excelled at the sport at school, often playing in sides much older

Summerbee weaves passed WBA substitute Alan Merrick during City's 6–1 1968 Charity Shield success.

than himself. At the age of 9 he captained his junior school side, which mainly contained 11-year-olds. By the time he was 14 he had more or less given up on any form of academic success but remained popular with his sports teachers simply because of his skill and commitment. According to Mike, he struck a deal with the headmaster whereby he would take a back seat with regular studies to concentrate on his football. 'Just keep coming back for the games,' his headmaster is alleged to have said.

Mike was given a trial at Bristol City, at the age of 15, in December 1957. It didn't work out – he was not happy with the surroundings and felt homesick – but it did prove that he had enough skill to consider seriously a professional career, and when Swindon Town offered him a trial shortly afterwards, Mike jumped at the chance. Within a couple of months of signing amateur forms, he was playing reserve-team football against the likes of Chelsea and Arsenal.

Two years after the trial at Bristol, Mike made his Football League debut for Swindon against Bournemouth. He was 17 years old and, over the course of the following 5 years, he scored 29 goals in 218 League appearances for the Wiltshire club. Those goals included one in a match that has entered the record books because it was watched by Manchester City's lowest League crowd at Maine Road. The match was a Division Two encounter in January 1965 and it was attended by a miserable Mancunian crowd of 8,015. Swindon won 2–1, with Mike scoring their second goal in the 64th minute. It was the lowest point City had ever reached and, fortunately for Mike, supporters demanded change. In July Joe Mercer arrived as manager, and life, for both the Blues and for Mike, changed considerably.

Destiny Fulfilled

Mike was actually the second player, after Ralph Brand, brought to Maine Road by Mercer in 1965 but Mercer had been keen on signing Mike for some time. He had kept a close watch on the player's career and had always felt that Mike would do an excellent job for him. The opportunity to sign him only really arrived once Mercer was in the manager's chair at Maine Road but once it did, Mercer couldn't wait.

'I knew that Joe had watched me when he was manager at Aston Villa and had fancied me as a player,' says Mike. 'Unknown to me, Swindon had sent terms of my contract on ahead of me but while I was driving up to Manchester I was telling myself that I was going to one of the top clubs; a club with great traditions and a superb ground. I told myself that I would get a few quid out of them and as I passed through Birmingham I was telling myself that I would ask for £50 a week. By the time I came through Sale I'd decided that I was worth £75. City had pots of money... were a "Super League" club... they could afford it. I pulled up outside Maine Road and found Joe in the trainer's room. Joe told me, "We're in the Second Division. We've had a bad time. We've won nothing for years and we're skint.

Mercer's second signing proved his commitment consistently throughout his ten-year Maine Road career.

Player Career Statistics
Appearances

MIKE SUMMERBEE

Position
Wing forward 1965–75

Typical Height and Weight
1.79m (5ft 10in)
72kg (11st 4lb)

Born
Preston, 15 December 1942

League Debut
Middlesbrough (away)
21 August 1965

	LEAGUE		FA CUP		FL CUP		EUROPE		TOTAL	
	App	Gls	App	Gls	App	Gls	App	Gls	App	Gls
1965/66	42	8	8	2	2	0	-	-	52	10
1966/67	32	4	4	2	2	1	-	-	38	7
1967/68	41	14	4	4	4	2	-	-	49	20
1968/69	39	6	6	0	3	2	2	0	50	8
1969/70	32 (1)	3	2	0	7	2	7	1	48 (1)	6
1970/71	26	4	2	0	1	0	6	0	35	4
1971/72	40	3	2	0	2	0	-	-	44	3
1972/73	38	2	4	1	2	0	1	0	45	3
1973/74	39	1	2	2	11	1	-	-	52	4
1974/75	26 (1)	2	0	0	2	0	-	-	28 (1)	2
TOTAL	355 (2)	47	34	11	36	8	16	1	441 (2)	67

'Inspired by Mike Summerbee, they ground relentlessly on towards Division One with a ruthless display of soccer that demoralised North End.'

You are on £35 a week at Swindon and we'll give you £40." I accepted like a shot!'

Mike's arrival attracted a great deal of interest. Despite City having suffered so much earlier in 1965, the appointment of Mercer and, shortly afterwards, Allison, had brought excitement to Mancunians and so, inevitably, the first transfers were important. Mike impressed from the start. His debut came in the opening match of the season at Middlesbrough and the *Daily Mirror* reported, 'Mike Summerbee was value for his £35,000 price tag from the kick-off. With his first contact with the ball he put Jimmy Murray through for a run which Ian Davidson ended with a desperate late tackle and from then on, Summerbee was City's danger man.

'He did not always have understanding with his team-mates, naturally, but he clipped over an inch-perfect lob for Murray to head City's goal early in the second half. Fed properly, the new No. 7 will be a frequent matchwinner for the Maine Road club.'

During the weeks that followed, many headlines were written about Mike's performances for the Blues, and it seemed that week after week local journalist Peter Gardner was proclaiming Mike's latest performance to be his best since his arrival in Manchester. Perhaps the greatest performance of the opening months of the 1965/66 season came at Preston in October. The Blues totally dominated Preston and won 3–0 with a goal from Ralph Brand and two from Neil Young. It was Mike, though, who received most praise. 'Mighty Mike has the touch of the master' and 'A touch of Matthews magic from Summerbee' read the headlines as Mike was compared to Stanley Matthews and to the great Preston hero Tom Finney.

Peak Performance

Mike often talks of that match against Preston as his greatest City game and there's no doubt that all

supporters who attended Deepdale that day do remember his scintillating performance. It was perhaps the first match of the season to convince fans that the Blues really were destined to climb out of Division Two. Reporter David James recognised the transformation and for most of his match report he commented on Mike and on the supporters. 'The arrogant singing of Manchester City's thousands of faithful fans boiled to fever pitch in a white-hot second half. "We're going up," they chanted – and on this showing they must be right. For City confirmed that they are as complete a team as will be found in the Second Division. Inspired by Mike Summerbee, they ground relentlessly on towards Division One with a ruthless display of soccer that demoralised North End.'

Despite some memorable and superb performances Mike only managed eight League goals during his first season. Some suggested this was playing on his mind but Malcolm Allison and Joe Mercer were not concerned. They recognised that his all-round performances had helped the Blues to push forward. Those performances had already pushed Mike into England consideration. During the early part of 1966, letters appeared in various local and national papers urging Alf Ramsey to consider Mike for England. Ramsey had developed a reputation for playing without wingers, so calls for Mike to appear seemed to fall on deaf ears until April, when Alf Ramsey picked Mike for the England Under-23 match with Turkey. A year later, Mike was selected to travel to Canada as part of an official Football Association party.

At the age of 25, in February 1968, Mike became the first City player since Don Revie, in 1956, to appear for the full England side. Considering the quality of players available and the fact that Ramsey had an aversion to wing play, this was a major achievement. The game was a European Nations

Cup qualifier against Scotland at Hampden Park, watched by an incredible 134,000. It ended 1–1 and Mike performed well enough to keep his place for the next qualifying round, which was against Spain. Shortly after the Scotland game, he admitted that it had been a worrying international debut. 'I was nothing short of a nervous wreck. I was England's centre forward that afternoon. I would rather have been playing anywhere but Hampden Park that day, as Bobby Moore led us out on to the pitch. Yet as soon as the game began, all my worries melted away and I felt the same kind of elation and disbelief I had when I was first selected. This really is what playing for England is all about. This is the pinnacle of a player's career.'

Better Than Best

In total Mike made eight international appearances and scored once – a vital goal in England's European Nations qualifier with Switzerland in November 1971. The game ended 1–1. Ramsey's reliance on his 'wingless wonders' restricted Mike, but the fact that he was the first of City's side selected for England proved that his skills were recognised across the country.

One man delighted with Mike's England selection was City manager Joe Mercer. He had predicted a great future for the player several years earlier and he loved telling others of Mike's qualities. 'Now, he is an attacking player; in fact, I would say that he is one of the best players there

Summerbee and Best chase for possession during the thrilling 3–3 draw in November 1971. Summerbee scored City's equaliser in the final minute.

Mike's Prime Time

Newcastle United 3 Manchester City 4. Football League Division One – 11 May 1968

Goalscorers Summerbee, Young (2), Lee

City Team Mulhearn, Book, Pardoe, Doyle, Heslop, Oakes, Lee, Bell, Summerbee, Young, Coleman

Attendance 46,300

The 1967/68 League Championship was one of the most closely fought campaigns of all. City, United, Leeds and Liverpool were in sensational form and each side had, at one time or another, seemed certain to win the Championship. The Blues had been the outsiders and few had given them any hope of success, but Mike Summerbee and those who had joined Mercer and Allison's merry band while they were in Division Two had recognised that there was something special about their development. Mike says, 'We suddenly woke up that season. Everyone expected us to go straight down after promotion, but here we were fighting our way forward. The club had changed almost overnight and that was down to Joe and Malcolm.'

So much has been written about the game itself and the build-up to it that this has become one of football's most chronicled matches. Nevertheless, it's crucial to explain the importance and role played by Mike that day. Although he would probably not call this his greatest match, his performance did much to ensure victory came City's way. 'I remember everything about that day because it was such a special moment,' says Mike. 'Colin Bell, Peter Blakey, the physio, and I travelled up on our own because Colin and I were both nursing injuries. We arrived at the hotel in Gateshead, had a meal and so on, and went to bed at about 11.

'The atmosphere was so relaxed, but I remember waking up the next morning with this roar outside the hotel. The road was full of City supporters in cars with their horns going – there must have been 500 outside our hotel. The atmosphere was brilliant and I was really looking forward to the game. We knew Newcastle were a good side, and by the time we got to the changing room the tension was growing. Ten minutes before kick-off, Joe cleared everyone out

apart from the players and backroom staff. Joe's team talk was something simple like "Get out there and sort it out!"'

City needed to achieve a better result than Manchester United to win the title and with the Reds at home to lowly Sunderland it was clear City needed to put in a fine performance. After 13 minutes Mike set up the Blues for victory. 'It was a lovely day and, while the surface was good on the wings and in the middle, it was bumpy in the goalmouths. After about ten minutes, this ball came through from the right. If it had been a flat surface, I would have struggled to score but, as Willie McFaul came out of his goal, the ball bobbled and I was able to flick it over him.'

From that point on, the Blues surged forward at every opportunity but Newcastle were also committed and before City could score a second, the Geordies had equalised. After 32 minutes, it was 2–1 to City after Young had scored from 22 yards (20m), but three minutes later Newcastle were level again. A Francis Lee effort was disallowed, leaving it 2–2 at half time.

Despite the scoreline, the Blues were confident. 'There was no way we were going to lose that game; no way!,' says Mike. 'If they'd scored six, we'd score seven. That's how it was always going to go.'

In the end Newcastle scored three and City scored four and had two 'goals' disallowed. The Blues became champions for the first time since 1937. Mike had helped to restore City pride: 'We won 4–3 and had a couple disallowed but the most satisfying element for me was putting City back to the top. That Championship, particularly taking it from United, gave City their credibility back and meant our fans could walk with their heads held high. That's what gave me the greatest pleasure.'

Summerbee in control at Maine Road during the 1973–74 season.

is with his back to the game. It is more difficult as a forward because, basically, one is receiving the ball the wrong way. And the hardest thing in football is to turn round with the ball, especially with defensive football as it always is, where they mark tight. Mike is the best, or the bravest player with his back to the game that I have ever seen. Jimmy Logie was good, and so too was Alex James; George Best is another but Mike is the best I have ever seen.

'He is strong when he is going past them. When he is buzzing he takes them all apart. He is very positive and quite a character.'

Another man to recognise Mike's qualities was United's George Best: 'At centre forward, he's a different class. One of the best in the country. He does work for the other players that the fans don't see. I'd like to play a game in the City attack just to see what it's like.'

Fans' Favourite

The 1968 season ended with the Blues as League champions and over the course of the following two seasons Mike helped City to win the FA Cup, League Cup and European Cup Winners' Cup, although he was unfortunate to miss, through injury, the European Cup Winners' Cup final in Vienna. He had played in seven of the eight European games leading up to the final and certainly deserved to be recognised for his part in City's first European success.

In addition to his exploits on the pitch, Summerbee often entertained the Blues with practical jokes and his performances in the annual club pantomime. To fans, he always seemed to enjoy his time at Maine Road and he quickly became a favourite with a large proportion of supporters. Because of his surname and his footballing style he was understandably nicknamed 'Buzzer', and there seemed to be nothing more enjoyable than the sight of him buzzing up the wing, ready to set up another goal for Francis Lee or Neil Young. The 1969 Cup-final goal owes much to Summerbee's determination and understanding of the game. That goal was scored as a result of him gathering a throw-in from Lee, racing down the right, slipping the ball past Leicester's David Nish and centring for Young to crash the ball past Shilton. It was an important goal, created by a popular player. He was so popular that he was voted the Supporters' Club Player of the Year in both 1972 and 1973, thus becoming the first man to win the award twice.

Mike's City career lasted until 1975, by which time the great Mercer-Allison side had broken up. A year before his departure he played in the 1974 League Cup final, alongside other greats Bell, Lee, Law and Marsh, but success evaded the Blues. He moved to Burnley for £25,000 in June 1975, then went to Blackpool, before becoming player-manager at Stockport under chairman Freddie Pye.

Away from football, Mike developed a shirt-making business and he also made an appearance in the seminal footballing film *Escape To Victory*, with Michael Caine, Sylvester Stallone and fellow former Blue Kaziu Deyna.

In 1994 he came back to City to work on commercial activities and, at the time of his inauguration into the City Hall of Fame, Mike was still a popular member of City's workforce. Always popular with fans, Mike has remained one of the Club's greatest ambassadors.

During the early 1970s Mike told supporters how much he loved being at Maine Road, 'Manchester City are the finest club in the world to play for. With them I have risen to heights which I never dreamed possible and if I had to give up football tomorrow I would have no regrets. I have done everything I could possibly have hoped for.'

Mike Summerbee collecting the Hall of Fame award in January 2004.

‘ Thank you, everyone, for this. I really do mean that. Thanks to all the fans for honouring me this way. It's a tremendous situation for me to be in and I do very much appreciate it. There are many people whom I must thank. First of all the players I played with, right the way through from 1965: Roy Cheetham, Glyn Pardoe, Alan Oakes, Johnny Crossan, Mike Doyle... they are the ones who were here when I first arrived in the Second Division with Joe Mercer and that great coach Malcolm Allison. More than anything, though, this is for a man who believed in me when I was 15 years old, playing for Swindon Town. He came in the car park one day when he was the manager of Aston Villa. He said, "You're going to come to me, son, one day." This is for Joe Mercer. ’

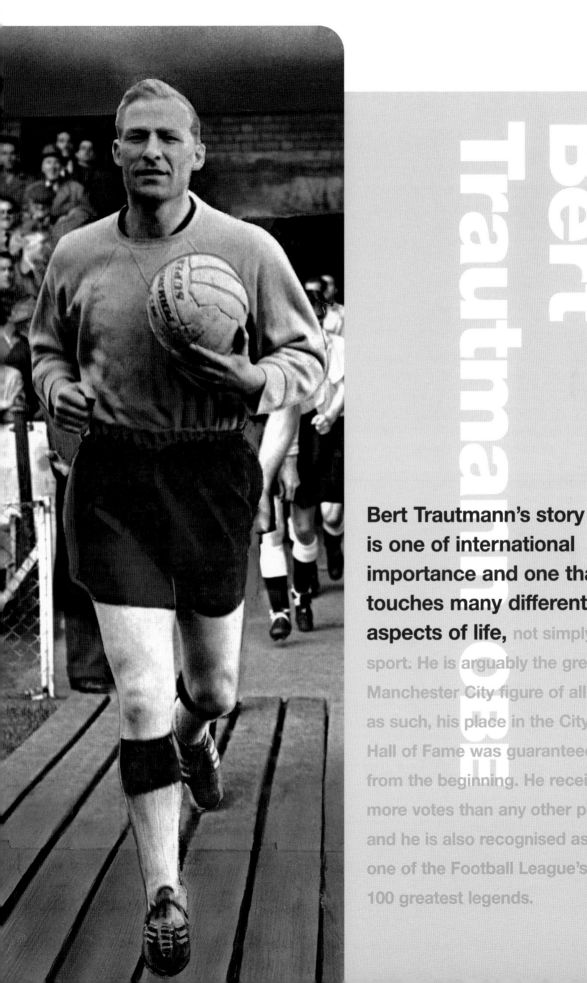

Bert Trautmann OBE

Bert Trautmann's story is one of international importance and one that touches many different aspects of life, not simply sport. He is arguably the greatest Manchester City figure of all and, as such, his place in the City Hall of Fame was guaranteed from the beginning. He received more votes than any other player and he is also recognised as one of the Football League's 100 greatest legends.

Bert Trautmann OBE
1958–1965 AWARD

Desperate Days

Bert's upbringing and early life have to be considered in the context of the country in which he was raised. Germany during the late 1920s and 1930s was, at times, a desperate place to be. The country was on its knees following the First World War and the early years of the Depression. It was an environment in which the far-right policies of Adolf Hitler and the Nazi party flourished and for many average Germans the new leader seemed to offer hope. Young Bert, already a keen sports enthusiast, became a member of the Hitler Youth. It wasn't as a result of strong political beliefs: he was simply following the route expected for anyone with his talents. It gave him the opportunity to play sport and the high-profile 1936 Berlin Olympics gave him the desire to excel.

When war broke out in 1939, Bert was an apprentice motor mechanic. He went on to join the Luftwaffe and served in Poland and for three years in Russia. As a paratrooper he was captured by the Russians and by the French Resistance, escaping on both occasions, and he won five medals for bravery, including the Iron Cross (first class). Bert saw the full extent of war. Some days he would kill; other days he would see his colleagues die. It was a nightmare existence, although Bert has always been quick to point out that it was no worse than the situation millions of others were in: 'There was tragedy and there was humour, as there was on every battle front.'

In 1945 he was captured by the Americans but somehow managed to walk free and then the British caught him. He spent a few weeks imprisoned near

A typical 1950s City scene showing a packed Kippax and a courageous Trautmann.

'People can boycott or not as they like...

From what I have heard of him he is not a good
goalkeeper; he is a superb goalkeeper.'

Ostend, then in Essex, before he was officially
classified as a Nazi by the British forces. The view
was that he had known nothing but Nazi
indoctrination from childhood and, together with his
bravery awards and his role as a paratrooper, this
meant he was to be transferred to a 'Nazi section' of
a prisoner-of-war camp in Cheshire. Later he moved
to a camp in Ashton-in-Makerfield, Lancashire,
where he was to live until 1948. It was at this camp
that, for the first time, he began to play in goal
during football matches.

Courting Controversy

Bert was officially released from captivity in February
1948 but elected to stay in Britain, as he saw no
immediate prospects in Germany. He was initially
given agricultural work and at the end of 1948 was
transferred to bomb disposal work in Liverpool and,
briefly, Bristol. By this time he was playing football
for St Helen's Town and proving very popular.

As the 1949/50 season commenced, several
League clubs were showing interest in him, most
notably Burnley but others, including Bolton,

Player Career Statistics
Appearances

BERT TRAUTMANN

Position
Goalkeeper 1949–64

Typical Height and Weight
1.88m (6ft 2in)
91kg (14st 5lb)

Born
Bremen, Germany,
22 October 1923

League Debut
Bolton Wanderers (away)
19 November 1949

	LEAGUE		FA CUP		FL CUP		TOTAL	
	App	Gls	App	Gls	App	Gls	App	Gls
1949/50	26	0	0	0	-	-	26	0
1950/51	42	0	1	0	-	-	43	0
1951/52	41	0	2	0	-	-	43	0
1952/53	42	0	3	0	-	-	45	0
1953/54	42	0	2	0	-	-	44	0
1954/55	40	0	6	0	-	-	46	0
1955/56	40	0	7	0	-	-	47	0
1956/57	21	0	2	0	-	-	23	0
1957/58	34	0	1	0	-	-	35	0
1958/59	41	0	2	0	-	-	43	0
1959/60	41	0	1	0	-	-	42	0
1960/61	40	0	4	0	2	0	46	0
1961/62	40	0	2	0	1	0	43	0
1962/63	15	0	0	0	1	0	16	0
1963/64	3	0	0	0	0	0	3	0
TOTAL	508	0	33	0	4	0	545	0

Doncaster, Grimsby, Liverpool and Everton, made enquiries. By the end of September Burnley were ready to make an offer but then City decided to make a move. The Blues desperately needed to find a new goalkeeper, as Frank Swift, who had been drafted back into first-team action, was desperate to retire and had promised to fill the void only for a few weeks.

The Blues signed Bert in November 1949 but the move was not a popular one. For at least a month prior to the transfer, Manchester-based newspapers were publishing letters from fans threatening to boycott the Club. City had a large Jewish support at the time and many believed the arrival of a former German paratrooper was one step too far. The national media soon caught on to the

story and considerable negative publicity came both City's way and the way of Bert. The Club could have pulled out at any point but chairman Bob Smith answered critics by saying, 'People can boycott or not as they like. I am very glad we have signed Trautmann. From what I have heard of him he is not a good goalkeeper; he is a superb goalkeeper. We had to get him in quickly or other teams would have taken him from under our noses.'

The players, including captain Eric Westwood – a Normandy veteran – soon made Bert feel welcome and, despite the threatened boycotts, City felt delighted to have signed such an exciting prospect. Bert's debut came on 19 November 1949 against Bolton. The Blues lost 3–0 but the goalkeeper had impressed. Bert remembers this period as one of

Bert is in total control against Arsenal at Highbury. Many of his best performances occurred in London.

transition. 'It was the first time I actually saw people protesting against me. But within a month, a lot of those same people who'd been against me were having a go at anyone having a go at me! It changed very quickly. When I signed for City the 'papers were full of discriminating headlines along the lines of "If City sign a Nazi, what next?" And then people realised I'd been digging unexploded bombs in their country. They started to see me as a person with a mother and father. It was all about the human touch.'

Positive Attention

Bert quickly established himself as a worthy successor to Frank Swift, and the former England captain went to great lengths to stress the quality of the German. City fans adopted Bert as one of their own and the goalkeeper became more important to the Blues after every game. The early 1950s were not particularly strong years for the Maine Road club but that helped to demonstrate the value of Bert, as he often found himself saving the Club with breathtaking performances.

The attention the player was now receiving was all positive and the German media were beginning to show interest. This led to attention from German League sides, including Schalke '04, who made an offer of £1,000 for the player. City rejected the bid but for a while Bert became keen to return to Germany. Fortunately for the Blues, the prospect of losing their star man had receded by April 1953.

Bert makes a spectacular dive despite being in agony during the latter stages of the 1956 final.

A Vital Role

Between April 1953 and May 1955 the Blues' fortunes altered significantly. Bert was finding that he was no longer simply trying to save the Club; instead he was setting up attacks. His long, powerful throws really set play moving and when the Blues started to develop a reputation as a strong team – team being significant, because City were very much a team rather than a group of individual

MCFC statistics

	1958/59	1959/60	1960/61	1961/62	1962/63	1963/64	1964/65	Significant Events
League Position	20	15	13	12	21	6 (in Div 2)	11	League Cup inaugurated at start of 1960/61 season. City's average attendance in 1964/65 was the Club's lowest of the 20th century.
FA Cup Round Reached	3	3	4	4	5	3	3	
League Cup Round Reached	-	-	3	2	5	Semi-final	2	
Average Attendance	32,568	35,637	29,409	25,626	24,683	18,201	14,753	

players – he was a fundamental part of that, both defensively and when the Blues were setting up an attack.

In 1955 Bert became the first German to play in a FA Cup final. 'Today, I don't think the occasion means that much any more in terms of the community spirit and everyone singing "Abide With Me" and so on. When I went there I enjoyed the whole thing – the build-up... the media attention... everything. I have never known nerves like I had that day. Even when we went back a year later, they were still bad.'

After the final whistle Bert, helped by Bill Leivers and Laurie Barnett, leaves the Wembley pitch in agony.

The Blues lost the final 3–1 and were desperately unlucky but at the civic reception that followed in Manchester Town Hall, Bert received enormous praise from all the attendees. His father had been flown over from Germany and felt delighted with the popularity of his son. At one point during the evening he turned to Bert and said, 'They seem to be very fond of you and you must never forget them and what they have done for you. Hitler never had a reception quite like this.'

A Fateful Day

A year later, Bert was back at Wembley to help City defeat Birmingham City. It was a memorable game but, for many, the significant aspect of the day concerns what happened to Bert. 'It was only years later I could piece together what happened that day,' says Bert. 'I have watched film of the match and you can see me coming out to intercept the ball. I was in the air and neither me nor Murphy, the Birmingham player, could stop. He tried to get over me, lifted his leg but caught me in the neck with his right leg. It was accidental. After that I was gone. Everything was grey until the final minute. I made a couple of saves but don't remember anything until our centre half, Dave Ewing, collided into me. The pain was intense and I really didn't know what I had done. I was only aware of this pain – like an extreme toothache in my neck.

'On Sunday morning I was taken to hospital in London where they took X-rays and told me it was nothing. But I could not move my head. If I wanted to turn I had to move my whole body. I knew something was wrong.'

Incredibly, Bert played his part in City's homecoming and footage of the day shows him travelling through Manchester on the open-top Finglands bus. He then made an impromptu speech at the Town Hall while the crowd chanted his name. 'I must have looked like death,' says Bert. 'We had the homecoming in a packed Albert Square and I had to speak. At the reception I remember Frank Swift slapping me with his enormous hands – it felt like I had been split right down the middle with an axe!'

Bert's Prime Time

Fulham 1 Manchester City 0. Football League Division One – 14 January 1950

City Team Trautmann, Phillips, Westwood, Gill, Fagan, Walsh, Munro, Black, Turnbull, Alison, Oakes

Attendance 30,000

Although many people regard the 1956 FA Cup final as Bert Trautmann's greatest match, the truth is that this meeting with Fulham during his first League season is actually the game above all others that helped to establish his name. 'The papers said we should have lost by nine or ten that day,' says Bert, 'but we only lost 1–0. In the context of the early days, it was the best game I ever had – an experience you cannot describe – and the game that had the biggest influence on my career.'

So why was this City defeat such an important moment in the player's career? The answer lies in the fact that this was Bert's first game in London and, as a former Luftwaffe paratrooper, he was a major figure of hate for the Londoners. Bert had already overcome significant abuse in Manchester but London was anticipated to be much worse. Bert remembers it well. 'I had been getting a good press in the North west by this time but Jack Friar, who was to become my father-in-law, pointed out that my first game in London would really test me because of the papers and publicity down there. He said I wasn't just playing against Fulham; I was playing against London. I needed to make a good impression to get the national press on my side and he told me he expected we could lose 7–0 or 8–0!'

As the players entered the Craven Cottage pitch shouts of 'Kraut' and 'Nazi' rang out. Bert received tremendous abuse and a lesser player would have buckled under the pressure but Bert seemed to see the venom as a challenge and he started to appear more confident and more determined than he had in any earlier City match.

The City side Bert found himself playing in was a transitional one and at the end of the season the Blues would be relegated. City's lack of success during this season ensured that the goalkeeper was under a great deal of pressure. He had to perform well and, despite the abuse emanating from the terraces, Bert put in a marvellous performance. Shot after shot came his way and Bert made save after save. Jack McDonald did manage to score for Fulham but the game would have been a total annihilation had it not been for Bert.

At the final whistle both sides lined up to applaud Bert down the players' tunnel. Young Fulham fan Jim Sims remembers the day vividly. 'The effect on us at the Cottage was magnetic. We were watching a supreme professional at the top of his trade – a real flesh and blood hero. I am absolutely certain his appearance in the First Division just four years after ceasing hostilities had a major effect on boosting and repairing our relationship with the Germans. He'd been a prisoner of war as a paratrooper and was engaged to an English girl, which all helped. But he gave you that warm glow. After the game, we all clapped like mad as they made a corridor for him. It was unique. It was as if we were trying to wash away the sins of the world and was pretty emotional.'

Bert says, 'I was at the Thames End of the ground and was the last player to come off. Both teams stood at the dressing-room entrance and applauded; a very emotional moment. In London, at that time, that was a testimony. I was lucky in later years to win the FA Cup; win the Player of the Year; and play for the Football League. But Fulham was my greatest moment.'

Today many remember Bert's Wembley heroics, but this was the moment his transformation into a major footballing hero began.

Bert's Finest Fellow Citizens

The late 1950s and early 1960s are sometimes seen as a transitional period for Manchester City. The closest the Blues came to success was in 1964, when they reached the semi-finals of the League Cup. The great Cup-final side had started to move on by 1958 but players, such as Trautmann and Hayes continued to impress with many memorable appearances.

BILL MCADAMS Inside-forward Billy McAdams was born in Belfast and joined City from Irish League club Distillery in December 1953. Injury affected his first few seasons but by 1960 not only was he an Irish international, he was also City's top goalscorer. During 1959/60 he netted 21 goals in only 30 League games. Earlier, between 9 October and 7 December 1957, he made national headlines when he scored in ten consecutive League games. He actually scored 11 League goals during that period (he netted twice against Everton) and he also scored in a friendly match played between those dates. McAdams left City in September 1960, after 65 goals in 134 League and Cup appearances.

JOE HAYES Legend has it that Joe Hayes arrived at Maine Road with his boots in a brown-paper parcel, scored four goals in a trial match and then said in a broad Boltonian accent, 'Ta very much for t'game. Can I 'ave me bus fare back 'ome please?' Within eight weeks he was making his League debut against Tottenham and by the end of the 1950s he had proved to be one of football's greatest goal-poachers.

In total, 5ft 8in (1.71m) Hayes scored 152 goals in 363 League and Cup appearances, a tally that includes the opening goal in the 1956 FA Cup final. Sadly, a serious knee injury sustained at Bury in 1964 reduced his opportunities and he moved to Barnsley on a free transfer. He later had spells at Wigan and Lancaster City, where he became player-manager. In 1999 he passed away at the age of 63.

BILL LEIVERS Centre-half Bill Leivers joined City for a fee of £10,500 in November 1953 and made his debut in August 1954 against Preston. Over the course of the following decade he was to make a total of 281 League and Cup appearances. A key member of the 1956 FA Cup-winning side, Leivers was a committed defender.

After leaving City for Doncaster on a free transfer in July 1964, Leivers moved into management, guiding Doncaster to the top of Division Four. Then, as manager of Cambridge United, he guided his side from the Southern League to Division Three. He later had spells with Chelmsford City and Cambridge City.

KEN BRANAGAN Full-back Ken Branagan arrived at Maine Road in November 1948 but had to wait until December 1950 for his League debut. In between those dates his career had to be put on hold as he had to do 18 months' national service in the Army. When he did make it into the first team he was regarded by many as a safe, dependable defender. He was unfortunate not to form part of the squad for the two 1950s FA Cup finals but he did manage to make 208 League and Cup appearances between December 1950 and October 1960. He moved on to Oldham Athletic after his City career came to an end and, together with fellow former City men Bobby Johnstone and Bert Lister, he helped Oldham to promotion in 1963.

DAVE EWING Perth-born Dave Ewing joined City in June 1949 but didn't make his debut until the 1–1 draw with Manchester United in January 1953. Over the following nine years he was to make 302 League and Cup appearances and feature in both FA Cup finals. Often described as 'one of the toughest centre-halves in football' Ewing was a big, powerful defender who became noted for his vocal encouragement.

After City he played for Crewe and then had coaching spells at a variety of clubs, including City. In 1977/78 he ran the City reserve side that won the Central League for the first time in the Club's history.

The blue and white flag proudly proclaims 'City FC' as Trautmann makes another thrilling dive.

Understandably, Bert wasn't happy with the doctor's initial findings and he chose to have a second opinion. He visited an osteopath, who told him he had five vertebrae out of place. The player was manhandled until the osteopath claimed four had returned to their normal position. 'He then put my head on its side,' recalls Bert, 'and hit me with the flat of his hand. The pain shot through me.'

Again unhappy with his treatment, Bert finally managed to see an expert at Manchester Royal Infirmary on the Tuesday after the final. That's when the true extent of Bert's injury became apparent as the doctor told Bert he had broken his neck. Extensive treatment followed. Some felt his career was over but Bert never contemplated the end of his involvement. 'I was in my early thirties, an age when you should think your career could end, but I never really thought of the injury being that serious. There was nothing I could do but lie there and do a lot of thinking. And never did I think that I would not play football again.'

A Terrible Blow

A few weeks after the final, tragedy struck when Bert's son was killed in a road accident. Life was tough, immediately after Wembley, but Bert tried to keep his spirits high. Then in December – only seven months after the injury – Bert returned to League action. He had played a few reserve games – the first watched by more than 8,000 fans – and Les McDowall, the City manager, urged him to make a first-team return. Bert was not quite ready and the pressure placed on him was perhaps too great but the goalkeeper gave it his best shot. His return came on 15 December 1956 – the first City League match filmed by the BBC at Maine Road – but City lost 3–2. 'It was very difficult coming back,' remembers Bert. 'I came back too quickly, really. I would stand there with the forwards coming at me, saying, "Come on, have a go. Let me show you I'm still good enough." But it never happened like that. I reckoned I was finished. I told McDowall so but he told me I was wrong. I told him I had cost City at least six points but he said, "Think of the number of points you've saved us over the years." I think it took me about 18 months before I was fit enough but, even today, my neck is still painful and restricted, especially in cold weather.'

Bert continued to play for City until 1964, when he was awarded a testimonial. The official crowd was approximately 48,000 but the actual attendance was more like 60,000, as Maine Road was packed to the rafters, with thousands of fans locked outside.

During the latter part of his time at City, Bert was viewed as the greatest goalkeeper playing in England and in October 1960 he was chosen to captain the Football League's representative side for a match with the Irish League. This was a major honour at the time and compensated, to some degree, for the fact that he had not been picked to play for the German national side. The reason he never appeared for Germany has been debated many times over the years. The most likely reason, and the one the majority of footballing people believe, is that the German authorities had simply chosen not to pick him because he was playing outside of his home nation. Had he joined Schalke in the early 1950s, it seems likely he would have been a regular for his national side.

Real Recognition

Regardless of the German view during his career, it's fair to say that England's leading footballing figures recognised Bert's greatness, especially in 1956 when he was awarded the Football Writers' Association Footballer of the Year award. This was significant not only in that Bert was the first overseas player to receive the award but also because it was awarded to him in the days leading up to the 1956 final: his heroics that day had played no part in the decision.

After leaving the Blues, spells at Stockport County and Wellington Town followed as player-manager, plus various spells working with the German Football Association. While with the German FA he had a significant role assisting Third World countries with the development of sport. Stints in Burma, Tanzania, Liberia and Pakistan presented him with many obstacles, but, as with his playing career, Bert was determined to succeed.

Perhaps because of the positive effect that the better weather has on his neck, Bert has spent the last few years of his life living in Spain, but he still visits Manchester whenever he can.

Significantly, in October 2004 Bert was awarded an honorary OBE in recognition of his promotion of Anglo-German relations, and to thousands of football fans he remains a true hero.

‘ I am delighted to win this award and I am grateful to the supporters of Manchester City for their great support over the last sixty years. Thank you. ’

Bert Trautmann OBE collecting the Hall of Fame Award in December 2004.

Roy Clarke

When the decision was taken to create a lifetime achievement award, Manchester City knew there would be many possible contenders. There are several examples of players, backroom staff and other contenders who have dedicated their lives to the Blues, but there was one man who has excelled in several areas over the years: Roy Clarke. Roy was a player, one of the founders of the Club's Development Association and, for many years, the manager of City's social club.

Roy Clarke LIFETIME ACHIEVEMENT AWARD

Sporting Youth

Born near Newport, Wales, in 1925, Roy was a typically sports obsessed-youngster. He loved football but he also proved to be a good rugby player and baseball enthusiast. Although baseball may not appear to be a major British sport, it was a very popular sport among youngsters in Wales during the 1920s and 1930s. Roy was so good at the game that he represented Wales at schoolboy-

international level in 1939. Roy enjoyed all team sports but he was also good at swimming and diving and he was also the Newport table-tennis champion.

Throughout his teenage years it seemed inevitable that Roy would enjoy a successful sporting career; the major question as he grew up was in which sport would he specialise? Of course, the outbreak of war had an impact and he, like many of his friends, was given a job working in the local coal mines. It was not a pleasant job but it at least kept him close to home and gave him the opportunity to develop his sporting career.

Football became Roy's main sporting outlet and he had enjoyed playing for Newport side Albion Rovers and the local services sides when Cardiff City developed an interest in him. They asked him to sign amateur forms in December 1942. Several years later Roy Paul, Roy Clarke's City colleague, and fellow Welshman, claimed that several clubs, including Arsenal, had shown an interest in Roy Clarke and that Roy Clarke had turned them down only because of his desire to remain in Wales.

At Cardiff, Roy developed quickly. Roy Paul was a fan from the beginning and in 1956 he wrote, 'There are not many inches and pounds to Roy Clarke. He is just over medium height, with a wiry frame. But that frame is tungsten steel on a football field. The cause is never lost... he would play till he dropped. I would rather have him on my side than any number of temperamental stars. The Roy Clarkes of soccer make the game truly great because they bring to it the boundless eagerness of the true enthusiast. When still only 19 he played against Moscow Dynamo during the tour they made of Britain in 1945.'

International Debut

Roy enjoyed his time at Cardiff and made 101 wartime appearances and scored 51 goals. Those performances on the left wing helped him to gain

Roy Clarke seen pre-match at Maine Road in 1956 with the old Scoreboard End in the background.

international recognition and his first appearance for Wales came in the Victory International against Northern Ireland in April 1946. He went on to make a further 22 appearances for Wales. The following season, the first postwar, Roy appeared in 39 Division Three games and scored 11 goals.

During that 1946/47 season Manchester City were keen to strengthen their squad as they pushed for promotion from Division Two. The City management came to watch a Cardiff inside forward called Billie Rees but couldn't help but be impressed by Roy. After a number of inspections the decision was taken to sign outside-left Roy instead. Rees later signed for Tottenham but as far as City were concerned, the signing of the outside left was a wise one.

For Roy the move was a major, life-changing experience. Roy's wife, Kath, who has also been a major part of Manchester City for around 60 years, remembers their arrival. 'It was funny when we first arrived. We'd been married about a month and moving to Manchester was a move into the unknown for us. In fact Roy was so worried it would be much colder than South Wales that he bought a heavy, thick coat. It seems silly now but back then you really did not have any concept of what Manchester would be like – it was cold in the north, we were told!'

Roy's uncertainty about the weather was matched by his concern over the welcome he would receive. Any worries he may have had were dispelled quickly. 'I was pretty impressed with Manchester and once I got to Maine Road I knew that I'd made the right move. I found the Mancunians very similar to the Welsh – everywhere you went at Maine Road there would be a cup of tea waiting for you. At first I was frightened to death to go into the dressing room because it was full of all these famous football stars but I soon got into the swing of things. We moved

Player Career Statistics
Appearances

ROY CLARKE

Position
Outside left 1947–58

Typical Height and Weight
1.75m (5ft 9in)
72kg (11st 5lb)

Born
Newport, 1 June 1925

League Debut
Newport County (home)
14 June 1947

	LEAGUE		FA CUP		TOTAL	
	App	Gls	App	Gls	App	Gls
1946/47	1	0	0	0	1	0
1947/48	36	5	0	0	36	5
1948/49	34	6	1	0	35	6
1949/50	37	9	1	1	38	10
1950/51	39	9	0	0	39	9
1951/52	41	9	2	1	43	10
1952/53	22	3	0	0	22	3
1953/54	35	7	2	1	37	8
1954/55	33	7	5	3	38	10
1955/56	25	6	6	0	31	6
1956/57	40	11	2	0	42	11
1957/58	6	1	1	0	7	1
TOTAL	349	73	20	6	369	79

Roy (far right) celebrates City's second goal (scored by number ten Jack Dyson) at Wembley in 1956.

up from South Wales and into a house on Victoria Road, Fallowfield. The house was just a short walk from the ground, although I sometimes caught a bus – or at least chased after it!...

'I remember getting to the ground on Kath's bike – a typical girls- or ladies-style – and the other players ribbing me a little. The truth was they were a little envious and I think if they'd had the chance they would have all rode a girl's bike rather than walk.'

Distinguished Company

Roy signed for City on 23 May 1947 and the following day the Blues were playing West Ham. With four games still to play, promotion was already guaranteed and so manager Sam Cowan asked Roy to attend the team meeting. 'At the meeting were all the great stars and I felt a bit apprehensive looking at all these wonderful players. I was still nervous about life at a big-city club and didn't know what to expect. I remember thinking about the players I would be with: Sam Barkas – the great prewar captain; Frank Swift – the best goalkeeper in the

world; Andy Black – a marvellous Scottish international; Bert Sproston – another international star; Alec Herd... Every player was either an international or at least a recognised star. I was invited to the team talk and I thought, "I'm going to learn some words of wisdom here."

'In walked manager Sam Cowan – a wonderful man who had picked me up from the station when I first arrived and had already made me feel very welcome – and he sat on a ball on the bench. I'm not certain why but it did lift him above the players. He said, "Right. It's West Ham tomorrow. Get stuck in and let's murder them." Then he got up and walked out. That was the team talk!'

Summer Football

The Blues won that match 2–0 but suffered two defeats in the following games so the decision was taken to give Roy his debut. City were already Division Two champions by this point but the two defeats had disappointed fans. It was essential that the final match ended in a convincing win to ensure

'The long trail of injuries would undoubtedly have broken a lesser man.

He broke his left foot...; he had a hand trodden on and broken; he had his ribs cracked; collar bone broken; cartilage trouble in both knees...'

that hopes were high for the following season. The game became one of City's most interesting matches of all and for Roy it was a significant moment for several reasons. 'Naturally, a League debut is always memorable,' he says, 'but this match was played on 14 June and it was against my home-town team, Newport County. The winter had been a bad one, with very few games played during January and February, and the season had been extended. So I guess my debut must be the latest ever made by a City player.

'As well as those aspects, the game was also significant for me because my previous match for Cardiff had been in Division Three and my next match for City would be in Division One – three different divisions in three successive games. It was a record.'

The game ended 5–1 to City, with George Smith scoring all five goals to equal a club record set by Horace Barnes in 1923 and Frank Roberts in 1924. For Roy it was a wonderful start and in his next match, the opening game of the 1947/48 season, he scored his first League goal for the Blues as they defeated Wolves 4–3 before a crowd of 67,782.

It was a good first season back in Division One as City finished tenth. Roy netted five goals in 36 appearances and had done enough to impress the fans and the management. Over a 12-year City-playing career he made 349 League appearances and scored 73 goals, but that total would have been significantly higher had it not been for the large number of injuries he suffered. Captain Roy Paul always believed that Roy's determination and fighting Welsh spirit kept him going when many other players would have given up. 'The long trail of injuries would undoubtedly have broken a lesser man. He broke his left foot... the one he has scored so many goals

Roy proudly lifts the base of the FA Cup in 1956 after City's victory over Birmingham City.

Roy's Prime Time

Manchester City 1 Sunderland 0. FA Cup semi-final – 26 March 1955

Goalscorer Clarke

City Team Trautmann, Meadows, Little, Barnes, Ewing, Paul, Fagan, Hayes, Revie, Johnstone, Clarke

Attendance 58,498

To reach the semi-final the Blues had beaten Derby County (3–1), Manchester United (2–0), Luton Town (2–0) and Birmingham City (1–0), with both Roy Clarke and inside-right Johnny Hart playing exceptionally well throughout the run. Roy had netted both goals in the victory over Luton, while his colleague Hart had scored the only goal of the quarter-final meeting with Birmingham. Sadly, fate was to play its hand, with both players unable to play in the final. Not only that but Johnny Hart missed this semi-final through an injury he had sustained in a League game against Huddersfield the week prior to the tie.

No matter what was to follow for Roy, the 1955 semi-final was one match that was to prove his dedication and determination to the Blues' cause. Roy says, 'The conditions were appalling and it looked as though the match would be off. A policeman came into the dressing room to tell us it was still on. Apparently, they were worried about the fans and didn't want them to make the journey again. I felt sorry for the supporters because they were soaking wet before the match had even started. So wet, it was awful really.

'Sunderland were the favourites but I thought the conditions might work in our favour and I think they did. Maine Road was usually a bit of a muddy mess at this time of year, so we got used to passes falling short and the like. You couldn't pass the ball properly, so you needed to think more. You had to use your mind and your skill.'

With the conditions poor, neither team made much headway in the first half. Both sides had chances but mastering the conditions seemed to consume most energy. Nevertheless, the quality players on both sides still managed to entertain. Goalkeeper Bert Trautmann enjoyed the spectacle. 'If City and Sunderland had not

been at peak fitness, they could never have lasted 45 minutes let alone 90 under such conditions. Not only did the players last the pace but they provided a game which for quality can seldom have been surpassed. There was none of the kick-and-rush stuff that might have been expected in the mud and water. Every critic agreed without reservation that the game was a classic – and the only goal worthy of the occasion.'

The goal was scored by Roy. 'It was about 11 minutes into the second half,' he says. 'Joe Hayes centred a free kick towards Bobby Johnstone. I was in the outside-left position near the back of the box and I just had a feeling that Bobby would miss the ball. I don't know why but it was clear as day to me that this would be my chance, not Bobby's. Before the ball even reached Bobby I started to dive. It passed him and I connected. I headed with such pace that the ball flew past the Sunderland 'keeper and into the far corner.

'There are a couple of photographs taken of the goal. One shows the mud and the wet; the other shows

the cold, wet fans stood in the Villa Park Main Stand paddock. They didn't celebrate or show any emotion because I think they were soaking wet and couldn't move!'

Not long afterwards disaster struck for Roy. 'I was tackled as I came to pick up a loose ball. The Sunderland player fell across my knee. That was it. My cup run was finished. Next thing I remember is Roy Paul lifting me up and carrying me off the pitch. He said a few things to encourage me but I felt awful. I didn't know how bad it was but I feared the worst.'

Roy Paul knew it would be a struggle for his fellow countryman but tried to encourage him, as Roy Paul recalled. 'He told me privately, "I don't think I'll make the Cup final, Roy." I turned to him and said as forcefully as I could, "Of course you'll be there." Incredibly, this never-give-up footballer did come back. Then, a week before the final, we played again on Aston Villa's ground. Almost on the same spot where he was injured against Sunderland, Roy was hurt again. It was the same knee!'

Roy Clarke missed the final but he had done more than most players to help the Blues reach that final stage. This semi-final in 1955 was both Roy's finest hour and perhaps his saddest moment while playing for the Blues.

Roy Clarke heads the only goal of the 1955 semi-final with Sunderland.

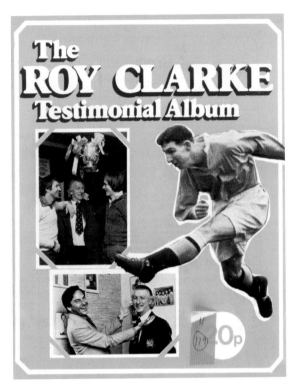

As social club manager, Roy successfully welcomed Bob Monkhouse and many other stars to Maine Road.

with; he had a hand trodden on and broken; he had his ribs cracked; collar bone broken; cartilage trouble in both knees; and a recurring thigh injury kept him in and out of the game. Then a mystery skin complaint struck him down. For weeks he lay in hospital, his face a mask of bandages.'

Cup Winner

Injury struck again in 1955. Roy netted the only goal of the FA Cup semi-final against Sunderland but missed the FA Cup final because of an injury sustained in the final League match before Wembley. Fortunately, the Blues reached Wembley again in 1956 and Roy deservedly won an FA Cup winners' medal.

Roy managed to achieve a great deal despite these injuries but there was a time, before he even reached his twenties, when it had looked as if a football career would not be possible. At that early stage, he had been told his knees were so badly damaged that he would never play football again and when he first arrived at City many observers had claimed he was too frail to make the top grade. Some questioned what he was even doing at the club. They quickly realised, though, that appearances can be deceptive. Eric Todd of the *Guardian* once said that Roy was 'built for speed rather than comfort'. That speed proved essential during City's Cup runs.

During the 1957/58 season Roy realised that he was nearing the end of his City career and he started to take an interest in coaching. For a while he acted as an assistant coach but realised that his team-mate Jimmy Meadows, whose career had ended as a result of injury in the 1955 final, was also keen on pursuing a coaching role at Maine Road. Generously Roy stood aside and in September 1958 he moved to Stockport County. The fee was £1,500.

City Gent

He spent about five years at Stockport before becoming manager of Northwich Victoria, but his heart wasn't really in management and in 1960 he returned to Maine Road to help improve City's non-matchday income via the Development Association. He had also developed his own business interests with a sports shop in Fallowfield, though he eventually took the decision to close his business and concentrate on his new role at City.

By the late 1960s this role had developed considerably as Roy became the first manager of City's social club. The club opened in 1966 and both Roy and his wife Kath spent considerable time and effort ensuring that the enterprise was a huge success. The social club won a host of awards and became recognised as a leading entertainment venue in its own right. Major stars of the period, such as Bob Monkhouse and Frankie Vaughan, enjoyed appearing there, and Roy certainly ensured that supporters were able to have closer links with the Club they loved. Players were encouraged to attend and, as time moved on, organisations like the Junior Blues were able to use the club, which strengthened the bond between the football Club and supporters.

Roy remained the social club manager for almost 25 years and then continued his love affair with the Blues by helping the Club to organize matchday hospitality. He also became one of the founder members, together with fellow 1950s stars Fionan 'Paddy' Fagan and Roy Little, of the former players' association.

The lifetime achievement award rightly recognises Roy for the joy he brought to spectators on the pitch and for the enormously successful efforts he made off the pitch to turn City into one of the friendliest, most approachable clubs in the world.

' We love City. We really love City! '

An emotional **Roy** and
Kath Clarke
collecting the Hall of Fame
award in January 2004.

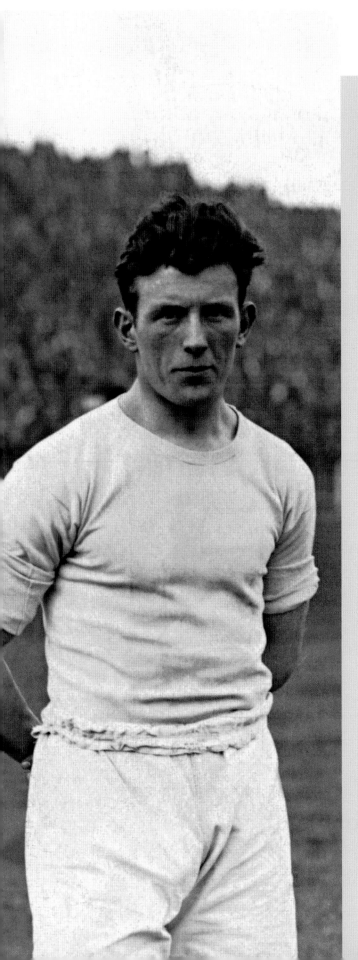

Sam Cowan

The second year of the Hall of Fame saw the development of two time-based awards: one for those who played pre-1950 and one for those who played post-1950. Contenders for both categories were extremely strong, but the winner of the pre-1950 category, Sam Cowan, was a clear favourite amongst fans. Known throughout football for the quality of his captaincy, Sam guided the Blues to two FA Cup finals and made three England international appearances at a time when internationals were few and far between.

Sam Cowan
PRE-1950 AWARD

Late Developer

As with so many footballers from the first 50 years of the Club's history, Sam grew up in a mining community. Born in Chesterfield in 1901, it seems Sam's family moved further north to the Doncaster area early in his life. Whether this was as a result of wartime necessity, or because of work commitments isn't known and there is some uncertainty on where the family settled, although research suggests they settled in the town of Adwick-le-Street, 6.4km (4 miles) north-west of Doncaster. It is known that Sam loved sport from an early age. Every spare moment was spent outdoors, however stories from Sam's early playing career claimed he didn't actually play football in childhood.

During the early 1920s much was made of Sam's footballing development and the story, as told during the period, claimed that at the age of 17 Sam was asked to take part in a local park game to make up the numbers. He borrowed a boot – just one – and enjoyed the game so much that the youngster allowed the sport to dominate the rest of his life.

Assuming Sam's first match came in 1918, it is clear that his development from that point on was rapid. He had spells with Adwick Juniors and another Adwick-le-Street side before receiving an approach from Huddersfield Town. The Terriers gave him a trial and, although again there is a little uncertainty on the length of his stay at Leeds Road, it does appear that he stayed for a few weeks. A spell at Denaby United and Bullcroft Main Colliery followed.

Thrilling Performances

Early in 1923 local League side Doncaster Rovers gave Sam a trial and in June of that year the 22-year-old joined the Division Three (North) side. Although

22 seems a relatively late age to join a professional club, it had only been a little over four years since that landmark moment in the Adwick park.

Sam immediately proved his worth to Doncaster with some thrilling performances. In March 1924 he scored a hat-trick of headers against Halifax Town and by December 1924 he had netted 13 goals in 48 League appearances. Considering Sam was, in theory, a defender this was a great ratio and it was inevitable that larger clubs became interested in the centre half. Several approaches were made but City manager David Ashworth was the most persuasive.

Ashworth had become City manager during the 1924 close season and had already recruited winger Billy Austin to improve distribution. Cowan was brought in to fill the void created by popular half-back Mick Hamill moving to Boston, in the United States, during the close season.

Exciting Developments

Eight days after signing, Sam made his City debut in a 2–2 draw on 20 December 1924 at home to Birmingham City and on 3 January he netted his first goal, in the 3–0 defeat of Nottingham Forest. Unfortunately he was also injured in the match and missed the following League game and an FA Cup tie with Preston. Despite the injury he had made 21 League appearances by the end of the season and had proved to be a popular, attack-minded defender. At this time in football, players such as Sam were leading a change in emphasis for midfielders and defenders. For most of the early years of football, players had been expected to perform one role – in simple terms, your position determined whether you defended or attacked. Defenders were not

'For Sam it was the first of his three FA Cup final appearances for City. To this day Sam is the only player to appear in three FA Cup finals while with the Blues.'

expected to make surging runs or even to move forward when corners were taken. They had to stick rigidly to their position. However, by 1924 football tactics were developing and Sam was one of a new breed of attacking centre halves. Fans loved this new approach and Sam's popularity increased as a result.

Sam Stars

The 1925/26 season saw Sam become a City star after several good performances during a rather strange season. In November 1925 manager Ashworth had resigned and the Blues spent almost all the remaining season without a manager. Vice-chairman Albert Alexander senior took on most of the manager's duties and even guided City to the FA Cup final but results in the League were mixed and City were relegated by a point on the last day of the season.

The FA Cup final ended in defeat but for Sam it was the first of his three FA Cup-final appearances

with City. To this day Sam is the only player to appear in three FA Cup finals while with the Blues.

Sam's second FA Cup final came in 1933, by which time he had taken over the captaincy from popular Scottish international Jimmy McMullan. Unfortunately this match also ended in defeat but afterwards Sam told the guest of honour, the Duke of York, that City would be back in 1934 to win the trophy. No one knew for certain whether this showed determination on Sam's part or whether this was simply his way of improving morale but shortly after the match Sam and his opposite number, the Everton captain Dixie Dean, were asked to take part in a filmed feature for Pathe News. The two men toasted each other and Sam stated that he was glad the Cup had been won by a Lancastrian team and that he hoped the trophy would stay in the county but find its way to Manchester City instead of Everton. He seemed determined to find success.

Player Career Statistics
Appearances

SAM COWAN

Position
Centre half 1924–35

Typical Height and Weight
1.80m (5ft 11in)
83kg (13st 2lb)

Born
Chesterfield, 10 May 1901

Deceased
Haywards Heath, 5 October 1964

League Debut
Birmingham City (home)
20 December 1924

	LEAGUE		FA CUP		TOTAL	
	App	Gls	App	Gls	App	Gls
1924/25	21	1	0	0	21	1
1925/26	38	2	7	0	45	2
1926/27	27	2	0	0	27	2
1927/28	28	0	2	0	30	0
1928/29	38	1	1	0	39	1
1929/30	40	1	5	2	45	3
1930/31	40	2	1	0	41	2
1931/32	31	3	5	1	36	4
1932/33	32	4	7	2	39	6
1933/34	32	3	8	0	40	3
1934/35	42	0	1	0	43	0
TOTAL	369	19	37	5	406	24

Sam's Prime Time

Manchester City 1 Manchester United 1. Football League Division One – 12 September 1925

Goalscorer Cowan

City Team Mitchell, Cookson, McCloy, Sharp, Cowan, Pringle, Austin, Warner, Roberts, Johnson, Hicks

Attendance 66,000

The largest derby attendance up to that time witnessed a truly memorable meeting between Manchester's two major sides. The attendance topped 66,000 once season ticket holders were added to the 62,994 who paid on the day, although initial reports had predicted the crowd would exceed the 76,166 who had witnessed a City cup tie with Cardiff in 1924.

For Sam the game was an important milestone. He had been with the Blues for nine months and had impressed, but the derby match was expected to provide Sam with his strongest test to date. This would be the largest crowd he had played in front of at the time, while the derby was always a testing match for any player. Recently promoted United had been a division below City for almost four years and had not won at a City ground since 1913. They were determined to break tradition and the talk leading up to the match was all about how United would embarrass their more popular rivals.

Such was the interest in the game that the *Manchester Evening Chronicle* focused its attention on the crowd. 'In the centre of the city large queues waited to board the innumerable tramcars, and there were similar scenes at all the outlying parts of Manchester, where the match cars started. Manchester must have almost tilted over by this migration of what was equal to the population of a large town to the Moss Side district of the city.

'The 200 tramcars were beginning to work, but the queues that waited on the entrances were quickly absorbed. One woman – it was the fair sex that seemed the more excited all the time – waved her City rosette and jigged her way to the turnstiles singing joyously. Hundreds came in their working clothes, and

as many munched meat pies in lieu of lunch. At 1.45 the "fans" began to arrive with coloured umbrellas, and waving all kinds of mascots. One large party mixed up of rival supporters carried bells.'

The derby was a significant event for all Mancunians at the time. For Sam this was the day he would become a Manchester hero. Pre-match he would have been as nervous as any of the players and may have contemplated what fate had in store for him. Interestingly, none of the pre-match papers commented on the player at all. Inevitably they mentioned the cult figure of Tommy Johnson and several of the other City players but Sam was not mentioned. Perhaps he had yet to convince neutrals of his strengths. Whatever the reasons, it was this game that was to make him a star.

The game turned out to be a classic encounter, with fans certainly gaining value for money. From the start City attacked, but United goalkeeper Alf Steward proved to be in excellent form as he performed a string of fine saves. Unfortunately, after a barrage from City's forwards, Steward managed to create a United attack from a save, and forward Clatworthy Rennox gave the Reds a shock opening goal.

City retaliated immediately. The *Manchester Guardian* reported, 'Nothing stimulates the City so thoroughly as a reverse, and within ten minutes Cowan restored equality with a most remarkable goal. Hicks took a corner-kick, a blue shirt sprang up near the extreme post and collapsed over the line near the rails. In some way ball and head had made contact, and the former object was reposing within the netting. The United protested on the way back to the centre of the field. Nobody quite knew why, although their amazement was easy to understand.'

The goal became the focus of all match reports as journalists tried to explain to those that had not been there the quality of Sam's header. The *Athletic News* commented, 'Cowan's headwork was a feature of the match. More he tackled with grim determination and effectiveness, and distributed the ball with discrimination and accuracy.'

The second half continued to be entertaining, with Sam and the rest of the Blues performing well. They came close to scoring a winner on several occasions but Steward, the United goalkeeper, was clearly playing at his best. The game ended 1–1 with Sam gaining most of the praise. The *Athletic News* stated, 'Cowan promises to be all that the City club expected when they brought him from Doncaster Rovers last season. He has all the physical requirements for a centre half-back, and judging by his display in this match, he has the temperament for the big event. His equalising goal was a masterpiece in headwork and judgement.'

Sam was now a key City man and during the course of the 1925/26 season he was to be one of the linchpins as the Blues reached Wembley – defeating United 3–1 in the semi-final. He was also part of the side that defeated United 6–1 at Old Trafford in the return League fixture. This remains the largest win by either side in the Manchester derby.

Matt Barrass separates boxers Sam Cowan and Len Langford in this 1932 training session.

Centre-half Sam takes a kick during a pre-match warm-up.

The 1933/34 Cup run did end with a marvellous victory over Portsmouth at Wembley. Newspapers in the days immediately after the final were full of photos of Sam carrying the Cup with a wonderful beaming smile. Together with the Frank Swift story, the face of Sam Cowan represented that 1934 success.

Sam's captaincy during this period was one of the key factors behind City's success and many players, in particular Frank Swift and Matt Busby, would later refer to Sam's captaincy with great affection. He was known for many qualities but, according to the other players, he excelled in making them feel at ease. He always spent time trying to calm players and reassure them of their qualities.

Keeping the promise he made to the Duke of York, Sam collects the Cup from king George V in 1934.

A Sideways Move

Sam's rapid development during the early 1920s, culminating in his first appearance at Wembley, gave him a national presence. His career was often featured in sporting papers of the day and it became inevitable that he would be brought into contention for an international appearance. There had been a rumour that he would be selected for England v Scotland in April 1926 at Old Trafford but with the match coming only a week before the FA Cup final it seems the authorities felt the time wasn't quite right. However, he did make his international debut in the next England match. Surprisingly, he played his first international as a left half, rather than at centre half. The game, against Belgium at Antwerp in May 1926, ended in a 5–3 victory with Sam performing well despite playing in a less familiar position. Sadly, the good

form of Burnley's Jack Hill with England – Hill went on to become England captain – limited Sam's opportunities. The City man made two further international appearances – against Austria (a goalless game in Vienna in May 1930) and Belgium (a 4–1 win in Brussels in May 1931) – but he gained representative honours with the Football League in 1934 and in a trial match against the England international side in 1931. It seems Sam was always in contention but was unable to create a permanent role. Nevertheless, three internationals was a major achievement for a man who hadn't kicked a ball until he was 17.

Leaving City

In addition to the success in the FA Cup, Sam's time at Maine Road saw the Blues win promotion as Division Two champions in 1928, finish third in Division One in 1930 and re-establish themselves as a hugely popular side that was always in contention for trophies. Sam, as captain, had guided the Blues to fifth place in the FA Cup-winning year and fourth in 1934/35 but by the summer of 1935 it was clear that his time was nearing its end. He was 34 by that point and the City management had to look to the future. A talented Scot, Bob Donnelly, was signed for £6,000 in the summer of 1935 as a direct replacement and, although Donnelly never did manage to fill Sam's role in the way expected, his arrival sealed Sam's fate.

The hugely popular City captain joined Bradford City for £2,000 – Bradford's second highest fee at the time – in October 1935 and he went on to make 57 League appearances for them before arriving at Mossley in July 1937 as their player-manager.

Long-Distance Manager

Sam was with Mossley for 11 months before an offer came from Brighton and Hove Albion to become their coach. The 1938 move to the south coast excited Sam and with Brighton he developed a strong interest in the well-being of players and in physiotherapy. His reputation grew and he became well known for the quality of his physio work.

Inevitably, his involvement in football also kept him in close contact with many key figures and, shortly after the Second World War, the resumption of League football brought an opportunity for Sam to move into management.

Wilf Wild had been the City manager since 1932 and combined his role with that of Club secretary. It was clear that this could not continue and so Wilf turned to his old captain to see if the role could be split. Sam, keen to prove himself, accepted the manager's position on 3 December 1946.

The Blues were challenging for promotion from Division Two and had lost only three of their opening 16 games. However, Sam's domestic arrangements were causing difficulties. Because of his physiotherapy interests and family commitments in Brighton, Sam had agreed with the City directors that he could commute from the south coast. He would arrive in Manchester midway through the week and return to Brighton after each match.

City forward George Smith remembers that the team tried to make this work. 'We'd have training sessions and meetings certain evenings so that Sam could arrive and talk with us. I don't think we thought there was anything strange, we just went along with it, although I do remember some of the tactical meetings were supposed to be voluntary – well some of the older players didn't like that. They wouldn't volunteer to stay in the evenings for tactical discussions back then.'

The Blues ended 1946/47 as Division Two champions. The final match of the season was on 14 June – the latest finish to any season – when George Smith netted all five goals against Newport. Eleven days later Sam was forced to resign. In later years it became clear that Sam's commuting did cause a great deal of debate within the Club. Most of the players seemed to accept it, but 1950s star Johnny Hart, an office boy at the club in 1947, remembers, 'There were a few mutterings around the place. There was one away game – it could have been Southampton in April 1947 – when Sam chose to stay with his family rather than be in the

hotel with the players. I think the directors were unhappy with that and I think that's the day when they decided things had to change.'

A Southern Outlook

Sam left Maine Road more popular than ever. Not only had he been a great player but he had also brought the Division Two Championship after only a few months as manager. Supporters were disappointed when he left – they felt he could have achieved the same sort of development that another ex-Blue, Matt Busby, was starting to see at United – but they didn't hold that against Sam.

After City he remained dedicated to sport and further developed his physiotherapy business. He worked with Sussex County Cricket Club, Brighton Ice Hockey Club and various other sporting clubs. In addition, whenever a singer, dancer or actor performing on the south coast suffered an injury,

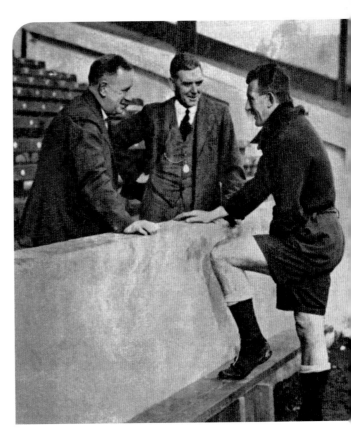

Manager Wilf Wild and trainer Alec Bell talk with Sam in front of the Main Stand at Maine Road in 1934.

Sam was always the man brought in to give advice. His face regularly appeared in the newspapers helping a celebrity to regain fitness.

Sam's granddaughter, Joanna Cowan, grew up on the south coast and is Sam's only living descendant. 'Sam passed away before I was born and so I never had the pleasure of meeting him. My father, Sam's son, had been hit really hard by Sam's death and so he never talked with me about him. I guess it was too emotional for him. My parents also divorced, so other topics filled the family time we had. Manchester was not at the forefront of my thoughts as a child, so as time went by I knew little about Sam's achievements. Eventually what little I had learnt from my grandmother – Sam's wife – became vague. So much so that when my own father passed away a few years ago I was shocked to find that locked away in his attic was a box containing scrapbooks, medals and international caps from Sam's career.

'At that point, I could remember nothing my family had told me, so it was all a surprise. I needed to find out more because, and I guess this is the strange thing, when you are confronted by this box of very important items and memories proving the importance of your grandfather, you still find it hard to accept. I went into bookshops looking for information and I found what became to me a very important book: *Manchester – The Greatest City*. I found a profile of Sam and couldn't believe how highly he was thought of. I contacted author Gary James and, within a few weeks, we'd mapped out Sam's life.'

Sam had passed away in October 1964 while refereeing a charity match in aid of Sussex wicketkeeper Jim Parks and in 2003 Joanna was invited to Maine Road during its final season. 'Simply walking into the dressing room was an emotional experience for me. I suddenly felt as if I'd come home. This was Sam's place and perhaps for the first time in my life I felt my grandfather's presence.

'I visited Sam Cowan Close, near to the ground, and I spent a great deal of time coming to terms with how important Sam was to Manchester. I've also found that other memories are starting to return, for example I now do remember sitting down with Sam's widow and creating a small scrapbook when I was a very young child.'

Seventy years after his debut and more than 40 years after his death, Sam Cowan remains one of City's most popular players, captains and managers of all time.

Joanna Cowan
Sam's granddaughter, collecting the Hall of Fame award in February 2005.

' I would like to say a big thank you to all you fans who voted for my grandfather Sam Cowan for a Hall of Fame award. Being able to accept the award was a great honour. Sam died four years before I was born, but with the help of family and Gary James at MCFC I have learned what a great man he was. His ability to motivate and help take the team to victory in 1934 has ensured that Sam's name will forever be in the history books, and I am extremely proud to be his granddaughter. '

Alan Oakes

The post-1950 category at the second Hall of Fame awards was always anticipated to be a tightly run contest. Almost every member of the great sides of the 1950s, 1960s and 1970s is worthy of a place but there could only be one winner. Loyal servant Alan Oakes gained most votes from supporters and clearly his record-breaking career provided many great memories for City fans.

Alan Oakes
POST-1950 AWARD

Coats for Goalposts

Born in Winsford, a beautiful Cheshire village south of Manchester, in 1942, Alan was interested in sport from the beginning. In the summer he would play cricket and in the winter he would play football. 'We all loved playing. I suppose there wasn't much else to do and so we did what all lads did in those days. We used our coats for goalposts and played wherever we could. My family was very sporty and so it was all very natural. Of course, my cousin Glyn Pardoe also became a City player, so I guess that shows our interest.'

As he grew, he started being noticed for his footballing abilities and in his early teens he was selected for the Mid-Cheshire Boys side. 'During a game at Broughton, Salford, I was spotted by a City scout called Albert Kavanagh,' remembers Alan, 'and he came around to our house to try and sign me as an amateur for City. It was a total and utter surprise because I really didn't think City would be interested. Other clubs had watched me but City were the team I wanted to join. I'd been to Maine Road and stood on the old Kippax before it had a roof – I guess that shows you how long ago that was – and I idolised players like Bobby Johnstone and Ken Barnes. So to get a chance to join City was incredible.'

A Sweeping Role

Alan left school at 15 and joined City's groundstaff in 1958. Naturally, he was there for football but his duties also included sweeping up and cleaning the boots of players. 'I had to clean Bert Trautmann's boots and I cannot describe how wonderful that felt. He was another hero and, in my eyes, the greatest goalkeeper of all time, so it was a real pleasure to clean his boots.

I loved being around the place. When it came to coaching we had Laurie Barnett and Fred Tilson working with us. They were two of the stars of the thirties side, so it was a great place to learn.'

Initially Alan moved into digs close to the ground but later he moved back to Cheshire and travelled by train. Once he'd passed his driving test and had started to earn enough money to buy a car, he did so. Settling in Manchester was a major culture shock for Alan. Although he'd watched games at Maine Road before joining the Club he was not a regular visitor to Manchester and although the big, industrial city was only a few miles from Winsford it was a significantly different way of life. Inevitably, he knew that the opportunity he had been presented with was one he had to take, and so he settled.

A Waiting Game

Although Alan was delighted at being a member of City's groundstaff it was clear to him that the opportunities to impress were limited. There were more than 50 professionals at the Club when he joined and dozens of other hopefuls waiting for their chance to come. Alan believed he would have a long arduous journey but then in November 1959 an opportunity came. 'Ken Barnes was injured, so I was drafted into the first team for my debut, at home to Chelsea. I was determined to give it my best shot because this, at the age of 17, was my big chance. I think I played okay but I handled the ball and gave away a penalty and I thought this was the end of my career. Fortunately, Bert Trautmann saved the shot and we ended the game 1–1. You can imagine how grateful I felt – I would have gladly cleaned his boots for the rest of my life!'

'I had to clean Bert Trautmann's boots and I cannot describe how wonderful that felt. He was another hero and, in my eyes, the greatest goalkeeper...'

Ken Barnes returned from injury and Alan's next chance didn't arrive until January 1960. After that he became almost a regular in the side, making 18 appearances in 1959/60, 22 in 1960/61, 25 in 1961/62 and 34 in 1962/63. Unfortunately, these were difficult times for City as the 1950s cup-fighting team had broken up, and the early-1960s side struggled to find consistency. There were some great players at Maine Road but the team lacked the drive fans expected and demanded. Relegation came in 1963. 'We had a lot of quality in the side,' says Alan, 'but seemed to be conceding too many goals. We knew we were struggling but we always gave it our best. After we were relegated in '63 Derek Kevan

and Jimmy Murray arrived. We were doing really well, then Jimmy did his cartilage in – that was a major blow – and we tailed off. We missed promotion, finishing sixth, and we couldn't get it going again until Joe Mercer and Malcolm Allison arrived in '65.

'It was a great lift, of course, but I know we were wary of Malcolm at first. He had all these ideas and it seemed so different to what we were used to but within a week or so he'd won everybody over. The transformation by the two men was so fast – before we'd completed our pre-season games we were convinced we would win promotion. We couldn't wait to get started. The confidence flowed and then

Player Career Statistics
Appearances

ALAN OAKES

Position
Wing half 1958–76

Typical Height and Weight
1.80m (5ft 11in)
82kg (12st 13lb)

Born
Winsford, 1 September 1942

League Debut
Chelsea (home)
14 November 1959

	LEAGUE		FA CUP		FL CUP		EUROPE		TOTAL	
	App	Gls	App	Gls	App	Gls	App	Gls	App	Gls
1959/60	18	0	1	0	-	-	-	-	19	0
1960/61	22	0	0	0	0	0	-	-	22	0
1961/62	25	1	0	0	0	0	-	-	25	1
1962/63	34	3	2	0	4	1	-	-	40	4
1963/64	41	3	1	1	6	0	-	-	48	4
1964/65	41	4	2	0	1	0	-	-	44	4
1965/66	41	1	8	0	2	0	-	-	51	1
1966/67	39	2	6	0	2	0	-	-	47	2
1967/68	41	2	4	0	4	1	-	-	49	3
1968/69	39	0	7	0	3	0	2	0	51	0
1969/70	40	3	2	0	7	1	9	1	58	5
1970/71	30	1	3	0	1	0	4	0	38	1
1971/72	31 (1)	0	2	0	0	0	-	-	33 (1)	0
1972/73	13 (1)	1	0	0	0 (1)	0	2	0	15 (2)	1
1973/74	28	0	0	0	5	0	-	-	33	0
1974/75	40	2	1	0	2	0	-	-	43	2
1975/76	38 (1)	3	2	1	9	2	-	-	49 (1)	6
TOTAL	561 (3)	26	41	2	46 (1)	5	17	1	665 (4)	34

Alan's Prime Time

Manchester City 1 Stoke City 0. Football League Division One – 9 November 1974

Goalscorer Marsh

City Team MacRae, Hammond, Donachie, Doyle, Barrett, Oakes, Summerbee, Bell, Marsh, Hartford, Tueart

Attendance 30,966

At first glance this match may not appear too important but as far as Alan Oakes' career is concerned this was a landmark moment and a prime example of Alan's importance to City and the Club's supporters. Prior to this game Alan was presented with a silver salver by chairman Peter Swales to commemorate his 500th League appearance for the Blues. This meeting with Stoke was actually his 501st match, with the 500th having come a week earlier at Everton.

Throughout his career Alan had proved to be one of the Club's most dependable players and the 1974/75 season was perhaps Alan's best. On the morning of the game with Stoke, newspapers were full of stories outlining his commitment and professional approach. Peter Gardner, writing in the Manchester Evening News, talked of his fine performance at Everton – City lost but Alan had been the only man to come out of the game in a positive manner – and then added, 'Oakes, never sent off or booked in his professional career will even turn down any approach from City manager Tony Book to hand him the captaincy for the day.'

Before both the Everton and Stoke games there had been calls to give Alan the captaincy either on a permanent basis or at least for a one-off match to mark reaching the 500 landmark. Prior to Stoke he turned down the captaincy and told reporters, 'I don't want any fuss. There's a job to be done with two points at stake. I regard this as just another important League game and want things to carry on as normal.' This was typical of Alan. He valued the team more than the individual.

In 2005 Alan admitted, 'The 500 landmark was important, I guess, and the presentation was nice but I just wanted to play. City were in a good League position and it was important for us to challenge. After

the Stoke game I did think about the record, which at the time was held by Bert Trautmann with 508 League games but because it was Bert I felt a little sad that I was about to take it from him. He was one of my heroes and I wish I hadn't taken it from him. I did feel, though, that I could play for some time still. I was enjoying the game more than ever and I really did want to go on forever. Obviously, I knew I couldn't but I certainly had no thoughts of retirement.'

The game itself was not a classic but City managed a victory, with Rodney Marsh scoring the only goal after 21 minutes. The win put City top of the table but it also strengthened Alan's place as one of City's true heroes. According to Peter Gardner, writing about the team the following Monday, 'Their Maine Road record is virtually without a flaw – eight wins and one draw – in topping the table as clear leaders for the first time this season. They went to the top on Saturday with the strength of a hard-earned 1–0 win over a Stoke side whose stifling tactics wrecked the game as a truly entertaining spectacle. Stoke clearly came for a point but were denied by a side who grasped supreme midfield command in a first half display that was one of City's best of all season. Altogether it was a solid, professional, performance and thoroughly deserved victory for the Blues. Alan Oakes crowned a consistent season by being the Man of the Match once again.'

After the match manager Tony Book was asked for his views on Alan, 'He's a model professional. The way he is playing at present there is no knowing what number of League games he is going to play for us. I think he is playing as well now as at any time of his career.'

On 18 January 1975 Alan passed Bert Trautmann's 508 League games record when he helped City to a 5–1 victory over Newcastle United. He went on to reach a total of 564 League appearances. It's a record that may never be beaten, although Alan hopes that one day it is. 'I'm looking forward to the day when the record's beaten. I know it will take a lot to beat but I hope somebody does it and if the person who beats it has the same sort of career and enjoyment at City that I have had, then he will have had a fantastic career. It will also mean he has had to dedicate himself to the Club, which can't be a bad thing.'

Thinking of the length of his career and the approach he used to take, Alan explains, 'I loved playing and whenever I hear people say I was a "good professional" I have to tell them that my aim was always to give my best. I used to simply get on with it. I was dedicated and tried to give everything for the Club. I believe I was a good, honest pro. If I was asked to do an interview, I'd do it, but I never sought the headlines. More than anything I wanted to make sure my role on the pitch spoke for me.'

Speaking in the mid-1970s, the great Liverpool manager Bill Shankly talked of Alan in glowing terms. 'The very best type of professional on the field and off it... exactly the kind of player youngsters should use as a model.' That solid, steady professionalism was as evident in his 501st match, against Stoke, as in the previous 500 and the 63 to come. Alan was always the model professional.

Malcolm tackled our fitness. Of course we won promotion easily and then held our own in 1966/67. Don't forget we had faced a couple of big tests in those first two seasons – we took a strong Everton side to two replays in the FA Cup while we were still in Division Two and narrowly lost to Revie's Leeds the following year. We lost 1–0 to Leeds through a Jack Charlton goal that should have been disallowed. So we came away from those games confident we could face any side. There was nothing for us to fear.'

Super Six

Alan became City's regular number six and played his part in every City success of the 1960s and early 1970s, although he was to miss the 1974 League Cup final. It was a great period for the Club and for Alan. 'Throughout this time we feared no one and were absolutely convinced we would win every game. The Championship and European successes were both very important but because I was there during the dark days of the early sixties, I think the most important success of the period had to be promotion in 1966. My reason is that without that, none of the rest would have followed. Joe and Malcolm didn't just get us promoted, they first stopped the rot. We were going downhill fast and they stopped that, changed gear and pushed us forward quickly and it wasn't done with negative play.

Player of the Year Alan photographed in action during his record-breaking 1974/75 season.

A lot of teams pack the defence and try to ensure they don't lose; we always went out to win and never contemplated holding out for a point.'

Manager Joe Mercer was always positive about Alan's contribution. In 1969 he commented, 'He has got the best left foot in the business. He is always dependable and a great fellow; very strong. He always gives you 90 minutes. Week in, week out, he is our best player. He is so direct and it is fantastic how he can hit a ball. I have seen him hit a ball from left half to outside right, which would have taken me three kicks to have got there. He's got a right foot which is as good as anybody's and he only uses it for standing on!'

Throughout this period City's progression in the various cup competitions meant they played an extremely large number of games each season.

Alan ready to face Spurs on 13 September 1969. Alan scored and City won the game 3–0.

In 1969/70 they featured in 61 first-team, competitive fixtures (excluding friendlies and tour matches) with Alan missing only two of those games. Inevitably there was great pressure on the players to perform at the highest level three times a week but Alan thrived on this. 'Nowadays the footballing authorities talk of limiting games, allowing clubs to field weakened sides in competitions, and even moving the FA Cup final to allow longer breaks et cetera but as a player I loved playing as often as possible. Playing was preferable to training and I would have loved to have played three or more times a week every week. That's what I'd wanted to do from being a boy and I think that's what every footballer really wants. We don't want to be training; we want to be playing.'

Time to Go

As the 1970s progressed, the team created by Mercer and Allison started to break up, yet Alan remained a key figure throughout the managerial reigns of Johnny Hart, Ron Saunders and then Tony Book. In 1974/75 he was voted the Supporters' Club Player of the Year and in 1976 he was a member of the 1976 League Cup-winning side, but shortly afterwards he chose to move on.

Supporters knew that Alan still had a great deal to offer, but he felt differently. 'I'd had a great season. I'd played 39 League games and won the League Cup and so there was no pressure to leave but I did think that I may have blocked some other gifted players coming through. Previously I had never considered leaving but then Neil Young had moved on and Mike Summerbee and Francis Lee had both been sold – far too early in my opinion as they both had so much more to give. I started to worry that I'd be dropped or the next one out but I never thought about choosing to leave. Why would anyone want to leave the best club in the country?

'I remember thinking that somebody would take my place and that I had to keep performing at the highest level. In some ways I liked to push myself by thinking of all the people who could take my place but I never, ever thought about leaving until after the League Cup final of 1976. I was aware that I'd be 34

Watched by goalkeeper Keith MacRae, Alan looks for a
way forward during the 1974/75 season.

when the new season started and that I may not be
up to it in the way I would normally expect. Chester
City were just up the road and keen for me to join
them. There was also the opportunity to move into
management there, so for me it was a nice move. I
do remember shortly afterwards thinking, "What
have I done?" because I'd gone from a First Division
palace to play at Third Division grounds but the
move was a good one. Looking back, though, I was
perhaps wrong to leave when I did. My advice to any
player now is to remain playing at the highest level
for as long as you physically can. Those days are
precious and should not be cut short.

'I also missed Maine Road a lot when I left and I
miss it even more now. In my view City lost
something when the Club moved but I guess in 80
years' time fans will feel the same about the new
stadium as I do for Maine Road. I regret the fact City
have left that ground though.'

A Matter of Survival

After City Alan became player-manager of Chester
City from 1976 until 1982, making 211 League
appearances, and later coached at Port Vale. He

even played a League match during an injury crisis
for Vale at the age of 42 and some fans commented
that he was fitter than the majority of Vale players,
but Alan chose to make this a one-off.

Alan remains very positive about his achievements
after leaving City. 'In the six years I was at Chester
we had a great time. Success is different for a team
like Chester – it's all about survival – and so I had to
do a lot of work in the transfer market. I had another
ex-City star, Cliff Sear, with me and we worked well
together and I loved every minute at Sealand Road.
Often I'd be trying to negotiate good transfer fees
and working hard to sell a couple of players to keep
us afloat and so I got satisfaction from that when it all
came right. I still got a lot of satisfaction from playing
as well, so it was a perfect role.

'We had several good players, and I was most
satisfied, I suppose, with Ian Rush – a great find. We
knew we had to sell him because of our financial
position and, because I am a Blue, I wanted him to
go to City. We were having a great cup run and Tony
Book and Malcolm Allison came to watch him. Rush
scored twice and I met up with Tony and Malcolm
afterwards. Tony was keen but Malcolm didn't rate

him for some reason and it all collapsed. He later went to Liverpool and the rest is history but I wanted him to go to Maine Road and I wish that deal had occurred. Of course, you never know how these things would have worked out.'

A Missed Opportunity

Alan's love of City was demonstrated further in 1983 when he applied for the City manager's job. At the time fans were unaware of his application. 'Billy McNeill was given the job in the end,' says Alan, 'but I desperately wanted the role because I loved the Club and because I believed I knew exactly what City needed. I'd also served what I thought was a good apprenticeship – six years at Chester taught me a great deal about survival and transfer negotiations. I knew City had financial problems and that someone with the right experience was needed... so I felt I was ideal for the role. Don't forget what I'd experienced as a player at Maine Road as well. Most importantly, I understood the Club and all about Manchester football fans and their expectations and needs. I got an interview at Peter Swales' house. A few directors were there and I thought I gave a very good interview. Unfortunately, I didn't get the job. I still wonder what might have happened.'

Son Shines

Alan's appointment would have proved immensely popular with fans but it didn't happen and the former City star now spends his days playing a variety of sports for relaxation. His contribution to football continues, though, via the exploits of his son Michael, who in 2005 was goalkeeper at Wolverhampton Wanderers. Alan tries to enjoy his son's games. 'It's a great game to be a part of and I love the fact he's involved. Joe Corrigan helped him a lot when he was young and so I'm grateful for that and when he joined Aston Villa I was delighted. Now he's at Wolves and I do try to watch him but I find it very difficult. I'm always in two minds as to whether I want the ball to be at his end of the field or not. If Wolves are attacking I know he's safe but I also know he can't demonstrate his abilities. If Wolves are on the defensive I want him to have to make a great save but I'm also worried he's going to be caught out. I think he's doing really well, though. I once replaced Bert Trautmann in nets – it was against West Ham and he was sent off, so I deputised. I can't remember much about it now but I don't think Michael would have learnt much if he'd seen it.'

Alan's 18-year City career remains an inspiration to all and his dedication, determination and confidence on the pitch were loved by supporters.

‘ This is a great club with terrific fans and I have enjoyed every minute of my time with the Club. ’

Alan Oakes
collecting the Hall of Fame
award in February 2005.

Ken Barnes

As with the first lifetime achievement award, there were many contenders from various areas of the Club who deserved to be recognised. Ken Barnes proved to be the deserved winner. He has been one of the major contributors to City's success for more than 50 years. Ken has been a player, captain, coach, assistant manager, chief scout and an inspirational figure throughout his long association with the Blues.

Ken Barnes LIFETIME ACHIEVEMENT AWARD

Street Football

Born in Birmingham in 1929, it was inevitable football was always going to be Ken's main preoccupation as a boy. 'I was born in St Andrew's Road, Birmingham, and spent my early life living in a flat that overlooked Birmingham City's ground. It was like being born next door to Maine Road: you couldn't help but get interested. As a boy I'd play football every minute of the day. Twenty-odd-a-side often. Whenever I got the ball I'd charge forward and head for goal because there was no way I'd pass it to another player – it'd be another half hour before you got it back!'

Inevitably, Ken went to watch Birmingham City play and he also started to be noted for his own footballing abilities. Birmingham made him a member of their Colts side but Ken wasn't quite ready to dedicate his life to a footballing career. 'I got into a lot of trouble with my dad because with the Colts I had lots of opportunities but I wasted them, or worse, missed them all together! I let myself down. Dad knew that I could have progressed and told me that chances only come once in a while. I was then called up for the RAF and Bolton Wanderers started to show interest but the RAF were insistent that my first responsibility was to them and so the Bolton opportunity disappeared as well. Eventually I started to play for Stafford Rangers. Dad wasn't happy again. "Why them?" he asked. Other sides had shown a lot of interest and then in May 1950 I joined City for a fee of around £750.'

Unsteady Progress

The first few years at Maine Road did not progress in the way that either Ken or his family would have wanted. He did make it into the first team in January 1952 when the Blues beat Derby County 4–2, but no further opportunities came until the start of 1954/55. 'I waited so long I had splinters in my backside from sitting on the bench.'

Once Ken did return to the League side in August 1954 he became a permanent fixture and one of the most important team members. At the end of 1954/55 City reached the FA Cup final but success eluded them. 'In football you have to make your own luck sometimes,' says Ken, 'but on that day against Newcastle the luck was against us. We couldn't shake it off despite a lot of hard work, which normally would have won any game. We conceded a goal within a minute. Jackie Milburn wasn't known for his heading ability but the first attack caught us on the hop. He wasn't picked up as he should have been and then he headed home. One goal down in less than a minute. It's very difficult to come back but we worked hard.

'Then, after about 20 minutes, Jimmy Meadows went down injured and we were down to ten men. You would expect the match to be over but we came back. Bobby Johnstone equalised with a wonderful goal but as the game progressed, the extra man made the difference. We still thought we could do it at half time but the second half was hard and we lost 3–1. I was very, very disappointed. Before the final I'd told myself we had to win because no one remembers the losers but the early goal and the injury worked against us.'

Twelve months later Ken helped the Blues reach Wembley again and this time they were successful against his home-town team Birmingham City, although Ken wasn't entirely happy with his role in the first half. 'Birmingham were the cup favourites

'Before the game McDowall had tried to stop me smoking but there was no way he could stop me smoking after we'd won!'

but we had to win. Before the game I always had a quick smoke and so I was hiding in the toilet having a cigarette when the manager Les McDowall came storming in. He had a go at me but I pointed out I always had one, then he told me I had to closely mark Birmingham's Peter Murphy. I said, "When I get the ball I'm attacking; I'm not going to worry about Peter Murphy!" He went on at me and, as he was the manager, I had to do as he said. It wasn't my game but I had no choice.

'In the first half we didn't shine as much as we ought. We took the lead but they came back at us and it was 1–1 at half time. Don Revie had a go at me, saying, "Where were you in the first half?" I told him about the discussion with McDowall and he told me to ignore that and play my own game. In the second half I did and the Revie Plan started to work. We went on to win a great final 3–1. Before the game McDowall had tried to stop me smoking but there was no way he could stop me smoking after we'd won!

'At the time you can't take it all in. You live through the drama and excitement of it all but you don't savour it. It's impossible to enjoy it in the way supporters can – you can watch it, enjoy it, suffer with it in some ways as well but for players you're working and can't pause to think of it as a significant historical moment.'

Serious Injustice
Success in 1956 was thoroughly deserved, particularly for Ken, and as the decade developed he remained one of the Club's most consistent performers. So much so that Mancunians and many neutrals believed he should have played for England. Competition was tough but key footballing figures, including Denis Law, believed Ken should have played for his country. Roy Cheetham, a young player with City during this period, remains convinced that England missed out on a major star, 'For me, Ken Barnes has always been one of the best – how could he never receive a cap? He was

Player Career Statistics
Appearances

KEN BARNES

Position
Wing half 1950–61

Typical Height and Weight
1.80m (5ft 11in)
69kg (10st 13lb)

Born
Birmingham, 16 March 1929

League Debut
Derby County (home)
5 January 1952

	LEAGUE		FA CUP		FL CUP		TOTAL	
	App	Gls	App	Gls	App	Gls	App	Gls
1951/52	1	0	0	0	-	-	1	0
1952/53	0	0	0	0	-	-	0	0
1953/54	0	0	0	0	-	-	0	0
1954/55	40	0	6	1	-	-	46	1
1955/56	39	1	7	0	-	-	46	1
1956/57	31	2	2	0	-	-	33	2
1957/58	39	11	1	0	-	-	40	11
1958/59	40	4	2	0	-	-	42	4
1959/60	37	0	1	0	-	-	38	0
1960/61	31	0	4	0	2	0	37	0
TOTAL	258	18	23	1	2	0	283	19

Ken's Prime Time

Manchester City 5 Sheffield United 2. Football League Division One – 25 August 1954

Goalscorers Revie (2) Hart (2) Clarke

City Team Trautmann, Meadows, Little, Barnes, Ewing, Paul, Spurdle, McAdams, Revie, Hart, Clarke

Attendance 23,856

Ken Barnes was very much a fringe player at the time of this game. He had made only one appearance for City – his debut in January 1952 – and with time moving on his chances seemed to reduce as the months passed by. Then, just as he looked likely to leave the Club, the use of the new, deep-lying centre-forward tactic known as the Revie Plan resurrected his career. The Blues had been defeated 5–0 at Preston on the opening day of the season after trying to use their new tactical innovation. Many felt the plan should be abandoned and that it would never work but the truth was that a vital ingredient was needed – Ken Barnes.

Ken had been a key figure in making the plan work in the reserves. 'It was perfect for me,' he says. 'Traditionally, forwards had to keep in their position, not roam around; and be there simply to score goals. The Plan changed that. It was first tried in the reserves, with Johnny Williamson and I, and it worked like a dream. Fred Tilson, who was in charge of the reserves at the time, allowed it time to develop. I remember McDowall talking with Fred Tilson and he wasn't convinced we'd get away with it in the first team. It was almost scrapped after the Preston game but Don Revie, apparently, stressed to McDowall that it had worked so well in the reserves because of my part in it. He urged him to give me a go.'

In the *Manchester Evening Chronicle*, journalist Eric Todd was also convinced the Plan should be given time. 'History is studded with names of people who, while experimenting in the interests of progress, have been blown to bits and generally have had a rough time of it. To that list can now be added Manchester City. It is far too early, however, to condemn City's experiments as failures and the fact that Revie is playing "deep" is no concession to the continental

fashion. They have tried similar tactics in the past in the second team with some success, and the roving centre forward is nothing new to them. The only thing continental about the team is Trautmann.'

In the days that followed there was no mention of Ken until the day of the game when Eric Thornton of the *Manchester Evening News* announced, 'The wing half who rarely gets a chance comes into the City team.' Thornton went on to point out how unlucky Ken was by quoting a story of how the player had been selected for an away game in place of an injured Roy Paul. 'Just as the coach was about to leave, the City captain arrived and Barnes was told to go home as he was no longer needed!'

The meeting with Sheffield United commenced with the Blues conceding a goal after only 40 seconds. Eric Todd commented, 'City turned in a Jekyll and Hyde act at Maine Road, so we still don't know what sort of a season they're going to have! A goal down while people were still paying to come in, and on level terms before those same people had received their change, City took control against a bewildered Sheffield United, produced near-faultless football and with a 4–1 lead at half time they went in to an ovation the like of which I haven't heard in years. And fully deserved by every man.'

Frank Swift, City's former goalkeeper, was in the press box telling all who could listen that the first-half performance was the best he had ever witnessed, while the *Manchester Evening News* reported, 'City were terrific – a display so snappy that one old timer was carried out fainting.'

The second half started with a fifth City goal after 49 minutes but the mood of the game changed as the Blades began marking Ken tightly. City had little chance of making the Plan work with Ken under so

From left to right (back row) Barnett (trainer), McAdams, Ewing, Barnes, Trautmann, Little, Branagan, Tilson (coach), McDowall (manager) (front row) McClelland (trainer), Fagan, Revie, Paul, Hart, Clarke. Interestingly, this side never played together in the League or Cup.

much heavy marking and so they played more of a long-ball game.

Sheffield United managed to score a second but City's first-half performance couldn't be matched. The game ended 5–2 with Ken and Johnny Hart receiving a great deal of praise. Eric Todd stated, 'Barnes was marvellous and thoroughly deserves an extended run and Hart for once was cheered on by his many critics. After that, I've heard everything!'

Ken did receive an extended run. Apart from injuries, he remained first choice for the following seven years. Ken puts the transformation in his career down to this meeting with Sheffield United: 'The circumstance was suddenly right. I could fit in. I wasn't a great tackler but I did have imagination... improvisation... I was a good passer. A wing half couldn't just be defensive in my eyes; they had to attack as well. It's an old saying but it's true that attack is the best form of defence. It really annoys me when coaches stress negative play. It doesn't matter how many goals you concede so long as you score more.

'From then on I became a regular and we started to get noticed as a team – it was a true team effort. Other sides had no idea how to combat it. They tried to get their wing half to mark Don but it still seemed to leave a man spare somewhere else.'

far better than some of the guys who did play for England. Ex-United man Walter Winterbottom was the England manager and I believe there were certain teams that had a better relationship with him and the selectors. Because of that, chances for players from other clubs were limited. Ken should definitely have played for England. He was the best in his position and everybody in football knew that.' The closest Ken came was when he was asked to be England reserve for a match with Wales in October 1957.

Captain Ken

As the 1950s progressed, Ken took over the captaincy from Roy Paul and helped to ease the transition between one set of players and their replacements. Many of the Cup winners had moved on and the City side became a mix of youth and experience. Ken helped the younger players to develop, including one Denis Law, a headline-grabbing 20 year old who joined the Blues in March 1960. 'It wasn't a great period for the club,' recalls Ken. 'The cup team had broken up and other players had been brought in but we were not at the standard we'd been at just a couple of years earlier. Clearly Denis Law was a tremendous signing but a good player needs other good players around him to make him a great player.

'In terms of my captaincy, I've always believed there should be 11 captains in a side. Every member of the team should be shouting, encouraging, helping, urging the rest of the team on. I can't abide sides that play as individuals. It's a team game and so when I was captain I tried to encourage the whole team to work for each other.'

A Welsh Interlude

In May 1961 Ken moved on to Wrexham. Until his transfer he had remained as City's regular number four but he realised that opportunities during the following seasons would be limited. In addition there was the possibility that he could move into management. 'I wanted to play football and so Wrexham offered me that opportunity as well as

Peter Murphy's no match as Ken Barnes is in control during the
1956 FA Cup-final victory over his home-town team Birmingham City.

the role of manager. We had some very good players and managed to play good quality football. I tried to encourage everyone. I enjoyed my time there – or at least most of it – because we had some good players and we won promotion. My only problem – throughout my life I guess – is that I always try to speak my mind and that worked against me at Wrexham. I'd been injured and wasn't able to play my part on the pitch. Results went against us and then I had a bit of a disagreement with the directors. One of them was having a go at me about team selections and styles of play and I interrupted him and said, "You're a farmer aren't you? I don't tell you how to milk your cows so don't expect to tell me how to manage the side." He didn't like that and a few days later I was on my way.' Spells at Witton and Bangor followed, before Ken joined the City coaching staff under Mercer and Allison in August 1970.

Coaching City

The return to Maine Road saw Ken fulfil a variety of crucial roles, including trainer, coach, assistant manager and chief scout. Each role put him into a position of influence at the Club and it's fair to say that City's development of good-quality, young players throughout the 1970s, 1980s and early 1990s owes a great deal to Ken's presence. 'Joe Mercer asked me to come back to Maine Road as a coach and I enjoyed working with him, Mal and the others. Football was my life and passion, so it was great to be back.

'For the next 30 years or so, it was wonderful to work with the Club. The only real problem was having so many managers. Each change caused us to lose too many young players. Look at the ones we've groomed and lost over the years. I had many, many arguments over the years when some of our great youngsters were put on the transfer list, or offers came in. Naturally, the manager would make the ultimate decision but I always made sure he knew my mind. Every major, successful side we've had over the years has always contained a good sprinkling of home-grown talent and I believe we would have achieved a great deal if we'd kept some of the lads we let go, particularly in the 1980s and early 1990s.'

A Popular Presence

Considering Ken's strengths and the managerial problems City suffered during his coaching years it may seem surprising that Ken never became manager, but this was his own choice: 'I was assistant manager to Johnny Hart and Tony Book at times but I never wanted the job myself. I was offered it once by Peter Swales but I remembered back to the days at Wrexham. I'm not saying there would have been any interference from anyone at Maine Road but I didn't want to be in the position to find out. I'd rather work on the positive aspects of

the game without worrying about saying the right things to the right people. The game's there to be enjoyed and you can't afford to worry about pleasing the directors.'

During the mid-1990s Ken retired from his role as chief scout but he continued to be a popular presence around the Club. During his retirement his opinions have been sought by many interested in the positive aspects of the game and although he is critical of the forced coaching regimes employed by footballing authorities over the years, he does remain positive about the game itself. 'Football is not a negative game. I remember listening to a coach one day telling young lads to stop the other side scoring because that way you won't lose. I said, "Yeah, and you won't win either." Football's about entertainment, excitement and goals. Every player should be encouraged to open up play, not kill it off. My philosophy is simple – you can do anything at all on a football field at a given moment, so try things out. If you have an idea, try it. Don't be afraid. Don't follow the rules of how not to concede a goal: follow the belief that you can do something exciting or that you can help another player shine. I hope all young players in the future get the chance to enjoy the game as much as I have. If they do, they'll blossom and football will be a better game as a result.'

' I love football and have spent my life being paid for something I enjoy. Few people can say that, and I just hope all young players in the future get the chance to enjoy the game. If they do, they'll blossom and football will be a better game as a result. '

Ken Barnes

collecting the Hall of Fame
award in February 2005.

Index

Alexander, Albert 79–80, 153
Allison, Malcolm 7, 28, 130
  and Alan Oakes 161–3, 164, 165–6
  and Colin Bell 79, 82
  and Francis lee 51
  and Joe Corrigan 10, 11, 12, 14, 17
  and Ken Barnes 172
  and Mike Summerbee 128, 132
  and Tony Book 30, 31, 32, 33, 34, 35, 38
Anderson, Viv 60
Ardiles, Osvaldo 14
Arsenal 102
Ashworth, David 152, 153
Astle, Jeff 55
Aston Villa 107

Bailey, Roy 61, 111
Balfour, Arthur 95
Ball, Alan 109, 111–13
The Ball of Fortune (film) 96
Barkas, Sam 48, 74, 146
Barnes, Horace 20, 24, 26, 147, 148
Barnes, Ken 56, 58, 66, 118–19, 123, 160, 161, 167–73
  career statistics 169
  prime time 170–1
Barnes, Peter 82
Barnett, Laurie 138, 160, 171
Barrass, Matt 154
Bass, Rosie 7
Beardsley, Peter 61
Beckford, Jason 59, 63
Bell, Alec 157
Bell, Colin 33, 34, 36, 37, 55, 65, 77–86, 130, 132
  career statistics 79
  MCFC statistics 80
  prime time 84–5
Benson, John 18
Berlin Olympics (1936) 134
Bernabéu, Santiago 76
Best, George 34, 104, 129, 131

Birmingham City 120–1
Bishop, Ian 62
Black, Andy 146
Blakey, Peter 130
Blanchflower, Danny 104
Blunstone, Frank 30
Bolton Wanderers 92
Bond, John 14, 16, 17, 18
Bonetti, Peter 96
Book, Tony 17, 29–38, 66, 84, 173
  and Alan Oakes 162, 164, 165
  career statistics 31
  and Francis Lee 52, 54, 55
  MCFC statistics 32
  prime time 34–5
Bookbinder, Susan 7
Booth, Tommy 10, 36, 37, 55, 82, 84
Bramble, Harry 45
Branagan, Ken 140
Brand, Ralph 128
Bray, Jackie 46, 102
Brightwell, Ian 58, 60, 65, 112
Brook, Eric 24, 39–48, 72, 102
  career statistics 41
  MCFC statistics 44
  prime time 44–5
Browell, Tommy 23, 24, 26, 27
Brown, Michael 111
Buchan, Martin 85–6
Burns, Francis 34
Busby, Matt 43, 44, 46, 72, 119, 155, 157
Byrne, Roger 119

Caine, Michael 132
Catton, Jimmy 92
Ceresoli (Italian goalkeeper) 40, 41, 42
Charlton, Jack 114, 163
Cheetham, Roy 132, 169
Clarke, Allan 81
Clarke, Kath 124, 145, 146, 150

Clarke, Roy 122, 123, 124, 143–50, 170, 171
  career statistics 145
  prime time 148–9
Clemence, Ray 18
Cocker, Les 15
Coleman, Tony 34, 36
Connor, David 36
Copping, Wilf 42
Corrigan, Joe 8, 9–18, 33, 54, 55, 166
  career statistics 11
  MCFC statistics 16
  prime time 14–15
Coton, Tony 108, 112
Cowan, Joanna 158
Cowan, Sam 43, 44, 45, 46, 72, 120, 146, 151–8
  career statistics 153
  prime time 154–5
Cox, Arthur 96
Crooks, Garth 15
Crossan, Johnny 38, 132
Cullis, Stan 82

Dale, Billy 44, 72, 73, 75, 102
Davidson, Ian 128
Davies, Wyn 53
Dean, Dixie 28, 153
Derby County 110–11
Deyna, Kaziu 132
Dickov, Paul 8
Doherty, Paul 104
Doherty, Peter 83, 97–104
  career statistics 99
  prime time 102
Doherty, Stephen 104
Donachie, Willie 82
Donnelly, Bob 156
Dorsett, George 94–5
Dowd, Harry 10, 36, 78
Doyle, Mike 11, 15, 30, 34, 36, 37, 55, 82, 83, 132
Drake, Ted 30
Dyson, Jack 120, 123, 146

Edinburgh, Duke of 121
Edwards, Duncan 119
Escape to Victory (film) 132
Everton 24–5

Ewing, Dave 123, 138, 140, 148, 170, 171

Fagan, Fionan 'Paddy' 122, 139, 148, 150, 171
Ferguson, Alex 60, 62
Ferguson, Bobby 53
Finney, Sir Tom 33, 70, 71, 76, 128
Fletcher, Eli 20, 24, 26
Forrest, W. 93
Friar, Jack 139
Frizzell, Jimmy 64
Fulham 139
Furniss, Lawrence 88

Gardner, Peter 34, 37, 55, 128, 162
Gascoigne, Paul 109
George V, King 20, 26, 27, 43, 72, 156
German Football Association 142
Gillespie, Billy 92, 94
Gleghorn, Nigel 110
Godwin, Harry 10
Goodchild, Jim 23, 26, 27
Gow, Gerry 14, 16
Graham, George 107
Greenwood, Ron 18
Gregg, Harry 11

Halford, Bernard 5, 6, 7
Hamill, Mick 152
Harding, John 90
Harford, Mike 111
Hart, Johnny 56, 81–3, 122–3, 148, 157, 164, 171, 173
Hartford, Asa 17
Hatton, Ray 10
Hatton, Ricky 10
Hayes, Joe 123, 140, 148
Healey, Ron 12
Hendry, Colin 59
Hepburn, John 76
Herd, Alec 44, 46, 47, 72, 101, 102, 103, 146
Heslop, George 34, 36, 54, 55
Hibbs, Harry 70

Hill, Jack 156
Hinchcliffe, Andy 58, 60, 62–3, 65, 66
Hitler, Adolf 134, 138
Hoddle, Glenn 14
Hodge, Peter 24
Hughes, Mark 62
Hurst, Geoff 53
Hutchison, Tommy 14, 17

Ince, Paul 62

Jack, David 21
James, Alex 131
James, David 128
James, Gary 76, 158
John, Roy 44
Johnson, Alan 20, 23, 28
Johnson, Alec 80
Johnson, Tommy 19–28, 48, 154
  career statistics 21–2
  MCFC statistics 22
  prime time 24–5
Johnstone, Bobby 120, 122, 123, 140, 148, 160, 168
Jones, Billy Lot 94
Jones, Tommy 82

Kavanagh, Albert 160
Keane, Robbie 114
Keegan, Ged 37
Keegan, Kevin 96
Kendall, Howard 57, 63, 64, 65, 107, 112
Kevan, Derek 161
Kidd, Brian 84, 85

Lake, Paul 5, 57–66, 109
  career statistics 58
  MCFC statistics 61
  prime time 62–3
Langford, Len 25, 72, 155
Law, Denis 34, 37, 79, 123, 132, 169, 171
Lawton, Tommy 71
Leake, Alec 91
Lee, Francis 26, 34, 36, 37, 49–56, 83, 114, 130, 132, 164

career statistics 50
prime time 55
Leighton, Jim 112
Leivers, Bill 123, 138, 140
Lifetime Achievement
  Awards 7
    Ken Barnes 167–73
    Roy Clarke 143–50
Lister, Bert 140
Little, Roy 120, 122, 123,
  148, 150, 170, 171
Logie, Jimmy 131
Lomas, Steve 111, 113

McAdams, Bill 130, 170,
  171
McCarthy, Mick 64–5
McDonald, Jack 139
Macdonald, Malcolm 106
McDowall, Les 117,
  118, 141–2, 168, 169,
  170, 171
Machin, Mel 57, 63, 64
Mackay, Dave 33
Mackenzie, Steve 14, 15
McMullan, Jimmy 46, 153
McNab, Neil 64
McNeill, Billy 64, 166
MacRae, Keith 13, 165
Maley, Tom 93
Manchester City
  Experience 6, 63
Manchester City Hall of
  Fame, aims and history
  6–8
*Manchester Evening
  Chronicle* 80, 154, 170
Manchester Evening News
  7, 34, 37, 81, 162, 170
Manchester United 34–5,
  62–3, 130, 154–5
Mangall, Ernest 20
Mann, Arthur 36, 55
Marsh, Rodney 83, 132,
  162
Marshall, Bobby 24, 44,
  72, 75
Match of the Day 113
Matthews, Stanley 33, 41,
  42, 44, 45, 128
Meadows, Jimmy 121,
  148, 150, 168, 170
Meek, David 12, 55
Mercer, Joe 7, 10, 12, 28,

49, 130
and Alan Oakes 151,
  163, 164
and Colin Bell 79–80
and Francis Lee 51, 52,
  55, 56
and Ken Barnes 172
and Mike Summerbee
  126–8, 129–31, 132
on Neil Young 37
and Peter Doherty 104
and Roy Paul 116
and Tony Book 31, 33,
  34
Mercer, Norah 7
Meredith, Billy 5, 20,
  87–96, 116, 124
  career statistics 89
  MCFC statistics 90
  prime time 92
Meredith, Sam 88
Meredith, Winifred 93, 96
Merrick, Alan 126
Milburn, Jackie 121, 168
Monkhouse, Bob 149,
  150
Moore, Bobby 129
Morley, Trevor 61, 62
Mortensen, Stan 70
Moulden, Paul 60, 64
Mulhearn, Ken 10–11, 12
Murphy, Peter 169, 172
Murray, Jimmy 128, 161
Mussolini, Benito 41

National Football
  Museum Hall of Fame
  103
Newcastle United 84–5,
  130
News of the World 76
Nish, George 132
Noad, Len 79

Oakes, Alan 36, 55,
  81, 83, 132, 139,
  159–66
  career statistics 161
  prime time 162
Oakes, Michael 166
Oldfield, David 62
Osborne, John 55
Owen, Bobby 36
Owen, Gary 82

Pallister, Gary 62
Pardoe, Glyn 36, 37, 55,
  66, 132, 160
Parker, Fran 44, 45
Parker, Kevin 6, 48
Parkes, Phil 18
Parkinson, Sir Lindsay 100
Parks, Jim 158
Parlby, Joshua 88
Paul, Roy 115–24, 144,
  147, 148, 170, 171
  career statistics 117
  MCFC statistics 118
  prime time 120–1
Players' Union 93
Portsmouth 72
Power, Paul 13, 14, 16,
  17, 84
Premier League 112
Pye, Freddie 132

Quinn, Niall 66, 105–14
  career statistics 107
  MCFC statistics 113
  prime time 110–11

Ramsey, Alf 55, 125,
  128, 129
Redmond, Steve 58, 60,
  64, 66, 110
Rees, Billy 145
Reid, Nicky 14, 17
Reid, Peter 64, 111, 112
Rennox, Clatworthy 154
Revie, Don 118, 119, 121,
  122, 128, 148, 163, 169,
  170, 171
Revie Plan 122, 170–1
Richards, John 83
Rimmer, Jimmy 15
Roberts, Frank 24, 27,
  147
Roberts, Graham 14
Robson, Bryan 61
Rosler, Uwe 112
Ross, Jimmy 95
*Rothmans Football
  Yearbook* 104
Royle, Joe 53, 82
Rush, Ian 18, 111, 165–6

Sagar, Ted 70
Saunders, Dean 110
Saunders, Ron 37, 164

Scott, Ian 65
Sear, Cliff 165
Shankly, Bill 51, 163
Sharpe, Ivan 22, 40, 42
Sheffield United 170–1
Sheron, Mike 112
Shilton, Peter 18, 110,
  132
Simmons, Arthur 102
Sims, Jim 139
Smith, Bob 136
Smith, George 74–5, 147,
  157
Smith, Tommy 80
Smith, Walter 94
Sproston, Bert 74, 75,
  146
Spurdle, Billy 123, 170
Stallone, Sylvester 132
Stapleton, John 7
Stepney, Alex 34
Steward, Alf 154
Stoke City 162–3
Summerbee, George 126
Summerbee, Mike 36,
  53, 54, 55, 80, 83,
  125–32, 164
  career statistics 127
  prime time 130
Sunderland 148–9
Swales, Peter 38, 56, 61,
  84, 162, 166, 173
Swift, Frank 12, 18, 67–76
  and Bert Trautmann 136,
  137, 138
  and Billy Meredith 96
  career statistics 69
  and Eric Brook 44, 45,
  46, 47
  and Ken Barnes 170
  MCFC statistics 75
  and Peter Doherty 102
  prime time 72
  and Roy Clarke 146
  and Sam Cowan 155
Symons, Kit 111

Talbut, John 55
Taylor, Tommy 119
Thornton, Eric 92, 123–4,
  170
Thurlow, Alec 74
Tilson, Fred 24, 72, 102,
  160

and Eric Brook 39, 43,
  44, 46, 47
and Ken Barnes 170,
  171
Todd, Eric 150, 170
Toseland 44, 46, 47, 72,
  102, 103
Toshack, John 53
Tottenham Hotspur 14–15
Trautmann, Bert 12, 18,
  50, 75, 133–42
  and Alan Oakes 148,
  160, 162–3, 166
  career statistics 135
  and Ken Barnes 170,
  171
  MCFC statistics 137
  prime time 139
  and Roy Paul 120, 123
  and Tony Book 29, 33
Tueart, Dennis 15, 82, 84,
  85, 86
Turnbull, Sandy 91, 94

van Aerle, Benny 114
van Breukelen, Hans 114
Vaughan, Frankie 150
Villa, Ricky 15

Wallace, Danny 62
Warhurst, Paul 59
Wark, John 13
Watson, Dave 15, 16
Webb, Neil 62
West Bromwich Albion 55
Westwood, Eric 75, 136,
  139
White, David 58–9, 60, 64,
  65, 66, 107, 111
Wild, Wilf 69, 157
Williamson, Johnny 118,
  122, 170
Wilson, Danny 7
Winterbottom, Walter 121,
  171
Woodley, Vic 70
Woosnam, Max 23, 27

Young, Neil 36–7, 52, 53,
  128, 130, 132, 164

Zamora, Ricardo 21

Acknowledgements

Picture acknowledgements

Action Images 11 centre left, 13 bottom, 17 bottom, 30 bottom left, 31 top left, 53 bottom, 54 top, 57 left, 58 bottom left, 59 top right, 68 top left, 79 centre left, 93 top right, 97 left, 105 left, 106 bottom left, 107 centre left, 109 bottom right, 111 top, 117 centre left, 123 bottom, 125 left, 141 top.

Colorsport 15 bottom left, 52 top, 60 top, 67 left, 69 centre left, 81 top, 99 centre left, 101 bottom, 103 top right, 115 left, 117 top right, 129 bottom, 131 top, 135 centre left, 143 left, 144 bottom left, 147 bottom right, 153 centre left, 155 top right, 159 left, 163 bottom right, 164 bottom left, 165 top, 167 left, 169 centre left, 172 top.

Empics 85 bottom left, 100 top.

The Manchester City Experience Archive (Museum & Tour) /Club Photographer, Ed Garvey/Gary James Collection 5, 8, 15 top left, 18 bottom left, 19 left, 24 bottom, 27 bottom, 28 bottom left, 36 bottom, 38 centre left, 41 bottom right, 42 bottom left, 45 centre right, 46 bottom left, 48 bottom left, 55 centre left, 56 bottom left, 62, 66 centre left, 76 bottom left, 77 left, 85 top right, 86 bottom left, 89 centre left, 91 bottom right, 95 top, 96 bottom left, 104 centre left, 108 top, 110 bottom left, 114 centre left, 121 centre left, 124 centre left, 132 centre left, 137 top right, 142 bottom left, 145 centre left, 148-149 bottom, 149 top right, 150 bottom left, 155 bottom left, 157 bottom right, 158 bottom left, 166 bottom left, 173 centre left.

Getty Images 2-3, 9 left, 33 top right, 37 top left, 49 left, 50 centre left, 51 top right, 70 top left, 71 bottom, 121 top left, 126 bottom left, 134 bottom, 136 bottom, 151 left, 156 top left, 171 top left.

Manchester Evening News 21 centre left, 23 bottom, 25 top right, 29 left, 35 top, 39 left, 41 centre left, 43 top, 63 top left, 65 top left, 65 bottom right, 73 top, 83 top, 87 left, 92 bottom left, 119 bottom right, 127 top right, 133 left, 138 bottom left, 146 top, 161 centre left.

Acknowledgements

I would like to thank all the players, their families, supporters, officials and other personalities quoted within this work. Many of these have provided assistance to me in several ways over the years, some of it obvious, most of it not. I have enjoyed every interview and every moment of my research.

I'd also like to thank John Riley and Johnny Williamson from the Former Players' Association – two men who work tirelessly for the Association – and Ed Garvey, a brilliant photographer and friend. Special thanks also to the staff of City's award winning museum and tour, the Manchester City Experience, who have provided a great deal of support, while the Experience's archive has assisted with much of the material contained within.

I am also very grateful, as always, to my wife Heidi and children Michael and Anna for all their support and encouragement. I would also like to thank my publishers Hamlyn, in particular Trevor Davies and Jessica Cowie for all their hard work.

Finally, thanks to City Chairman John Wardle for allowing this work to be published as an official record of City's Hall of Fame.

Executive Editor Trevor Davies
Editor Jessica Cowie
Executive Art Editor Geoff Fennell
Designer Darren Southern
Senior Production Controller Martin Croshaw
Picture Manager Liz Fowler